Seeing Red & Feeling Blue

Susan Aldridge was born in Lancashire. She graduated from Cambridge University with a BA in Natural Sciences and received her PhD in 1978 from London University for work on the chemistry of blood pigments. In 1983 she obtained a postgraduate certificate in science education and then in 1990 was awarded an MSc in biotechnology. She has many years' experience in both education and medical research, and since 1989 has worked as a science writer. A full-time writer and Medical Editor for *Focus Magazine*, Susan Aldridge is a Fellow of the Royal Society of Medicine. She lives in London.

Also by Susan Aldridge

Magic Molecules: How Drugs Work
The Thread of Life: from Genes to Genetic Engineering
Biochemistry for Advanced Biology
Practical Biochemistry for Advanced Biology

Seeing Red & Feeling Blue

Susan Aldridge

ARROW

Published by Arrow Books in 2001

1 3 5 7 9 10 8 6 4 2

Copyright © Susan Aldridge 2000

Susan Aldridge has asserted her right under the Copyright,
Designs and Patents Act, 1988, to be identified as the author of this work

First published in the United Kingdom in 2000 by Century

Arrow Books
The Random House Group Ltd
20 Vauxhall Bridge Road, London SW1V 2SA

Random House Australia (Pty) Limited
20 Alfred Street, Milsons Point, Sydney,
New South Wales 2061, Australia

Random House New Zealand Limited
18 Poland Road, Glenfield,
Auckland 10, New Zealand

Random House (Pty) Limited
Endulini, 5a Jubilee Road, Parktown 2193, South Africa

The Random House Group Ltd Reg. No. 954009

www.randomhouse.co.uk

A CIP catalogue record for this book is available
from the British Library

Illustrations by Rodney Paul

Papers used by Random House
are natural, recyclable products made from wood grown in
sustainable forests. The manufacturing processes conform
to the environmental regulations of the country of origin

ISBN 0 09 929690 X

Printed and bound in Great Britain by
Bookmarque Ltd, Croydon, Surrey

Contents

Illustrations

Acknowledgements

I am grateful to the following research scientists who have taken the time and trouble to answer my questions and provide me with useful material for this book: Terrie Moffitt, Paul Grasby, Chris Frith, Cary Cooper, Andrew Smith, Robert Sapolsky, Eric Brunner, Sheldon Cohen, Michael Rutter, Deborah Denno, Alan Kazdin, Hamazaki Tomohito, and Joe Hibbeln.

Discussions with the following clinicians have also been extremely important in shaping my knowledge of depression and how it is treated: Albert Persaud, David Baldwin, Robin Royston, Chris Manning, and Richard Maxwell. I would also like to acknowledge the help given to me by the Depression Alliance and Befrienders International. I am extremely grateful, too, to the late Glyn Jones and his wife Daphne for sharing their experience with me.

Staff at the Wellcome Library for the History of Medicine have been most helpful in providing bibliographic searches.

I also want to thank my agent, Caroline Davidson, for her immense help in developing the proposal for this book. Finally, I am grateful to Karen Ingram and my husband, Graham Aldridge, for reading the manuscript and making many helpful comments and suggestions.

Introduction

Many teenagers who celebrated the Millennium can expect to see the dawn of the 22nd century too. For if medical science continues to advance at its current breathtaking pace, a life expectancy of 120 (thought to be the natural human lifespan – but who knows?) will be the rule, rather than the exception. But how healthy and happy will their lives be? Unlike their counterparts from the last century they will have little to fear, on the whole, from infectious disease. TB, blood poisoning, diphtheria, and scarlet fever are not the major killers they were, and smallpox has been eradicated. Within the next 50 years too, we will find answers to those diseases which came to prominence as the threat of infection receded: heart disease, cancer, and Alzheimer's disease.

But what about the mental health of the up and coming generation? In the United States, suicide now claims as many lives as AIDS, and the World Health Organization predicts that depression will become one of the leading public health problems over the next 50 years. Meanwhile, rising material aspirations and profound socio-political change are leading to an explosion of crime in the former Soviet Union, and there is no diminution of criminal and political violence elsewhere.

However, we have the means to shed light on these problems, and find new solutions to them, through neuroscience and psychology. Traditionally, psychology has depended upon the study of human and animal behaviour. But increasingly this work is being complemented by more formal laboratory experiments, which look at biochemicals (the molecules of life, if you like), genetics, and brain imaging. All these approaches are yielding enormous amounts of fascinating data about the human mind; what is desperately needed is a synthesis which can bring practical benefits.

I have written about stress, depression and crime, because these are the key concerns facing us all today. Surveys show that most people know someone who has suffered from clinical depression and that one person in 20 is affected at any one time; similarly most people have felt the adverse effects of stress, and few of us are not touched, directly or indirectly, by crime or the fear of it.

I also believe that neuroscience will uncover some important links between stress, depression and crime. Intuition already tells us that depression and violence could be two sides of the same coin – aggression turned inwards, or outwards. But only time will tell if common neural circuits are involved, and whether their expression depends upon genetic and/or environmental factors. Stress may turn out to be the triggering factor which sends people down the blue path, to depression, or the red path, to aggression and bad behaviour.

Currently, however, there is little dialogue between the three areas of research. Biological psychiatrists don't really talk much to the police and stress experts think more about the management of the workplace than the workings of the brain. In a small way, this book attempts to build a bridge between these three areas of human concern.

In part I, I'll briefly point out some of the links between stress, depression and violence (which I believe will be firmed up by research within the next few years) before looking at those aspects of the brain and those technologies which are most relevant in exploring these issues. To show the worth of this research, we will also look at the extent, and history, of the problems. In part II, I focus on stress, depression, and violent behaviour as separate – though interlinked – issues. Then, in part III, I explore solutions – from drug treatments and therapy through to self-help. Part IV looks to the future – at where the new understanding of mood and emotion may lead us.

It is always difficult when writing any popular science book to strike the right balance between accessibility and over-simplification. I hope I have not erred too much in either direction. Cognitive neuroscience and molecular genetics are both quite young disciplines, although they are evolving very rapidly. So much of what is discussed here is not yet established fact in the way that, say, the laws of physics and astronomy are. Even so, discoveries over the last ten or so years already point to ways in which the burden of mood disorders and antisocial behaviour might be lightened, for the benefit of the individual and society as a whole.

PART I

The Biology of Emotion

CHAPTER ONE

Red Rage and Blue Gloom:
The Common Links

A boy of five and his seven-year-old sister were found dead with their mother yesterday on what should have been his first day at school. Michael Flitcroft, his sister Hannah and their mother Mary were found inside a car in woods at Harpsden, near Henley-on-Thames, Oxon, at 7.45 am. Police were treating the deaths as one suicide and two murders. The children were still in their nightclothes and it is thought that Mrs Flitcroft drove the family to the woods during the night. Mrs Flitcroft, 35, had separated from her husband, and he is believed to have been told of the find as he worked at Heathrow airport. He was driven to Reading, Berks, to identify the body. Mrs Flitcroft and the children lived in Woodley, Reading, but her husband left the house some months ago and moved to nearby Twyford. She was said by neighbours to have been suffering from depression for some time.[1]

A dispute over child custody has left two young brothers dead, apparently killed by their father when he connected a hose to the exhaust pipe of his car and killed himself alongside his sons. Detectives yesterday attempted to unravel the circumstances which led to the discovery of the bodies of Daniel Philpott, seven, his three-year-old brother, Jordan, and Julian Philpott, 29, in a car in woods in Beddau, near Pontypridd, South Wales. The children's mother alerted the police when she arrived to collect them from her estranged husband's home on Monday afternoon and found the house on fire. After extinguishing the blaze, firefighters found the property deserted and South Wales police launched a search for the missing father and his children. Their bodies were discovered later after passers-by spotted the missing white Ford Escort. The three were dead when they reached East Glamorgan hospital.[2]

Murder followed by suicide is more common than you might think and does not always involve a gun-crazed loner cutting down innocent strangers. The massacres at Dunblane and Columbine High School naturally hit the headlines; however, there are many other, more private, tragedies which devastate the families involved and shock their local community but are soon forgotten by the world at large.

The two cases described above, separated in time by less than a year, bear an uncanny resemblance to one another. Meanwhile, a study of 78 similar incidents reveals a characteristic pattern: individuals tormented by family and work-related stresses, slipping into a downward spiral of depression, and then exploding in one unprecedented act of violence directed both inwards and outwards, at the same time.[3]

All of this suggests that stress, depression, and violence are intimately linked. Thankfully the combination does not always push people over the edge in such a tragic and heartbreaking way – but it still exacts an enormous cost from the individual and society in terms of ill health, crime, and human misery.

Stress, depression and violence – setting the scene

Aggression and depression – red rage and blue gloom; both logically and intuitively, they do seem to be two sides of the same coin. In the first case violence is directed outwards, at society, and is often expressed in criminal acts. In the second, the rage is directed inside, at the self; indeed, one of the key features of depression is an inner tirade of self-criticism and negativity.

Sigmund Freud was the first to point out the links between depression and violence (he had nothing to say about stress – because the term was not around in his day):

> *We have long known, it is true, that no neurotic harbours thoughts of suicide which he has not turned back upon himself from murderous impulses against others, but we have never been able to explain what interplay of forces can carry such a purpose through to execution.*[4]

Since Freud's era, we have brought the power of modern psychology and the new tools of molecular biology to bear upon the problems of depression and aggression. Slowly we are beginning to uncover the scientific reality behind Freud's 'interplay of forces'. So, in this opening chapter, let us just take a brief look at some of these exciting discoveries, to set the scene for what is to follow.

First, there are the sex differences. Men are seven times more likely to commit a violent crime, while women are at least twice more likely to suffer from depression. In a general population-based study of adolescent boys and girls, 68 per cent of the boys admitted involvement in at least minor delinquency, compared with 57 per cent of the girls. When it came to depression, the trend was reversed, with 56 per cent of girls reporting a tendency to blue moods compared with only 36 per cent of boys.

Twenty-three per cent of both the boys and the girls seemed to be happy and well adjusted, reporting neither delinquent behaviour nor depression. This suggests that emotional disturbance is equally likely in both sexes, but is most likely to express itself outwardly in boys and inwardly in girls.[5]

Depression and aggression are not always mutually exclusive. When American psychiatrists asked their depressed patients about aggressive and even murderous thoughts (something which is not usually done), a surprising number admitted to homicidal impulses[6] which, alarmingly, they said they would act on, given the chance (we will return to the controversial link between mental illness and violence in chapter 6).

More recently, a new type of depression characterized by irritability and tantrums has been identified. Up to one-third of the depressed outpatients seen by a team of psychiatrists at Massachusetts General Hospital[7] were suffering from this 'angry' kind of depression. Drugs that lifted mood also made the rage subside, suggesting that depression and aggression may, sometimes, have the same origin within the brain.

Where exactly does stress fit into all this? It may seem obvious that stress can lead to depression – but it is actually rather difficult to prove that this is the case. One of the best pieces of evidence for the link comes from a Canadian research study of the fortunes of people suffering from the chronic stress of physical disability. People with heart disease or arthritis were found to be two to three times more likely to suffer from clinical depression than those in the general population.[8]

Moreover, the depression could not easily be explained away as being part and parcel of the disease which was causing the disability, or as a side effect of the medication used to treat it. This seems to suggest a genuine link between stress and depression which may also occur in many other situations.

There is also a kind of depression which, like 'angry' depression, is very strongly linked with stressful experiences. People who are vulnerable to 'stress' depression do not start out by feeling low; instead their aggression is initially directed outwards, and their behaviour gets increasingly cranky and irritable. Only later do they report the blue mood which is typical of depression.

Strangely, these individuals actually reported fewer stressful events in their lives prior to the onset of depression, compared with the average depressed person.[9] This fits with their inability to cope with everyday stress; minor stressors such as a disappointing date, a social slight, or minor criticism from the boss were seen as major catastrophes, underlining pre-existing feelings of inadequacy, loneliness and isolation. What is especially interesting is that this group also had a characteristic biochemical abnormality which we will examine later.

Disordered thought patterns

People who are prone to depression or aggression view the world through differently tinted spectacles from the rest of the population. One experiment, in particular, shows that children who are depressed and children who are aggressive (as rated by their teachers and classmates) both tend to see the world as a hostile place.[10] Where they differ is that depressed children tend to blame themselves for others' hostility, while aggressive children blame someone else. The two groups of children also differ in how they respond to this perceived hostility; the depressed children feel helpless in the face of adversity and tend to favour withdrawal, while their aggressive counterparts, as you would expect, place more value upon an aggressive response. Knowing how depression and aggression colour thinking patterns is important; we will see in chapter 8 how cognitive therapy can change thought patterns, and help people see their world in a brighter and better light.

There is more; in adulthood, depressed patients tend to score higher than normal when it comes to general measures of hostility, like suspicion, resentment and irritability (maybe, like the patients described above, they were even harbouring homicidal impulses).[11] Aggression and depression even go together in people who are not clinically depressed, at least according to a recent small study from the University of Texas.[12] Forty-two women and 23 men were asked to rate themselves on standard psychological tests of both aggression and depression. There was a significant correlation between the two for women, though not for men, which led the researchers to speculate that there might be some common mechanism underpinning the extreme ends of the spectrum of human emotion. Again, it makes a lot of sense. Does your uptight, hostile next-door neighbour really seem like a happy person?

But why are aggression and depression linked? To learn more, we need to look at the chemistry of the brain, for it is here that we find increasing evidence of two important connections – one between stress and depression, and another between violence and depression.

Stress and depression: the cortisol connection

Mention hormones and most people immediately think about sex in some form or another. We blame hormones for the annoying personality changes in adolescent children, for our sexual desires, for pre-menstrual tension, the baby blues (or, worse, post-natal depression) and for the changes that occur with menopause. But when it comes to looking at stress and depression, the hormones we are interested in are quite different ones.

A hormone, put simply, is a chemical messenger, released by one organ in the body in response to some environmental cue or pressure. It travels through the bloodstream to its target organ, where it causes some physiological change, like increasing the heart rate, through a complex set of biochemical reactions. Hormone-orchestrated changes normally act to keep the body in tune with its environment throughout life.

Stress hormones put the body on red alert in response to an immediate threat. Their physiological effect is to boost the three A's – attention, arousal and aggression (commonly known as having your wits about you). Without, at this stage, going too deeply into the way the brain works or the fine detail of the stress response, this is how hormones make the body respond to stressful stimuli.

First, the stimulus is perceived by the brain which sends a hormonal message to the adrenal glands, located on top of the kidneys. The adrenals respond with the release of cortisol, the major stress hormone. Cortisol alters the body's biochemistry, temporarily, to cause the breakdown of carbohydrate, protein, and fat – the major constituents of our diet – into readily utilized fuel molecules which gear the body for action. Cortisol is not the only player in the stress reaction, however; another important component is the hormone adrenaline, which is released at the same time. Adrenaline revs up the body's sympathetic nervous system, producing those 'flight or fight' responses which are familiar even to the most laid-back person. You experience racing heart (more oxygen and fuel to the muscles), pale face (blood diverted to the limbs for a quick getaway or stand and fight), sweaty palms, dry mouth and so on in response to a pulse of adrenaline.

All this had fantastic survival value thousands of years ago, when our human ancestors had to battle over territory with other predators. Somehow, the annual work appraisal or the car that cuts in on the inside lane does not really pack the same lethal threat as a sabre-toothed tiger, yet we may produce as much cortisol as if they did.

To put it bluntly, we have to negotiate our way through the 21st century with a brain and nervous system that have not altered their response to threat since the Stone Age. No wonder we have mental health problems. Our saving grace is that some parts of our brains have developed the capacity to work out what is going on, and do something about it.

Because it is primitive, the cortisol response is only meant to act short-term, dealing with immediate threat. In normal circumstances, cortisol acts in what is known as a negative feedback loop. Once it is in the blood, it signals the brain to turn off its own production. It is a bit like feeling full after a meal; you do not go on eating for ever because a signal goes to your brain telling it you have had enough for now. Negative feedback is a powerful, universal mechanism which keeps life, at all levels, in a stable condition.

But negative feedback does not always work as well as it should. If cortisol production is not turned off quickly enough, the hormone can act as a slow toxin to the body and brain. There is extensive evidence that people suffering from depression have elevated levels of cortisol in their blood.[13] In other words, they are in a permanently stressed-out state at the mercy of an ancient alarm system. This may even lead to shrinkage of part of the brain (see Box 1), also seen in patients with Cushing's syndrome. People with Cushing's syndrome, in which cortisol is overproduced because of a tumour somewhere in the hormonal system, are also vulnerable to depression. Depression is a well-known side effect of steroid drugs, closely related to cortisol, which are prescribed for inflammatory conditions like arthritis and eczema. For instance, the suicide of the British photographer Terence Donovan in 1997 was attributed to steroid medication. All this suggests that cortisol overproduction, from stress, is a risk factor for depression and even a shrinkage of brain tissue. In other words, cortisol is the biochemical link between stress and depression.

BOX 1   *Stress shrinks the brain*

It has long been known that overexposure of rats to cortisol causes long-term effects on the hippocampus, a part of the brain which is involved in memory and learning and which has many molecular targets (known as receptors, of which more in the next chapter) for cortisol. So the hormone naturally heads for this area. The problem is that when there is too much cortisol around it weakens brain cells (neurons) in the hippocampus by making them, first, less able to survive damage, such as oxygen deprivation (as may happen in a stroke, say, or as a part of normal ageing). It also causes loss of dendrites, the thread-like projections which neurons use to connect to other neurons (for more, see chapter 2). Eventually, the hippocampal neurons are lost – resulting in an actual shrinkage of the brain.[14] Furthermore, you can produce the animal equivalent of depression if cortisol itself is injected into rats.

Throughout this book there will be similar references to experiments with animals. Whatever your ethical stance on this matter, it just is not possible to appreciate what is going on in the world of brain science as applied to the spectrum of human emotion and its disorders without looking in some detail at the animal work. For the present purposes, we will work on the commonly (but not universally) held assumption that these experiments are relevant, because it can be shown that animals have emotions and also that the parts of the brain we will be talking about also exist in animals such as rodents.

In the case of cortisol, stress and depression, what has been found in animals has now been replicated in humans. Recent brain-imaging studies show a significant reduction in the right and left hippocampus of female patients who had suffered clinical depression,[15] but were not depressed at the time of the experiment and otherwise in good health.

The extent of the shrinkage was dependent in a remarkably consistent way on how long the subjects had been depressed. And note, this work was done with people who had recovered from their illness. Similar hippocampal shrinkage has also been noted in people suffering from post-traumatic stress disorder, either from combat stress[16] or childhood abuse.[17] Now, none of this proves that cortisol actually shrinks the brain (put it this way: what if people born with a smaller than normal hippocampus tend to get depressed, or end up on the front line?). But it is a vital pointer to future research.

Depression and violence: the serotonin connection

You may have heard of the brain chemical serotonin in connection with the antidepressant drug Prozac (fluoxetine), which lifts mood by raising serotonin levels. (We will examine this fascinating topic in chapter 7.) In this chapter I want to look at the growing weight of evidence that links abnormal serotonin metabolism in the brain to impulsive behaviour. (Metabolism, by the way, is just the scientific term given to the chemical activity within the body.) This is important, because lack of impulse control so often leads to violence, whether it is directed inwards (suicide, attempted suicide, and self-mutilation) or outwards (murder, arson, and assault).

Serotonin is a 'master' chemical, which has a profound influence on both our physiology and our behaviour. For instance, it is involved in controlling the action of the heart and circulation, respiration, and body temperature. Serotonin also helps govern appetite, sensitivity to pain, learning, movement, sexual behaviour, mood and, as we are about to discover, impulse.

Box 2   *A marker for serotonin*

At present, it is too difficult to access the brain directly to measure the levels of chemicals inside it. So researchers have to rely on indirect methods instead. They look for 'marker' chemicals elsewhere in the body which reveal what is going on within the brain itself.

Brain serotonin is often measured using a marker chemical called 5-HIAA (short for 5-hydroxyindoleacetic acid) in the cerebrospinal fluid (CSF, the fluid which bathes and protects the brain and spinal cord).

5-HIAA in CSF is formed when brain serotonin breaks down. This is a perfectly natural process, because molecules in the body are being formed and broken down all the time – a certain amount of turnover is a normal part of metabolism (like staff turnover in a large company). The normal range of values for CSF 5-HIAA are well known; lower than normal values are reckoned to be indicative of lower than normal brain serotonin levels.

However, taking samples of CSF from volunteers in a research study is not very pleasant for them, for it requires a process called lumbar puncture. This involves inserting a large hollow needle into the lower part of the spinal canal to withdraw the fluid, and often gives people a

---

bad headache afterwards. For this reason, most of the serotonin studies to date have been done on patients and prisoners (still with their permission, of course) and have involved relatively small numbers of people. This means we need to be cautious about generalizing from the results.

You can also find out what is going on with brain serotonin by using a test called the fenfluramine challenge. Fenfluramine is a drug that prods brain cells into releasing serotonin. This has a knock-on effect; the serotonin sends a message to the pituitary gland, resulting in the release of a pulse of a hormone called prolactin into the blood stream. It is the prolactin (used for milk production after childbirth under normal circumstances) which is measured. Low levels of prolactin suggest the fenfluramine–serotonin–prolactin circuit is not functioning as it should.

Researchers are just beginning to measure serotonin levels in blood, and link levels reliably to levels within the brain (the relationship is quite complex, which is why this simple test has not been much used until now). This is an important step forward, because it means many more serotonin studies can now be done, and on larger groups of people.

We will start with a few animal studies – for animals have brains, they have emotions, and they exhibit many behaviours, like aggression and social climbing, which have human equivalents. If rats are depleted of brain serotonin, they suddenly develop an alarming tendency to kill mice (not their normal behaviour).[18] There was good news for the mice, though, when the rats' serotonin levels were topped up again by the experimenters; the killing stopped. Meanwhile, in adolescent male rhesus monkeys, low serotonin was linked with high aggression and risky behaviour.[19]

In humans, low serotonin is associated with similarly impulsive behaviour. Disruptive children – such as those with attention deficit hyperactive disorder (ADHD, of which more in chapter 6), conduct disorder, and oppositional defiant disorder (pathological naughtiness, put in plain terms) – have also been found to have low serotonin levels.[20]

Box 3   *Serotonin and the cruel child*

A 12-year-old girl came to the attention of Swedish researchers because of conduct disorder that seemed to be linked to low blood sugar and carbohydrate craving. She was given the standard behavioural questionnaire and answered 'no' to the question 'Have you ever injured or killed a small animal such as a cat or a squirrel just for fun?' However, she then described having found a baby bird, and throwing it in the air repeatedly to watch it attempt to fly until it died.

Her parents revealed that the child had mistreated her pet hamsters by attempting to cram them into confined spaces, such as the interior of toys. And when her adoptive mother was asked to rate the girl's behaviour, she gave the maximum score possible for aggression and cruelty.

The girl had, as expected, low brain serotonin levels, and this turned out to be a sinister pointer to her future life. Only four years later she was in a detention centre for cheque fraud and now had a history of cutting herself and making other suicidal gestures.[21]

In adults, a growing number of studies links serotonin dysfunction to a wide range of antisocial and criminal behaviours. A study in France showed low serotonin levels among 47 very difficult prisoners, whose history of bad behaviour included temper outbursts, death threats, arson, alcoholism, assaults, fights and cruelty to animals.[22]

A particularly important piece of research, carried out in Helsinki, Finland, focused on 36 violent offenders,[23] and suggested that low serotonin is associated with impulsivity rather than with violence *per se*. Twenty-one of the men had killed, while the remaining 15 were guilty of attempted murder. There was a marked difference in their serotonin levels depending on whether the crime was committed on impulse or was premeditated. The 27 impulsive offenders had significantly lower levels. Moreover, those who had committed more than one violent crime (17 of the group, of whom 14 were impulsive offenders) had lower levels than those who had offended only once. It was not only others that the impulsive offenders hurt – 17 of the 27 also had a history of suicide attempts and these men had the lowest serotonin levels of all.

So what was officially wrong with these men? The impulsive offenders had all been diagnosed as having either intermittent explosive disorder (like the childhood diagnoses above, this is exactly what it sounds like, and accounted for 20 of the group) or antisocial personality disorder. We will return to these important diagnostic categories in chapter 6, but for now it is worth remembering that none of these men were suffering from a treatable mental illness like schizophrenia or a mood disorder.

The link with suicide is particularly interesting, for this has been seen before. The earliest work, by Swedish researchers, linking serotonin and depression noted that patients with low serotonin were more likely to have attempted or completed suicide using particularly violent means than those who, although depressed, still had normal levels.[24] More recent research has confirmed this: for instance, in American patients suffering from depression, low serotonin was associated with suicide attempts that resulted in greater medical damage.[25]

These are extreme cases, and until quite recently it has been assumed that dysfunctional metabolism of serotonin leading to violence is confined to a small minority of people (although naturally, the ripples of their violent acts spread out to touch the lives of many more). But now we have evidence that low serotonin levels are also found in the population at large. Terrie Moffitt and her team at the Institute of Psychiatry in London surveyed a large population of young people in Dunedin, New Zealand (part of an ongoing study which we will return to in chapter 6) for aggressive behaviour. They studied court records and gave out questionnaires so the subjects could assess themselves. They found a small, but significant, increase in blood serotonin in aggressive men (but not women) compared with the normal population.[26] This is the first study to look at serotonin in the general population – it is unlikely to be the last.

Low serotonin has also been found in a condition which has strong links to both depression and violent behaviour: alcohol abuse. In one study, 37 clinic in-patients who were alcoholics had their serotonin measured immediately after intoxication and then after a period of supervised abstinence.[27] Just after drinking, their serotonin levels were the same as those in a control group of non-alcoholics, but as abstinence progressed, the levels plummeted.

This suggests that alcohol is used as a form of self-medication by certain vulnerable people to normalize their serotonin levels. Alcohol appears to release serotonin, and the person feels better for a while, but once alcohol is withdrawn, levels fall again and a vicious cycle starts up, as he or she turns to alcohol in an attempt to relieve the discomfort. Given the obvious downside of using alcohol in this way, maybe those affected should be offered more constructive ways of raising their serotonin levels.

A more recent report [28] confirmed that abstinent alcoholics have low serotonin; it also divided the patients into two types on the basis of their serotonin levels. Those with early onset of alcohol addiction (earlier than 25), who also showed signs of antisocial behaviour, had lower levels than those who began to abuse alcohol later in life and who blamed stress and anxiety for their lapses. The first group also tended to have a family history of alcohol abuse. Here serotonin acts as a pointer telling us that sometimes alcohol abuse is a biological problem, with strong genetic influences.

We have only touched upon the mountain of studies which links low brain serotonin to both depression and violence. The area is still controversial, particularly because the low serotonin involved in depression is probably not in the same part of the brain as the low serotonin involved in poor impulse control. For instance, the newly identified 'angry' and 'stress-driven' forms of depression, described above, appear to be driven by serotonin dysfunction – but no-one is yet sure which brain circuits and regions are involved.

However, the serotonin story, with all its variants, is beginning to be one of the most replicated findings in the area of biological psychiatry.[29] Moreover, the first hints are now emerging of a link between the serotonin story and the cortisol story. Treatment of rats with Prozac-type drugs not only normalizes serotonin, but also restores balance to the cortisol system.[30] One day soon, the next chapter of the serotonin saga will be written and the links between stress, depression and violence will become even clearer.

We will close this chapter with another visit to Sweden. (Incidentally, do not be surprised if a lot of the research mentioned in this book comes from Northern Europe. The Scandinavians are rated very highly for the quality of their work in biological psychiatry. They are not afraid to delve into the murkiest recesses of human behaviour. So perhaps it is no coincidence that the former Norwegian Prime Minister, Gro Harlem Brundtland, has made mental health top priority on taking office as Director General of the World Health Organization.)

We end in the same difficult and sad territory where we began this chapter – with the story of three attempted suicides who had killed (or tried to kill) their children.[31]

A 29-year old married mother of three was admitted to a mental hospital after drowning her four-month-old son. A few days earlier she had tried to strangle the same child and then threw herself downstairs. After treatment she returned home. Twenty years later, she again became depressed and convinced that her two surviving sons were dead. She tried to hang herself in hospital, and has since attempted suicide twice more.

A 36-year old man stabbed his 10-year old son, his wife and himself. The son died. The man had previously suffered acute depression, precipitated by marital conflict and gambling debts, taken a drug overdose, and had been scheduled for readmission to hospital on the day of the murder.

A 38 year old man tried to gas himself and the 4 year old daughter he was caring for after his divorce. They were both found unconscious by the girl's mother and resuscitated.

All of these patients were found to have abnormally low serotonin levels after the event. None of them had a previous history of violent behaviour, or of alcohol abuse, and we still cannot say whether the low serotonin was causal or not. But finding out more about serotonin is one important way forward in the prevention of further such tragedies (and lesser versions of them).

Before we can go any further in appreciating the colours of the human mood spectrum, we must first visit the place where they are created. In the next chapter, then, we will take a quick tour around the brain, and learn something of the tools of neuroscience.

CHAPTER TWO

Windows into the Brain

The whole spectrum of human emotion, from rage to despair, is generated by processes going on in the brain. And currently a revolution is underway; we can study the structure and activity of the brain in ever increasing detail, and so start to understand, as never before, what drives our behaviour and perhaps even find new ways of modifying it.

Before we examine that, though, we need to look at some of the structures, cells, chemicals, and circuits which will underpin the discussion that is to follow. We will also review some of the experimental techniques researchers use these days to take a look inside the brain.

This branch of science, by the way, is generally called *cognitive neuroscience*. *Cognition* comes from the Latin word *cognere*, to think. But brain scientists tend to use the term *cognition* in a broader sense to cover emotion, perception, thought and behaviour. This makes sense, because it is becoming ever more apparent that you cannot really separate these different mental functions. You may get scientists working in specific areas, like language or memory. But the challenge now is to integrate all these discoveries to create a true understanding of how the human mind works. Incidentally, we will not be looking at the relationship between the brain and the mind, nor the nature of human consciousness, here. We will just say that the brain is the organ of the mind, and leave it at that.

The basic brain

We live in a world increasingly dominated by communications and information technology, yet the most complex and sophisticated system of all resides inside our heads. The brain and nervous system process information from the outside world and arrange an appropriate (or sometimes, as we shall see, inappropriate) response.

At this superficial level, the analogy between the brain and a computer maybe has some validity (though as a working metaphor it is insultingly simple). Sensory stimuli – light, sound, touch and so on – are picked up by the outposts of the nervous system (known as the peripheral nervous system) and turned into electrical signals. These are conveyed along communication cables called nerves, through the spinal cord to the brain (together brain and spinal cord are called the central nervous system, or CNS).

These signals are processed via the interaction of many different areas of the brain. A response signal is generated, which is conveyed back through the nervous system, usually ending up in a muscle or an endocrine gland. Muscles generate movement, of course, so we can, for example, run away from danger. The endocrine glands secrete hormones, which act on target organs. The liver might be prompted to release stored glucose, say, to fuel the flight from danger (see Figure 1).

The interplay between the endocrine and nervous systems keeps us in tune with our environment throughout life. It is particularly important in the autonomic nervous system (ANS), which is involved in responding to stress. The ANS is divided into two branches: sympathetic and para-sympathetic. The sympathetic nervous system, which is kicked into action by stress (as mentioned in the last chapter) generates a state of 'red alert' – diversion of blood supply to the muscles, increased heart rate and breathing and so on – while the parasympathetic nervous system acts in the opposite way (we will examine this in chapter 4). Think of them like the controls of a car: the sympathetic branch is the accelerator, revving up the action, while the parasympathetic puts the brakes on things. They complement one another, adjusting your performance to what is happening outside.

The atoms of the mind

The basic unit of the nervous system is the *neuron* or nerve cell (just as atoms are the basic units of matter). The brain alone is reckoned to possess up to 100 billion neurons. They are supported by another type of cell called *glial cells*, which are even more numerous. A neuron has three parts: the cell body, a long fibre (up to one metre long in some neurons) called an axon, and numerous small projections called dendrites. Information passes from one neuron to another down the axon of one neuron to the dendrites of another (exactly how, we will discuss below).

Since each axon may divide into many thousands of branches at its terminus, and each neuron typically has around ten thousand dendrites

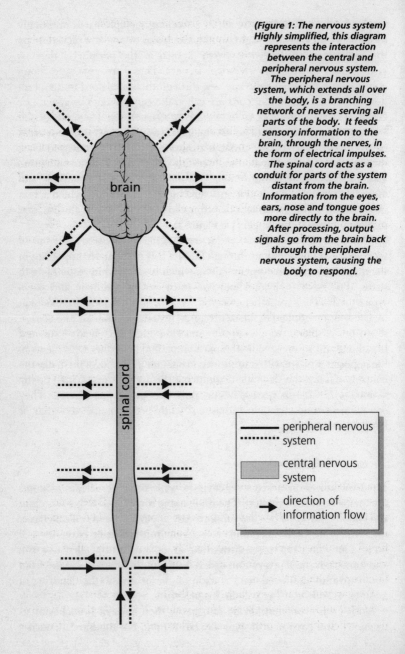

(Figure 1: The nervous system)
Highly simplified, this diagram represents the interaction between the central and peripheral nervous system. The peripheral nervous system, which extends all over the body, is a branching network of nerves serving all parts of the body. It feeds sensory information to the brain, through the nerves, in the form of electrical impulses. The spinal cord acts as a conduit for parts of the system distant from the brain. Information from the eyes, ears, nose and tongue goes more directly to the brain. After processing, output signals go from the brain back through the peripheral nervous system, causing the body to respond.

brain

spinal cord

——— peripheral nervous system
········· system

central nervous system

➤ direction of information flow

(each of which may receive input from many different neurons) the patterns of information flow through the brain are extremely complex, with trillions of possible connections.

The brain revealed

A naked brain looks very vulnerable; it consists of about one and a half kilograms of creamy porridge-like tissue (its consistency arising from being 75 per cent water). You can distinguish dark and pale areas of tissue, known as grey and white matter (hence the term 'grey matter' sometimes used to describe the brain or the intellect). Grey matter consists of cell bodies, while the white matter is an aggregation of axons.

Fortunately for our survival and well-being, the brain is the best-protected organ in the body. It is wrapped in three membranes called the meninges (these become infected in meningitis) and it floats in a bath of cerebrospinal fluid (CSF), which cushions it from shocks. CSF is found in the space between the inner and middle meninges, and also within spaces in the brain called the ventricles, which are useful landmarks when looking at brain scans.

The brain is vulnerable in another way too. It only occupies 2 per cent of the body's mass, but it consumes oxygen and glucose at ten times the rate of other tissues when the body is at rest. It relies on delivery of glucose via the bloodstream, for it has no fuel reserves of its own. Deprive a brain of oxygen for more than four minutes, and it may become irreversibly damaged. This is why cardiopulmonary resuscitation is so important if the heart stops pumping for any reason – you must keep the blood flowing to protect the brain.

The landscape of the brain

You probably know the town where you live pretty well: its streets, shops, green spaces, and landmarks. By the end of the next few pages, I hope you will be as familiar with the landscape between your ears. The language we use may be unfamiliar (the early brain anatomists were not exactly user-friendly in their terminology), but it will be well worth the effort, for you will then have (at the very least) a sketch map of the brain to hand for the discoveries which follow.

We start with a bird's eye view. From the top, you can see how the brain is divided into two hemispheres, like a walnut. It is bridged by a band of tissue called the *corpus callosum*, across which information flows from one hemisphere to the other. All the structures we will discuss are duplicated on the left and right hemispheres; however, for simplicity, they will be referred to in the singular.

And there the walnut analogy ends. Slice through a brain vertically and there are all manner of fascinating structures to be discovered, all of which derive from the two different ways in which the grey matter can be organized. In cortex tissue, the neuron bodies are stacked in layers. Alternatively the grey matter is organized in groups of spheres, called nuclei. Most of the structures we will mention are composed of nuclei.

There are four floors in our upward journey through the brain (see Figure 2). The basement is the *brain stem*, which connects the brain to the spinal cord. In evolutionary terms this is the part of the brain that appeared first, and it is sometimes called the reptilian brain because it resembles the

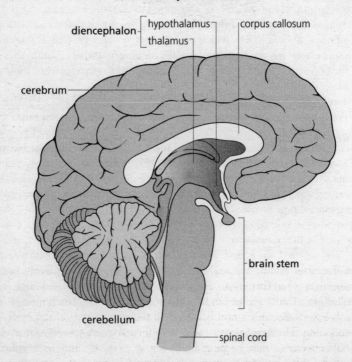

(Figure 2: The four storeys of the brain)
A vertical section through the human brain reveals the brain stem (basement), cerebellum (mezzanine), the diencephalon (ground floor) and the cerebrum (first floor). The corpus callosum is the thick band of tissue which joins the right and left hemispheres of the brain.

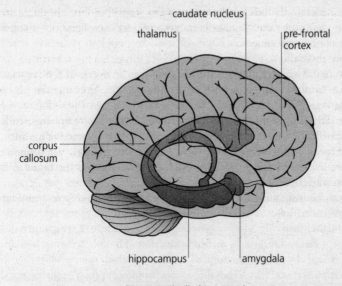

caudate nucleus

thalamus

pre-frontal cortex

corpus callosum

hippocampus

amygdala

(Figure 3: The limbic system)
Lying deep inside the brain, beneath the cerebral cortex, the limbic system
is a collection of structures, some of which are important in the generation
and processing of emotion. Here (in vertical section) the hippocampus,
amygdala and thalamus are shown, along with the caudate nucleus,
which is one of the basal ganglia. The prefrontal cortex is also shown; connections
between this region and the limbic region are (put simply) for the civilised
and appropriate expression of emotion.

brain of modern reptiles. The brain stem is common to all animals, and it regulates the most basic functions like breathing, heartbeat and state of consciousness. Indeed, the clinical definition of death is the cessation of all activity in the brain stem.

The ground floor is known as the *diencephalon* or, sometimes, the mammalian brain, because it first appeared with the evolution of mammals. Our first stop on the ground floor is at the *thalamus*. This collection of nuclei is the brain's relay station; all information from the body passes through it and is routed to the correct part of the brain for processing. The *hypothalamus* – which, as the name suggests, lies beneath it – is concerned with keeping the body in a steady state – regulating appetite, thirst, responses to stress and so on. Close by is the hippocampus, which was mentioned in the previous chapter. Next to this you find the almond-shaped *amygdala* which, as we shall see, is important in the generation of fear and maybe other emotions (see Figure 3).

The mezzanine floor houses the *cerebellum* (Latin for 'little brain'), that part of the brain which controls movement and co-ordination: alcohol affects neurons in the cerebellum which is why people may stagger when they are drunk.

The first floor, just underneath the skull, is the home of the *cerebrum*, which accounts for 85 per cent of human brain tissue. The large size of the cerebrum is the most striking difference between human and other animal brains. The outer layer of the cerebrum is made up of cortex tissue, which accounts for the majority of the brain's surface. It is around 2 mm thick, and deeply fissured and wrinkled (back to the walnut analogy). If you were to smooth out the human cerebral cortex, it would be the size of about four A4 sheets of paper.

Deep fissures, known as *sulci*, divide the cerebral cortex into four sections called lobes. Further fissures within the lobes themselves divide them further into ridges called *gyri* (singular *gyrus*), some of which turn out to be significant landmarks in brain function. The lobes themselves are marked out by brain anatomists into numbered areas, following a numbering system first used in the famous Brodmann map of the cerebral cortex, produced in 1908. Many of the Brodmann areas are merely structural landmarks, but some also have a functional designation, like the speech areas.

Now we will visit the various departments of the first floor, starting from the rear. The *occipital lobe*, at the back of the head, deals with visual signals. Moving forwards, the *parietal lobe* at the top of the head is concerned with body awareness, orientation and movement. The *temporal lobe*, above the ear, deals with sound, speech and some aspects of memory. Then we come to an area you will be hearing a lot more about but which, in a way, is the most mysterious – the *frontal lobe*. The higher mental functions, such as reasoning, planning, self-expression and maybe even consciousness itself, rely upon whatever happens in the frontal lobes (see Figure 4).

The pre-frontal lobes of the human brain, just behind the forehead, have increased dramatically in size during the course of mammalian evolution. Measurements on skulls ancient and modern show around 29 per cent expansion in the volume of the pre-frontal lobes in humans, compared with 17 per cent in chimps and only 3 per cent in cats. A large amount of the association cortex, involved in higher processing of sensory input, appears to be located in the pre-frontal lobe.

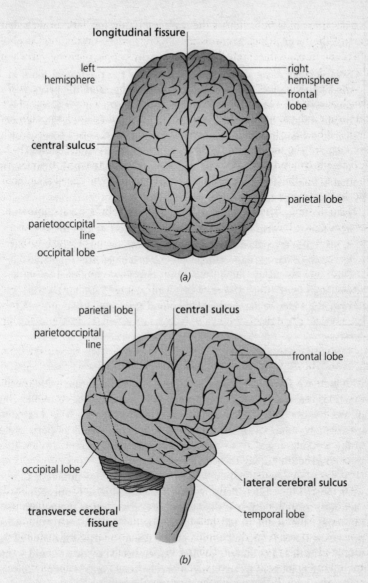

(Figure 4: The lobes of the cerebral cortex)
The outer surface of the cerebral cortex is divided into four main areas, as shown: frontal, parietal, temporal and occipital. The fissures which are the anatomical borders of the lobes are also shown. A is a view from above, while B is a vertical section.

BOX 4.   *A knife in the head*

Some of our ideas about the importance of the pre-frontal lobes in modulating human thought and behaviour come from the practice of psychosurgery, which was once used as a treatment for intractable mental illness. The usual operation that was performed, known as leucotomy (or *pre-frontal lobotomy*), involved cutting the nerve fibres which connect the frontal lobes to the rest of the brain. It was introduced in the 1930s by the Portuguese neurologist Antonio Egas Moniz; he had seen that a 'neurotic' monkey had calmed down after undergoing the procedure and thought it might be a good way of sedating difficult humans. Between 1936 and 1978, 35,000 people in the United States had leucotomies. And in the UK, it was quite common (at least in the 1970s), to see long-stay patients with the telltale scar on their forehead. But leucotomy did more than calm people down: it had a drastic and terrible effect on personality, for it left patients devoid of emotional response. Although Egas Moniz was rewarded with a Nobel Prize for his work in 1949, the widespread practice of leucotomy gradually died out.

Circuits and systems

Although we have just linked various parts of the brain with specific functions, the reality is far more complex. Brain 'mapping' is useful – but please do not get carried away with this metaphor. It is becoming increasingly apparent that it is more appropriate to think of parts of the brain working together to achieve a particular function, rather than isolated structures doing the job by themselves.

As far as we know, the best way to look at brain functioning is to start with the neuron. Each neuron *can*, in theory, make connections with thousands of others. But if they were all connected up to one another, randomly, the result would be chaos, not the sophisticated, organized processing that lets you talk on the phone while you assess the state of the weather outside, feel hungry (or not), remember who you are, and so on. In practice, it looks as if each individual cell makes contact with (relatively) few others, through its dendrites and neurons. The neurons it 'talks' to could, however, be in other brain regions (the hippocampus talking to the temporal cortex, for instance, when long-term memory is laid down). These circuits connect brain regions to form systems, which are concerned with various mental functions. The vital thing to remember is that we do not understand *any* of these systems in any great detail at the current time. All we can say is that, maybe, we have tabs on some parts of a fairly complex jigsaw.

What we can say is that information flow between the cerebral cortex and various structures in the diencephalon (the 'ground floor' of the brain), like the amygdala, is extremely important in consideration of moods and emotion. The structures thought to be involved in emotion are often considered together and called the limbic system. Put simply, the raw emotion is generated within these areas and then acted upon by the more rational cerebral cortex. (However, some brain researchers feel that the limbic system is an artificial construct, for the idea that emotion is actually 'generated' there is probably a gross over-simplification, if not downright misleading or even wrong, and merely a reflection of our current state of ignorance on the subject. Nevertheless, we will continue to take the liberty of using the term, just for convenience.)

The chemical brain

The flow of information throughout the nervous system is electrochemical in nature. Electrical impulses travel down axons, but they cannot leap from the end of an axon to the dendrite of the next neuron in the circuit. The gap between the neurons is known as a synapse, and communication across it happens via chemicals known as neurotransmitters.

BOX 5   *Bridging the gap*

The axon of a resting neuron is like an unconnected battery. It has a negative charge inside, and a positive one outside, the charge separation being known as a potential difference. This comes about because of the differing concentrations of ions (electrically charged atoms and molecules) on either side of the axon. In particular, the concentration of sodium ions is 25 to 50 times higher outside the axon than inside.

When an electrical impulse arises within the cell body of a neuron, the effect is a bit like connecting up a battery. The impulse starts to travel down the axon, and as it does so, ion channels within the axon membrane open up, allowing sodium ions to rush in. This alters the potential difference between the outside and inside of the axon membrane: the inside is now positively charged relative to the outside –

---

a change which propagates the wave of electrical activity along the axon until it reaches the terminus. The whole process is known as the firing of the neuron. After firing, various ion channels open and close in the membrane to restore the neuron to its resting state, ready to fire again.

Then what? The axon termini contact dendrites or, less commonly, cell bodies or even other axons in neighbouring neurons. At one time it was thought that the networks of neurons in the brain were continuous, like a railway system. Then the Nobel Prize-winning Spanish neuroanatomist Santiago Ramón y Cajal (1852–1934) showed that there was a distinct gap, known as a synapse, between the axon terminus of one cell and the next neuron.

Later research showed that the electrical impulse does not leap, as a spark, across the synapse. Instead the pre-synaptic neuron releases a chemical called a neurotransmitter into the synapse from a small storage compartment called a vesicle.

Neurotransmitter molecules travel across the synapse and then bind tightly to receptor molecules on the surface of the post-synaptic dendrite, like a key fitting into a lock (see Figure 5). The act of binding is like a switch, turning the post-synaptic neuron on or off. There are two types of neurotransmitter – *excitatory*, which turn a neuron on, and *inhibitory*, which turn it off. Once binding has occurred, the neurotransmitter's job is done, and it is cleared away by one of a number of mechanisms. Some neurotransmitters are broken down by enzymes, while others are recycled by being transported back to the pre-synaptic neuron.

There may be around 200 different neurotransmitters in the brain, but only around 50 have so far been identified. Each one is confined to specific brain circuits, and can home in on any one of a range of receptors, depending upon the particular circuit it happens to be servicing (there are an estimated 300 different subtypes of receptor; identifying them is currently one of the hottest topics in brain science). Indeed, it is the neurotransmitters which make the circuits come alive, and which give brain systems their complexity and versatility. The same neurotransmitter may flow through many brain areas, and the same brain area can use several neurotransmitters.

As we shall see, neurotransmitters are of major importance in mood disorders (we have already touched on serotonin in the last chapter) and most psychiatric drugs, such as antidepressants, work by modifying neurotransmitter action in some way.

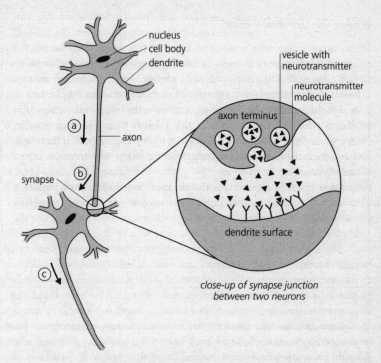

(Figure 5: Transmission across a synapse)
Two neurons are shown on the left-hand side of the diagram, with the direction of transmission of the information shown by arrows. An electrical impulse passes down the axon of the top neuron (a), triggering the release of neurotransmitter across the synapse (b) which causes the electrical impulse to travel through the dendrite, cell body and axon of the lower neuron (c). A close-up of the neuron is shown to the right-hand side of the figure. The electrical impulse causes excitatory (or inhibitory) neurotransmitter molecules to spill out of their vesicles into the synapse. They dock onto specific receptor molecules on the dendritic surfaces of the second neuron, causing the neuron to fire (or not) as they do so.

What is more, levels of neurotransmitter molecules in various brain circuits go up and down, and so too do the numbers of receptor molecules available to interact with them. So the circuits that carry information around the brain are in a constant state of flux; sometimes buzzing with activity, other times sluggish. So the anatomy and chemistry of the brain interact to create a level of sophistication which is quite breathtaking. The fine details of neural connections will vary from one person to another: your brain is truly unique.

Where the emotions rage

Before we go any further, we need to try to pin down what we mean by emotions, feelings, and moods, before we can even begin to discuss how they can be explained in terms of brain science. A useful working definition of emotion is a state of mind, generated at an unconscious level by specific systems within the brain. Feelings are the conscious realization of our emotions, while moods are perhaps best thought of as a kind of emotional colour filter through which we see the world – blue for sad, red for angry and so on. It is hard to distinguish between mood and emotion because even psychologists tend to use the terms interchangeably (thus clinical depression is, strictly speaking, a mood disorder, which correctly labels it as a state that persists over time, but you will often hear it called an emotional disorder too).

On the other hand we *can* (and should) make a clear distinction between emotions and feelings. For emotions are not the exclusive preserve of human beings. Charles Darwin, as part of his studies of biological evolution, noted that humans and animals both have emotions, which can be seen by a study of their facial expressions (if you have a pet you probably already know this). In 1872 he summarized his conclusions in *The Expression of Emotion in Man and Animals*. Of course, Darwin would have been interested in emotions because they have survival value; fear and anger drive behaviours which allow escape or confrontation of threats to any living organism. We cannot really comment on whether worms, prawns, spiders or even plants, have emotions because they do not possess a true brain (that is, a specialized organ located at the top of a spinal cord as is found in all animals with backbones). But they certainly exhibit defensive behaviour when the occasion calls for it (incidentally, so do bacteria – in the most ancient version of chemical warfare, they secrete antibiotics to defend their territory against competing species).

The basic emotions are thought to be hard-wired into the brain: in other words, they are produced automatically in response to the appropriate stimulus. We cannot help our emotions, although we may be able to control them (and when we cannot, it creates trouble, because modern human survival skills do not have a great deal to do with evading sabre-toothed tigers).

In the last 40 years or so, psychologists have produced various lists of these basic emotions. One of the most useful comes from Paul Ekman[1] who cites surprise, happiness, anger, fear, disgust and sadness as the emotions common to all species with a brain. What is especially useful for our discussion is the link Ekman makes with the various facial expressions of emotion, for the brain mechanisms linking to these in humans are now being studied, as we will see.

Naturally, the spectrum of human emotional experience contains many more subtle hues than those laid out in Ekman's palette. Psychologist Robert Plutchik[2] has a very appealing way of putting it: mixing the emotions like colours on a paint chart, so we get guilt from blending fear (of the consequences) and disgust (at oneself), alarm from a mixture of fear and surprise and so on. These blends of emotion, such as gratitude, shame, and pride, according to Richard Lazarus of the University of Berkeley in Southern California, are probably uniquely human.[3]

How a feeling is produced is complex, and barely understood by psychologists. Put simply, an input – which could be visual (something on the TV news), auditory (a phone conversation) and so on – will register in the cortex (via the thalamus), make links to memory areas, and so be processed, sent back to the emotional centres (which produce accompanying bodily sensations, like a chill up the spine), and then, finally, make you feel something on a conscious level.

What is more, different people can have a spectrum of feelings in response to the same stimulus. Take guilt, and a simple antisocial act like fare-dodging. One person might be tempted to do this occasionally, on a quiet train route where inspectors are rare and the station is deserted. Yet they will be aware of a nagging sense of discomfort all through the journey and feel relieved when they reach their destination. For someone else, avoiding paying a train fare (and income tax, too, perhaps) might be a way of life. If they are caught they will bluff their way out of the situation if they can. They will not feel guilt; in their view, it is the fault of the train operator (or the tax man) if the money is not collected. Being unacquainted with guilt is a key feature of having an antisocial personality (we will discuss this further in chapter 6).

Some people, though, are at the other end of the spectrum – pervaded by a vague feeling of having done wrong, even though they have never dodged a fare in their lives or fiddled their tax. Yet they may feel as uncomfortable within themselves as that occasional fare evader who is worried about getting caught. This kind of discomfort is a hallmark of depression.

Looking at how different people see the world through filters of different emotional colours is, of course, one of our main themes. It is all very subtle and complex, so it may seem rather demeaning that we have to start our investigations with the experimental activities of rodents. You will be surprised, however, by how much has been discovered about human emotions by studying rats.

The anatomy of fear

The only emotion that is at all well understood in terms of the brain is fear, and even that has only been studied to any great extent in rats, thanks to the research of Joseph LeDoux and his contemporaries.[4] Fear is a universal emotion which plays a key role in survival. In modern humans it also lies at the root of many psychological disorders, such as post-traumatic stress disorder and panic disorder.

In animals, you can elicit the emotion of fear by conditioning; that is, rats are given an electric shock and exposed to a particular sound at the same time. So they learn to associate the sound (harmless in itself) with an unpleasant experience (the shock). Soon, they will respond with the physiological characteristics of fear – increased heart rate, blood pressure, raised fur, all of which can be measured – to the sound alone.

BOX 6   *Tracing the origins of fear*

To get at what is happening in the brain during fear, Joseph LeDoux, of New York University, followed a standard experimental procedure, which is to make lesions at various points on the supposed information flow circuits in the brain. Since the fear stimulus was a sound, LeDoux knew it would travel via the thalamus to the auditory cortex, in the temporal lobe. Making lesions in the cortex did not extinguish fear, so the fear response originated lower down in the brain, he reasoned.

He found that making a lesion in the thalamus, or even lower down in the brain, did prevent the fear from occurring. So it seemed that the thalamus was routing the emotional content of the sound stimulus (fear) elsewhere; the signal was being split into two streams – one to the cortex for identification, perception, and understanding, and one to a region where the emotional content would be registered.

But how to work out where the second output from the thalamus was going among the millions of possible routes? Fortunately, there is a way. LeDoux injected a tracer during his experiments – a chemical that travels up and down axons, piggy-backing upon substances like neurotransmitters that normally go the same route. A tracer is linked to a coloured molecule, so its progress can be followed by studying microscopic slides of the tissue involved (inevitably, this does involve sacrificing the animal).

The technique shows what the connections are between neurons. In

---

this case it revealed what had hitherto not been known – that the second output from the thalamus led to the amygdala. What is more, when the flow of information between these two sites was interrupted by making a lesion in the rats' brains, fear conditioning was prevented.[5]

The key message here is that there are two response routes to an emotional stimulus. One, which Joseph LeDoux calls the 'quick and dirty' route, goes via the amygdala which orchestrates a range of physiological outputs, such as the secretion of cortisol from the adrenals, increase of heart rate, blood pressure and so on. These can feed back into the cerebral cortex at their leisure, inducing an awareness of the emotion of fear; meanwhile, however, the stimulus has also been relayed by the thalamus to the pre-frontal cortex where a slower, more considered response is assembled. This involves memory (links to the hippocampus), reasoning, and language. The body may have begun to respond to the stimulus via the amygdala – a strategy which has an obvious primitive survival value – but there are links from the prefrontal cortex to the amygdala which can override this response. This kicks into play if you are tempted to run away from a rustling sound in a city park: it might be a deadly snake, but your cortex summons up your past experience via the memory area in the hippocampus, and tells you it is not.

Where humans run into trouble is if these feedback links from the pre-frontal cortex to the amygdala are not strong enough. What works for rats is turning out to work for humans as well. People with damage in the amygdala have impaired fear responses, for instance. They cannot be conditioned to feel fear and they have problems in recognizing fear expressions in others.

Moreover, the amygdala has been also been pinpointed as one place where anger flares; abnormal electrical activity here can trigger violence. Perhaps this is not so surprising if we think in terms of survival; you can either run away from the threat (fear) or fight it (anger).

It is too soon (and probably too simple) to say that the amygdala is the seat of emotion; other brain areas are probably also important.

Emotional molecules

Brain regions are only part of the story underpinning emotion and its disorders because, as you remember, they are connected together by circuits powered by neurotransmitters. For the purposes of our discussion we are going to focus upon the big three: *noradrenaline*, *dopamine* and *serotonin*, the neurotransmitters of the emotional circuits.

Malfunctioning of these circuits goes hand in hand with mental illness, particularly depression and schizophrenia. Nearly all the drugs which act on the mind do so by intervening, in some way, in the action of the big three.

The main noradrenaline, dopamine and serotonin circuits were all worked out by Swedish researchers Kjell Kuxe and Annica Dhalström in the mid-1960s.[6] They exposed slices of rat brain to formaldehyde vapour, which makes both noradrenaline and dopamine glow with a green fluorescence, therefore neurons containing these neurotransmitters can easily be seen under a microscope and their location in the brain pinpointed to give the actual pathways. Further chemical treatment can distinguish between noradrenaline and dopamine neurons. A similar technique was used to trace the serotonin pathways.

This work revealed that all three neurotransmitters trace out complex, highly branched circuits in the brain, involving a high density of neurons in the mid-brain areas, like the amygdala, which are important in emotion.

The noradrenaline circuits originate in a tiny area (containing just 3000 neurons) in the brain stem called the *locus coeruleus* (from the Latin for 'blue place' because this structure does look blue when dissected out under a microscope). Noradrenaline neurons in the locus coeruleus branch out far and wide over the brain – to the hippocampus, the amygdala, the cerebellum and to the highest portions of the cerebral cortex. It is reckoned that they may make contact with as many as one-third to a half of all neurons in the brain. Noradrenaline seems to be involved in a major way in our emotional response to the world, in general levels of arousal and energy; lowered levels are associated with depression and topping them up with antidepressant medication improves mood. Dopamine circuits were also found to originate in the brain stem, in an area called the *substantia nigra* (again, Latin, meaning 'black substance', because it is heavily pigmented with melanin, the substance that gives colour to skin and hair). From here, one circuit leads to a region called the *corpus striatum*, which is concerned with co-ordination of movement. Too little dopamine can affect this circuit and lead to the uncontrolled movements of Parkinson's disease. Another circuit starts in a structure called the *tegmentum*, close to the substantia nigra, and branches into emotional areas like the amygdala and the *nucleus accumbens*, a small region which could be a crucial point in a circuit which generates pleasure after food, sex or taking drugs, like cocaine. Too little dopamine is linked with schizophrenia, and maybe some forms of depression.

Finally, serotonin pathways also begin in the brain stem, in a grouping of cells called the *raphe nuclei*. Connections ramify all over the brain, but are especially concentrated in the emotional areas, including the amygdala and the pre-frontal cortex. Serotonin tends to have a generally inhibitory effect on impulse, and promotes a general feeling of calm and well-being. Peter Kramer, who has written extensively about Prozac, likens serotonin to a molecular police force, creating feelings of safety, security and courage, and promoting orderly and sensible behaviour.[7] However, we are far from having a firm understanding of exactly what role each neurotransmitter plays in the generation of different mood states.

Spying on the brain

Animal experiments, such as those described in Box 6, have brought us a long way in understanding the brain, but they have obvious limitations. We really need to study human brains – preferably live ones. Until fairly recently, this was confined to investigating people who had contracted some form of brain damage, such as a stroke or tumour. But this is a rather hit and miss method: you cannot really will someone to have a stroke in the pre-frontal lobe because you would like to know what this region does, and how the patient will manage if it is wiped out. Instead, the researcher has to rely on an 'interesting' patient being in the right place at the right time (and being willing, of course, to be poked at by curious doctors in the interests of science).

A skull gives up its secrets

One classic example, which is quite relevant to our discussion, is that of Phineas Gage, a 19th-century railway worker in Vermont, whose frontal lobe was pierced by a steel rod during an explosion. Remarkably, he survived and was pronounced fully recovered within two months of the catastrophe. But as time went on, it became apparent that although his speech, memory and other faculties were intact, something had gone horribly wrong.

Formerly a popular, responsible and law-abiding worker, Gage became a foul-mouthed, drunken drifter, unable to discipline himself or plan ahead. He even found a job as a circus attraction, displaying the hole in his head along with the iron bar. (Remember, in the 19th century, human 'freaks' were displayed in a way that would horrify us today.) He appears to have developed epilepsy, and died of a major convulsion, aged 38, in 1861.

No autopsy was performed at the time, but more than 130 years later, Hanna Damasio and colleagues at the University of Iowa returned to Gage's skull. They took measurements, and recreated a three-dimensional image of the skull and the famous iron bar on a computer. From this, they could work out the possible routes of the bar through Gage's brain. It turned out that most of the damage was probably to the ventromedial region of the frontal lobe.[8] *Ventro* means underside (from the Latin *ventrus* for belly) and *medial* means close to a midline. So you have to imagine this important region being behind the forehead (the frontal lobe) but on the underside, towards the middle (a couple of inches behind the space between your eyebrows would be a good approximation). This area is now known to be important both in rational decision making and, through its connections to the limbic region, in the processing of emotion. No wonder poor Gage was precipitated onto the road to destruction.

A 20th-century Phineas Gage has been described by leading neurologist Antonio Damasio.[9] Elliott had been a successful businessman, until a large tumour began to grow from the meninges, compressing his frontal lobes upward, from below. The tumour had to be cut out, to save his life, but a chunk of pre-frontal lobe was also removed along with it – in just the areas where Gage's brain had been damaged.

Elliott appeared to be intellectually normal, but could no longer hold down a job, because he was completely incapable of managing his time or making decisions. He also admitted to being emotionally numb. The brain damage he had sustained had severed connections between the frontal lobe and the limbic region, including the amygdala (the effect being similar to a pre-frontal leucotomy). Gut feelings could no longer drive his decisions so, in short, he could not make any that made any sense.

Other patients with damage to the amygdala were unable to assess people they did not know on the basis of their facial expressions; they were unable to recognize angry expressions, or to assess people for approachability or trustworthiness. One woman in the experiment commented that in real life she could not judge people for character, and had a tendency to be indiscriminate in her contacts.[10] But although informative, these cases are rare. A fuller understanding of human emotions and moods can only come from brain scanning – technologies that give a window onto the brain, its structure and its activity.

Images of the brain

There are now three main techniques for obtaining images of the living brain, without cutting into it. These are magnetic resonance imaging (MRI), positron emission tomography (PET) and functional magnetic resonance imaging (fMRI). (For more details of the different technologies involved, see Boxes 7–9.) When people talk about brain scanning or brain imaging, they are generally referring to the use of any one of these three techniques.

You may already be familiar with MRI, as most large hospitals now have an MRI scanner. It is used in routine diagnosis of neurological conditions, such as brain tumours and multiple sclerosis, and for examination of the joints (most top football clubs use a portable MRI scanner to investigate knee and ankle injuries on the spot). MRI is used to look at the structure of the brain. Remember, evidence that stress and depression are linked with shrinkage of the hippocampus was gathered from MRI scans. But it cannot reveal anything about the brain's activity.

BOX 7 *Magnetic resonance imaging (MRI)*

MRI provides images of the brain's structure, although it does not reveal anything about the activity of the brain. It uses the magnetic properties of the water molecules in brain tissue. The nuclei of the hydrogen atoms in the water act like tiny bar magnets. When a strong magnetic field is applied to the brain, during the scan, the hydrogen nuclei line up in the direction of the field. Then they are exposed to a magnetic pulse from a transmitter which is built into the scanner. This momentarily kicks them out of alignment, but they soon 'relax' back to their original position, emitting energy in the form of radio waves as they do so.

An antenna picks up these radio signals and feeds them back to a computer for analysis. The strength and timing of the signals depends on the type of tissue they come from. The computer uses this information to create a set of images which correspond to 'slices' through the brain and these in turn can be built up to give a three-dimensional picture.

For the patient, or research volunteer (except for people with metal parts, like pacemakers, which are affected by a magnetic field), MRI is completely safe and painless. The only drawback is that some people find the scanner a bit claustrophobic, and those of a nervous disposition will not like the series of loud clicks that occur as the scanner goes through its paces.

PET scanning is generally only used in research. It involves injecting a chemical with a radioactive 'tag' which can be monitored by the scanning, and it can do two things. If you inject glucose, the parts of the brain which are most active can be revealed (they 'light up', in scanspeak) because they take up the most glucose. So researchers can look at which regions of the brain 'light up' (or stay dark) during routine mental tasks, by getting volunteers to stick their heads in the scanner while they are memorizing poems or counting backwards in sevens, and so on. It is also possible to investigate the brain activity in mental disorders like depression or schizophrenia with PET scans (we shall look at this later). This application is known as functional mapping – looking at which parts of the brain do what. As we pointed out above, this approach should not be taken too literally, for we should be thinking of parts of the brain working as a co-ordinated system, rather than assigning tasks to specific regions.

The second, and more up and coming, application of PET is for functional neurochemistry; that is, looking at how drugs act upon neurotransmitter receptors within the brain. This allows researchers to see brain activity at a molecular level and may lead to better drug treatments, although it is still in its early stages.

Box 8 *Positron emission tomography (PET)*

PET scanning monitors the activity of the brain, in real time. To map areas of increased neuronal activity, the scan looks at what is known as regional cerebral blood flow (rCBF). Since the blood carries glucose, rCBF is mapped by injecting radioctive glucose and then monitoring the radiation it gives off (in the form of particles called positrons) with a device called a gamma camera. This radioactive marker reveals the pathway of the rCBF. Naturally, many parts of the brain are going to be active at any given time, so the scanner's computer compares control images with rCBF in the region of interest. The strikingly pretty PET images that appear in scientific journals have been subjected to a great deal of computer processing.

With PET you can inject any chemical you like, so long as it has a radioactive 'tag' that enables it to be tracked on its journey through the brain. Advances in radiochemistry (making chemicals with the appropriate radioactive tags – no mean feat) have extended the scope of PET scanning to allow the study of what goes on at neurotransmitter level: so-called functional neurochemistry.

For instance, researchers are looking at both dopamine receptors (in schizophrenia) and serotonin receptors (in depression). They inject chemicals called *radioligands* which bind to the receptor and allow it to be visualized on the camera, via the radioactive tag. This gives us some idea of the state of the receptors (up- or down-regulated, and in which areas of the brain) in these mental disorders, although the research is still preliminary.[11]

Finally, fMRI can, like PET, measure brain activity, but it is completely non-invasive, as no injection is involved. fMRI gives sharper, more detailed images than PET. It is also a research tool, and is not currently as widespread as PET. However, it will probably become more useful than PET in the future, because volunteers will be able to have more scans (no radioactivity) which means more data will be available.

BOX 9   *Functional magnetic resonance imaging (fMRI)*

The drawback to PET scanning is that it does involve injection of a radioactive substance. While the dose is very low, the technique is still restricted, for safety reasons, to one session per patient per year (during which a maximum of 12 scans might be done). That severely limits the amount of data available.

fMRI is another way to get the same (or even better) information, without the risks and restrictions. The oxygenated blood which permeates an active region of the brain acts as a probe in fMRI because the magnetic properties of oxygenated haemoglobin (the protein which carries oxygen in the blood) differ from those of deoxygenated haemoglobin. The image is obtained in the same way as an MRI image.

Genetics and brain science

It is all very well that a scan can reveal that someone has an underactive pre-frontal cortex, or too many serotonin receptors. But imaging cannot tell us the *reason* for brain dysfunction. Sometimes the cause is obvious, as in the cases of Phineas Gage, or Elliott, described above. But sometimes the cause may lie hidden in a person's genetic make-up.

We are on the verge of uncovering the entire map of the human genome (the sum of our genetic material), and soon everyone's genetic secrets will be out of the closet. Indeed, it is already impossible to ask any question in biology or medicine without considering the genetic angle.

But the area of genes and behaviour is extremely controversial. Yes, mental illnesses do appear to run in families, but the original idea that a single gene may be involved now appears to be totally wrong. Over the years, single genes have been linked to schizophrenia, manic depression, and alcoholism, and in each case the discoveries have not been independently replicated.

What now seems likely is that there are many different genes which govern brain function and behaviour, acting in combination with one another. This could explain why there are so many different types of depression, for instance. Maybe each type corresponds to a different collection of behaviour genes?

It might also shed light on why a mental illness sometimes occurs when there is no family history. Supposing one parent had several of the relevant genes, but not enough to cross the threshold to illness, and the other had a similar complement. If a child inherited both sets, this could be sufficient to tip the balance and cause the child to have problems.

Finally, the way in which genes interact with the environment is also important, so two people could have a similar complement of genes that predispose to, say, violent behaviour, but only one gets into trouble – because they have different backgrounds. These (largely undiscovered) genes are best viewed as susceptibility genes for mental disorders: they increase the risk of developing problems but are not the sole, or even the major, cause of them.

With all these caveats, it is still possible to look forward to getting new insights into aggression and depression from genetic studies. Already three relevant genes have been discovered, and there will be many more. A variant of the dopamine receptor called DRD4 appears to be linked with novelty-seeking behaviour (the media could not resist calling this the gene 'for' cheap thrills, but of course this is just wrong: there is no single gene 'for' anything in the behavioural arena).[12] It has also been shown that this gene variant is more common in people with attention deficit hyperactivity disorder (ADHD) and less common in those with major depression.[13] A variant in the serotonin transporter (a molecule that takes the neurotransmitter for recycling) has been linked to anxiety[14] and to manic depression.[15] Finally, a variant in one of the serotonin receptors has been implicated in schizophrenia.[16]

These genetic studies will be discussed in more detail later on. But now we move to considering why these scientific studies are so important, by considering how far stress, crime and depression have affected people both today, and throughout the course of history.

BOX 10   *Gene hunting*

Gene hunting in a complex disorder like depression (where you have no idea what gene you are looking for) starts with looking at the patient's family. Medical records are used to construct a family tree, which reveals how the disease has been passed down through the generations.

Next, DNA samples from living family members are analysed. The aim is to look for patterns within the DNA which are the same among family members who have the disease and different from the patterns found in those who have not got it. In other words, the researchers look for the 'signature' of the disease within the DNA; this technique is called linkage analysis.

To understand how linkage analysis works, it also helps to know just a little about the nature of DNA. (You will then also be in a position to appreciate the next media announcement that the gene 'for' a particular disease has been discovered: you will know what has actually been done.)

DNA is the chemical from which our genes are made – a gene is just a stretch of DNA. Physically, genes are located within the nucleus of each cell of the body, within tiny thread-like structures called *chromosomes* (which can be seen under a microscope). Humans have 22 pairs of chromosomes, plus a pair of sex chromosomes, which are the same in females, and named XX, and different in males, where they are labelled XY.

The DNA molecule is built up of a chemical code, consisting of four chemical units called bases. There are four kinds of bases, known, for short, as A, C, T and G, and it is the sequence of the bases in a gene which gives it biochemical meaning.

For each gene 'maps' onto (or, as it is often put, codes for) a different protein molecule. Proteins are the master molecules of cells: most of them are enzymes, biological catalysts which facilitate the synthesis of other important molecules like neurotransmitters, hormones, and all the other chemicals the body needs to keep going.

Proteins, in turn, are built up from chemical sub-units called amino acids and these must be assembled in the correct order for the protein to function correctly. The correspondence between a gene and its protein

---

involves reading off the bases in sets of three, each 'triplet' corresponding to a given amino acid. So you can translate the sequence of the gene into the sequence of the protein (this is all done, in practice, by enzymes in the cell). The gene therefore has the sequence of the protein written into it in the form of a chemical code.

Mistakes, known as mutations, in the gene sequence (an A where there should be a C, for example) may translate into mistakes in the protein function, and this in turn could (although it does not always) cause biochemical havoc. Back to the brain for a second: if there were a mutation in a gene that codes for an important brain protein, then you could get brain dysfunction as a result.

As it happens, the human genome varies a lot in its sequence between individuals, even if you discount actual mutations. (One more complication: we have a lot of DNA that does not actually code for proteins, so any differences in this would not be classed as a mutation, but it is still useful for identification purposes.) So at one point along the genome, let us say that some members of your family may have a C, where others have a G. The existence of such variations is known as *polymorphism* (from the Greek meaning 'different forms').

Now back to the linkage analysis. Suppose A is the gene involved with the disease in our hypothetical family. We start off with no idea what A is, where it is, or what it does – so there is no point in looking for it directly. This will be a gene which everyone possesses but, like all genes, it comes in a number of variants known as alleles, which are slightly different in sequence. Let us say that one allele we will call A1 is associated with the disease. Family members with A1 have the disease, while those with another allele A2 do not. Close to A1 is a polymorphism, known as a marker, which we *can* detect by DNA analysis of the samples. We find the people with the disease have the polymorphism, and the healthy ones do not (or the other way round – it does not matter; the important thing is that in the marker we have the first 'letter' of the disease signature in the DNA). This is exciting, because now we are on the track of A1. The closer it is on the chromosome to A, the more likely it is that the polymorphism and A1 are inherited together. The two are said to be linked. Further analysis will eventually reveal the identity of A.

Once a linked marker has been defined, it can be used as a diagnostic test even though the susceptibility gene itself has not been identified. However, great caution needs to be used in interpreting results. The closer a linked marker is to the suspect gene on the chromosome, the higher the possibility that an individual has inherited the gene along with the marker. But, finding a linked marker is only a staging post on the way to finding the gene itself. Initially it reveals on which of the chromosomes the gene of interest lies. Then, further studies, with more markers, narrow down the region of the chromosome where it is located, until the gene itself is actually pinned down. Sometimes it turns out that the gene is already known, but the surprise could be to find it involved in the disease of interest. Or it may be a completely new discovery. Whichever is the case, the final task is to sequence the gene and confirm that there are differences (i.e. mutations) in the sequence between people with the disease and the general population. This stage may mark the end of the search for the gene – but it is just the beginning of understanding what the gene does in the disease

BOX 11 *Twin studies*

Our understanding of the role which genetics plays in disease owes much to the goodwill of various groups of twins who have let researchers monitor their health over a period of many years. There are two types of twins. Monozygotic twins arise when the same fertilized egg splits in two. Therefore these twins share an identical set of genes. Dizygotic twins come from the fertilization of two separate eggs with two separate sperm – so they are no more alike genetically than any other pair of siblings.

We can look at the frequencies of disease in both types of twins to get an idea of the relative contribution made by genetic factors. For instance, in a single gene disorder, if one monozygotic twin has the disease then the other must have it too. When both twins have the disease like this, they are said to be concordant. In fact geneticists would say that here they are 100 per cent concordant, because you can have various degrees of concordance. The higher the concordance, the greater the genetic input in the disease. In a single gene disorder, if a dizygotic twin has the disease, the other will not necessarily have it, for they do not share all their genes. A large difference in concordance between monozygotic and dizygotic twins also underlines the importance of genes in a disease. Where a disease has no genetic input you would expect no difference in concordance between both types of twins. The twin approach is, as we will see, as applicable to behavioural disorders as it is to physical disease.

CHAPTER THREE

Counting the Cost

Aggression and depression are universal problems; they always have been, and they probably always will be. Over the years, of course, the words used to describe human anguish have changed; for instance, what was called shell shock in World War I is now known as post-traumatic stress disorder.

But the problems are the same the world over: bullying that causes workplace stress is as debilitating in Japan as it is in the UK. Moreover, as life expectancy increases around the world, and people become less concerned with basic survival issues, the significance of mental health problems increases. The World Health Organization (WHO) predicts that depression will be the number two global public health problem, after heart disease, by the year 2020. There is another dark aspect to improvement in quality of life and aspirations, for this nearly always goes with an increase in crime.

The universal nature of these problems has its positive side, however. First, we might be able to learn something from other times, and other places. Reading Robert Burton's classic *The Anatomy of Melancholy* (1651)[1] could possibly comfort someone suffering from depression, and studying the positive effects of banning smacking in Sweden may provide a new idea for tackling youth violence in British or American society.

Secondly, the emergence of the same types of human behaviour at different eras, and around the world, underlines the importance of the brain studies outlined in the previous chapter; biology is independent of history or culture.

Stress and distress

From railway spine to post-traumatic stress disorder

> We didn't have counsellors rushing around every time somebody let off a gun asking 'Are you sure you don't have a ghastly problem?' You just got on with it. (The

Duke of Edinburgh, being interviewed on TV about his wartime experiences).[2]

It has become fashionable to decry the efforts of counsellors trying to help people bear the immediate effects of great emotional and physical stress. Yes, counselling may at times be ineffective, or even harmful, as we will see in chapter 8. But it is undoubtedly better than being executed. In World War I, 346 British soldiers were executed for a variety of reasons, including cowardice and desertion.[3] Some of these men refused to fight, or obey orders, not because they were unpatriotic or lacking in moral fibre, but because the stress of war had sent them crazy. Even now, the stigma still hurts their families, which is why they still campaign for the record to be set straight.

Even before World War I, it was known that the stress of war often drove soldiers over the edge.[4] The history books show that it hit French soldiers during the Napoleonic Wars, especially during the retreat from Moscow. In the American Civil War, too, the Northerners were forced to withdraw up to 7000 men from combat for psychological disorders. But all this was before Freud, the father of modern psychology, and military campaign leaders had other medical priorities, such as dealing with wounds and the toll of infectious diseases like typhus and cholera.

It was the advent of the railways and increased industrialization in the 19th century which finally pushed the idea of stress-related illness to the forefront. In these early days, serious accidents were common and the idea of holding someone responsible, who could hand out compensation, became popular. Previously it was put down to bad luck if you fell off your employer's rickety ladder and broke your neck.

Doctors began to notice a pattern of psychological symptoms – sleeplessness, anxiety, flashbacks – which often persisted after physical problems had healed. They searched for a physical cause for these symptoms, and came up with the idea of 'railway spine': a form of inflammation of the nervous system resulting from severe jolting in an accident which could be used as a basis for gaining compensation from the railway owner.

This set the scene for a more serious consideration of the damage inflicted by the stress of war. The term 'shell shock' was first used in a report to the *Lancet* in 1915 by Charles S. Myers, a British doctor with the Royal Army Medical Corps. He described three cases, with similar symptoms of memory loss, blindness, paralysis, hearing and speech disorders, and exhaustion. One, a 20-year-old, had become entangled in barbed wire on his way to his trench, when three artillery shells had exploded behind him. The second, who was 25, was buried in a trench after direct shell hits nearby. Myers' third case was a 23-year-old soldier, traumatized when a shell went off in the vicinity of a wall he had been sitting on.

Myers went on to collect hundreds more cases of shell shock. At the height of the war, in the period between July and December 1916, which included the Battle of the Somme, there were 16,138 cases of shell shock in British soldiers,[5] and a total of around 80,000 in the war as a whole – about 4 per cent of the fighting force.

The puzzle for the military doctors was that these men often had no physical injuries. They sought a physical explanation, though, and, drawing on the old idea of 'railway spine', said that the explosion of a nearby shell damaged the nervous system, possibly creating microscopic haemorrhages in brain tissue. Then cases came through of victims suffering the symptoms of shell shock who had not been exposed to artillery fire – so that theory fell apart.

However, the French neurologist Jean-Martin Charcot had put forward the idea of hysteria, late in the 19th century, which showed that psychological trauma could produce a range of symptoms, without any physical cause being involved. Then Sigmund Freud developed the hysteria concept, arguing that it had its origins in childhood trauma.

These ideas filtered down onto the battle field, and some doctors found them useful; certainly Charcot's and Freud's methods – psychoanalysis and hypnosis – were used in the treatment of psychological casualties. The hysteria concept also gave them an excuse to move away from the term 'shell shock', which was disliked by the authorities, as they thought it might encourage malingering. With hysteria, the blame could be shifted back to the soldier, who either had a pre-existing mental weakness, or was perhaps expressing an unconscious desire to get out of the war.

The number of psychiatric casualties would probably have been lower if recruits had been properly screened before being sent to the front. But the military authorities became increasingly desperate for troops as the war progressed, such were the losses sustained in the early campaigns, and they gave no more than a cursory (if any) medical examination.

William Rivers, a British neurologist, was one of the few to develop any real understanding of the condition. He argued that the shock of a bursting shell should be seen as the last straw that caused a man to break down from the cumulative stress of war. Dr Rivers treated many shell shock casualties, including the poets Wilfred Owen and Siegfried Sassoon (the latter had been hospitalized not for shell shock, but for speaking out against the war) at Craiglockhart War Hospital, just outside Edinburgh. Rivers' treatment was not dissimilar to modern counselling – he emphasized the relationship between doctor and patient, and encouraged the latter to talk through and face up to his traumatic experiences.

Although the House of Commons was assured (on more than one occasion) that it was virtually impossible for a soldier to be executed for cowardice or desertion if it was known he had suffered from shell shock, the reality was rather different. In 1917, for example, Commander-in-Chief General Douglas Haig confirmed the death sentence on two men whose court martial papers showed quite clearly that they had been treated in hospital for shell shock; several similar cases followed in 1918.

It was widely assumed, too, that the casualties would recover rapidly once the war was over. However, by 1921, 65,000 British soldiers were still getting pensions for nervous disorders. Moreover, new cases were seen after the war, and by 1939, 120,000 ex-servicemen were either receiving pensions or had been paid a lump sum for psychiatric disability, which accounted for 15 per cent of the total disability caused by the 1914–18 war.

In World War II, a similar level of psychological casualties was seen. There was no talk of shell shock this time (although the term is deeply embedded in our culture – how often do you hear someone say, 'I was completely shell shocked', in response to an unpleasant surprise?). Instead, the term 'combat exhaustion' or even just 'exhaustion' was used, reflecting the nature of the campaign, where much of the fighting was done by foot soldiers. The condition was especially marked in the soldiers being evacuated from Dunkirk, and over the whole war accounted for 23 per cent of all casualties. Doctors were better informed this time round, and those affected were, on the whole, evacuated from the front line pretty swiftly.

However, our modern understanding of traumatic stress comes from the Vietnam War. Here the experts were surprised, and pleased, at the low level of psychological casualties while the war was being fought (although these may have been masked by a high level of substance abuse). During the war, only three soldiers in 1000 seemed to suffer from combat-related stress. Problems only really emerged once the soldiers returned home. Around 15 per cent of Vietnam veterans reported psychological symptoms such as depression, explosive aggression, exaggerated startle responses, flashbacks and emotional numbing.

After much discussion among psychiatrists, the term post-traumatic stress disorder (PTSD) was finally adopted in 1980. It therefore earned itself a place in the *Diagnostic and Statistical Manual* (DSM). This is the psychiatrist's 'bible', now in its fourth edition (DSM-IV), which gives a check list of symptoms for all mental disorders.

Further studies on war veterans suggest that PTSD may be a long-term problem (as was shell shock for many British soldiers). The prevalence of PTSD among New Zealand Vietnam War veterans was still 10 per cent several years after the conflict[6] and around the same level has been reported in Gulf War veterans.[7] In contrast, only 2 per cent of the British soldiers wounded in the Falklands War were psychiatric casualties, probably because the conflict was relatively brief (and Britain was victorious). The continuing burden of traumatic stress disorders in war veterans suggest that it is part of a universal human response to the conflict of battle.

Soldiers are not the only psychological casualties of conflict, however. Recent research studied a group of 364 children who had been involved in the war in Bosnia. They had endured physical hardship and bereavement and had witnessed the sights and sounds of combat; almost 94 per cent were suffering from PTSD, with those in the Sarajevo area being most severely affected.[8] Another study carried out by the international medical relief organization, Médecins Sans Frontières, looked at a small group of Tibetan refugee children who had settled in India, and found around 11 per cent suffering from PTSD, although the prevalence of the problem appeared to decrease with time.[9] Meanwhile, Kuwaiti children are still suffering from fear symptoms associated with Iraqi aggression in the Gulf War, over five years after the end of the conflict.[10]

The modern epidemic

Most of us will never be involved directly in a war (although the effects of nightly TV bulletins on conflicts around the world on our mental health is not known). For many, the battle zone where stress-related problems arise is now the workplace. Being 'stressed out' (without descending into full-scale PTSD or slipping into depression) is not a measurable or notifiable disease, so it is hard to be sure of the costs in terms of lost production.

In Britain, however, it has been estimated that 40 million working days a year could be lost to stress-related illness, accounting for 60 per cent of all absence[11] and costing employers £7–£9 billion in sick pay and lost productivity[12]. More recent estimates have put the figure higher than this – at 91.5 million[13] or even a massive 180 million days.[14]

Figures compiled by the Health and Safety Executive seem to support the popular idea that we have been hit by an epidemic of stress. The 1990 Labour Force Survey revealed that 182,700 people – about one per cent of the workforce – believed they were suffering from work-related stress, anxiety or depression.[15] Five years later, the survey showed that this figure had risen to 280,000, a 30 per cent increase, and a further 250,000 people reported a physical illness linked to stress.[16]

These figures make stress-related illness the second most important cause of occupational ill health, after back pain. A survey by Yale University suggested that around 30 per cent of American employees feel 'quite a bit or extremely stressed at work'.[17] Meanwhile, research in Japan points to a similar epidemic of workplace stress: up from 50.6 per cent of the workforce in 1982 to 57.3 per cent a decade later.[18]

But the stress burden is not spread uniformly over the workforce. Some jobs are definitely more stressful than others, with those in public service taking most of the strain. In 1985, *The Sunday Times* commissioned occupational stress expert Cary Cooper of the University of Manchester Institute of Science and Technology (UMIST) to rate 104 different occupations for stress. The exercise was repeated in 1997, and revealed that stress ratings in nearly all jobs had increased.[19] The scale, based on the results of a stress check-list, ranges from 1 (least stressful) to 10 (most stressful); Cooper rated 7 plus as being 'extremely stressful', 6 plus as 'very stressful' and 5 plus as 'average stress'.

Prison officers topped the poll, with a score of 8.8, followed by the police with 8.7, and social workers with 8.5. Meanwhile, the professional contemplation of nature evidently makes for contentment: astronomers have the least stressful occupation, with a score of 2.3, while nature conservancy, horticulture and forestry average a score of 3. Maybe prison officers and social workers should go for long country rambles on their days off?

Farmers have a tougher time though, with a score of 6.3; this is backed up by a recent survey, which suggests that farmers in England and Wales are plagued by financial worries and the BSE crisis, burdened with paperwork, and bewildered by rapidly changing legislation.[20] No rural idyll here: small wonder the suicide rate among farmers is now 50 per cent higher than it is in the general population.

The concentration of occupational stress in the public service sector has resulted in two high profile compensation cases. The litigation landscape changed for ever when social worker John Walker succeeded in claiming £175,000 damages from his former employers Northumberland County Council, after proving in court that they had exposed him to a workload which had damaged his mental health (he suffered two nervous breakdowns, and was dismissed on ground of ill health in February 1988).

Policemen involved in the Hillsborough disaster of 1989 were allowed to proceed with claims for damages related to PTSD. This was significant, because it showed how our attitudes towards emotional problems have changed. Even so, critics pointed out that exposure to trauma is a policeman's lot. Does this mean they should just take it in their stride – or are we wrong to expect them to be superhuman? By 1995, in the United States, nearly one half of the states allowed worker compensation claims for emotional disorders, and disability due to stress on the job. Again, critics complain that such claims encourage a compensation culture and 'victim politics'.

All this has pushed stress up the health and safety agenda – and rightly so. If the statistics *are* correct, the costs of stress to society and individual are enormous, and growing. But there is an urgent need to confirm the widespread belief that we are in the middle of a global stress epidemic.

Here are some of the difficulties. First, although we know quite a bit about the physiological changes that are associated with stress – high cortisol in the blood, sometimes a shrinkage in the hippocampus – there is no quick and reliable screen you could apply to the whole population (as you might screen for HIV infection, for example). Instead, you have to rely on asking people questions. Since there is currently no general agreement among the experts about what stress (and occupational stress in particular) actually is, even compiling the questionnaire is fraught with difficulty. Conducting surveys is time-consuming and expensive, so they need to be designed to extract maximum data; the right questions need to be asked about the possible causes of stress, too. Finally, the way in which occupational stress interacts with other forms of life stress needs to be probed, as do the costs in terms of mental and physical ill health.

When responses come in, you have to think about the people who have taken the trouble to reply. Are they representative of the general population? Perhaps the really stressed-out people are those who *didn't* reply because they were too busy, angry, or disorganized. So the results of the survey would be an underestimate. Or the conscientious people who replied are more subject to anxiety, and so you have an overestimate (those who did not bother to reply are easy-going, take life as it comes, do not suffer from stress, and so on). Then again we have to be careful about linking cause and effect. There appears to have been an increase in occupational stress between 1990 and 1995, but we do not know how real this is. People may be more aware of stress, more willing to admit to it, than before. The same could apply to the stress profile of different occupations:

maybe stress-prone people are more likely to become teachers, or perhaps social workers do not mind admitting to being stressed, whereas foresters are in denial? We really need to know the answers to these questions before being certain that conditions in the workplace have worsened to the extent that increasing numbers find themselves unable to cope.

From this baseline, Andrew Smith and his colleagues at the University of Bristol have been commissioned by the Health and Safety Executive to carry out a major new study on the extent of occupational stress in the UK. They are surveying 17,000 people in the West Country. Results from a pilot study of 200 people suggest 2 per cent are extremely stressed at work, 15 per cent very stressed, while 50 per cent show at least moderate amounts of stress.[21] The high-stress group showed a marked increase in physical and mental health problems. They identified factors such as poor physical working conditions, heavy workload and long working hours as particular stressors. However, the results have to be interpreted with caution, because the sample is so small; the larger study will be far more informative (preliminary results suggest a similar level of stress-related problems, however).[22] Later, Smith and his team will also collect some physiological data, measuring cardiovascular and immune systems, and doing some biochemical tests. They will also do some tests of mental performance – for example, looking at selective attention, which is known to be impaired by both acute and chronic stress. This should tell us whether the reported stress effects have some biological basis.

According to Cooper of UMIST, it is the changing nature of the workplace which is now the root cause of occupational stress (while overwork, still a major factor, tended to dominate in the 1980s).[23] The concept of a job for life has become practically extinct as we move towards a short-term contract, freelance culture. For people in their 30s, 40s, and 50s this is hard to accept (although young workers will probably take this in their stride). In a recent ongoing survey, which is tracking the progress of 5000 British managers over five years, Cooper learned that 61 per cent of managers in companies of all sizes had coped with organizational restructure in the previous year.[24] Perhaps the most worrying aspect of this is that people perceive – usually correctly – that it is out of their control, especially when their organization places little value on communications. Lack of control, as we will see in chapters 4 and 5, makes stress-related health problems worse, and is a potent factor in depression.

Another important stressor which is peculiar to the 1990s, and is likely to become even more significant, is information overload. Of course, industry and business have always been subject to technological change and people generally learn to adapt, but information technology is something else. Voicemail, pagers, mobile phones, email and the Internet all mean that people are being inundated with data faster than they can ever hope to assess and process it. Similar pressures are being experienced throughout the Western world; for instance, a study of Swedish employees in the social security sector linked anxiety and exhaustion to concern about organization restructuring.[25]

Of course, stress is not confined to the workplace. You may be familiar with the stress scale which assigns points to various life events (it appears in most books on stress management, and we will look at it in more detail in the next chapter). Richard Rahe, one of the psychologists who devised the original scale in the 1960s, recently took the opportunity to update it. In so doing, he asked 427 volunteers to assess the stress in their lives, and compared the results with his earlier work. He discovered that there had been a 45 per cent increase in stress, from all causes, over the past three decades.[26] We still cannot be sure how real this increase is, for at least part of it could be due to greater awareness of stress-related problems, and a greater willingness to admit to them.

We tend to think that stress is a big problem only in Western society. That is not the case, however. Recent work by David Mumford and colleagues at the University of Bristol shows that people in rural Punjab[27] and in the mountain villages of Pakistan[28] suffer anxiety and depression related to stress, especially if they were illiterate or of low socio-economic status. In Pakistan, 46 per cent of women and 15 per cent of men suffer anxiety and depression, and in Punjab, the figures are 66 per cent and 25 per cent respectively.

Women the world over suffer more mental health problems than men, particularly in relation to stress, but the gap is widest of all in poorer countries, as the above figures show. Meanwhile, on the other side of the world, 30 per cent of all reports of illness in rural Brazil are attributed to a condition called '*nervos*', marked by insomnia, aches and pains, dizziness, trembling, weakness and emotional states ranging from feelings of sadness to anger.[29] One-third of those affected linked their problems to overwork and the resulting stress.

So, hard as stress is to define and investigate, it is worth the effort, for it may help lighten the burden on the individual, and on the economy. And, as we saw in chapter 1, stress often leads to depression. Fortunately, depression is a recognizable illness, which can be diagnosed with some degree of certainty. So there are some good data on which to base an assessment of its global importance.

A melancholy burden

The roots of depression

The earliest known description of clinical depression, attributed to the Greek physician Aretaeus, who lived around the second century AD, would not be out of place in a modern textbook of psychiatry:

> *The patients are dull or stern: dejected or unreasonably torpid, without any manifest cause: such is the commencement of melancholy. And they also become peevish, dispirited, sleepless, and start up from the disturbed sleep. Unreasonable fears also seize them . . .*

Even then, almost two thousand years ago, melancholia (and its counterpart, mania) were seen as serious mental disturbances, rather than as part of normal human experience. Descriptions like that of Aretaeus appeared throughout the Middle Ages and the Renaissance, culminating in Robert Burton's classic account *The Anatomy of Melancholy* in 1651. But it was not until the second half of the 19th century that melancholia came to be called depression (modern writers, such as William Styron, writing of their own experience, have commented that the term depression does not really capture the anguish of the condition and that melancholia was perhaps a more apt word).

In late Victorian times a condition which overlapped with depression, known as neurasthenia, became almost fashionable. The term was introduced as early as 1869 by the American neurologist George Beard. The hallmark of neurasthenia was overwhelming fatigue on the slightest exertion, which was not relieved by rest. No physical cause for the exhaustion could be found, although some doctors noted it often followed an infection, particularly influenza.

As with railway spine and shell shock, the search for a physical explanation continued for some time – remember, this was when psychology had not yet been established as a formal discipline. The prevailing view was that neurasthenia was a disease of modern life. Beard himself insisted that the disease was brought on by overwork, too much study, and exposure to new technology, such as wireless telegraphy and mass-circulation newspapers.

The term fell out of favour over the course of the 20th century with the growth of modern psychiatry. Those who would formerly have been diagnosed with neurasthenia were instead said to be suffering from depression. The word neurasthenia had all but disappeared in the United States and UK by 1960. But it is still used in the Netherlands, Eastern Europe, the former Soviet Union, and in China, where neurasthenia is viewed as a physical illness, which carries no stigma.

Simon Wessely, of the Institute of Psychiatry in London, has traced the history of neurasthenia, and suggests that its modern equivalent could be chronic fatigue syndrome (CFS, formerly known as myalgic encephalo-myelitis or ME).[30] The parallels are indeed striking: the link with the stress of modern life, the apparent lack of a physical cause, and the profound, inexplicable exhaustion.

But what we call a disease is important to those suffering from it. People with CFS do not like to be given a psychiatric label (even though many do benefit from antidepressant therapy and may perhaps reasonably be supposed to be suffering from depression). They continue to hope that a physical cause for their distress will be found. It will be interesting to see whether history repeats itself and CFS disappears only to re-emerge towards the end of the 21st century with a new name.

The parallels between railway spine, shell shock, and neurasthenia – where, a century ago, doctors sought (in vain) for a physical cause – and current preoccupations with the biology of mental illness are fascinating; the hope is that today's attempts to pin down the biological factors are rooted in hard science.

Suicide through the centuries

Just as depression has always afflicted the human race, so, too, has suicide. You might think that all people who attempt suicide are depressed, but that is not always the case. It has long been realized that great emotional upheaval can precipitate suicide in the absence of any mental illness.

Although in the Christian tradition suicide has been seen as a bad way to die, going against divine and natural law, the ancient Greeks and Romans were quite tolerant of it. At one time it became almost romantic (like neurasthenia). The appearance of Goethe's best-selling novel *The Sorrows of Young Werther* in 1774 inspired a wave of copycat suicides across Europe.[31]

During the second half of the 18th century, there were also a number of political suicides linked to the French Revolution.[32] But the British public were shocked when Viscount Castlereagh, the Foreign Secretary, was given a state funeral and buried in Westminster Abbey, in 1822, after committing suicide.

In many countries suicide was illegal until quite recently (often this meant the suicide's property was forfeited to the state, leaving the family without their inheritance). However, then, as now, coroners would avoid the suicide verdict if they possibly could, to spare the feelings of loved ones.

An important figure in the understanding of suicide was Emile Durkheim, the French sociologist who argued in his famous work *Le suicide: Étude de sociologie* (1897) that suicide was a response to the deficiencies and injustices of society (rather than being a result of an individual's psychology). He talks of three types of suicide: *egotistical* suicide seen in 'loners' who somehow fail to integrate into a family, or other social group; *altruistic* suicides who sacrifice themselves for the good of a group; and *anomic* suicides, which occur when the needs of the individual are not met by society.

There is some evidence that the suicide rate increased in the 19th and early 20th centuries, a trend which could be linked to the social disintegration caused by the Industrial Revolution, coupled with the writings of the philosophers of the era, including Schopenhauer and Kierkegaard, which encouraged melancholic thoughts; other writers have suggested a suicide epidemic in the Tudor period and in the 18th century. In the 19th century it does appear that the suicide rate varied markedly between countries; it was 3.1 per 100,000 in Italy, and 25.9 per 100,000 in Denmark.

Unfortunately, the historical data on suicide are complex and it is hard to pick out any reliable trends to compare with current figures. All we can say, with any confidence, is that suicide has always been less common among women than among men (although women attempt suicide more often than men do) and it has always tended to peak in the spring and summer months, and to fall in the winter. Furthermore, suicide has always been less frequent during war time, which underlies the theme developed in chapter 1: when aggression can be directed outward, to a common enemy, people are less inclined to destroy themselves.

A growing burden – depression and suicide today

According to the World Health Organization, the current global prevalence of depression is 10.4 per cent[33] – in other words, it affects one person in ten around the world at the current time, topping the list of mental disorders. That does not include illnesses like panic disorder, or alcohol dependence which are quite likely to have a depressive component (nearly 10 per cent of the global population suffers from two or more mental disorders concurrently). In fact 24 per cent of the population suffers from some kind of mental disorder, in which depression and adverse responses to stress are likely to play a major part.

Going further into this WHO study reveals that a further 10 per cent had what is termed 'subthreshold' psychological disorders. In other words, they were not ill enough to fulfil the DSM diagnostic criteria (and may never have sought help) but still had symptoms like anxiety. Another 31 per cent had an even milder form of psychological disability, marked by one or more isolated symptoms. Only 36 per cent of the population were classed as being mentally healthy. This might be just about acceptable if those affected were getting the help they needed. However, the WHO study had to conclude that these vast numbers of people with depression and related conditions were 'neither recognised nor treated sufficiently'.

Furthermore, mental ill health is linked to a greater level of disability, with those affected more likely than average to suffer from common chronic diseases such as hypertension (high blood pressure), diabetes, arthritis and back pain (one question the study does not answer is whether the mental illness causes the physical disability or vice versa).

These statistics set the agenda for the future global health scene. Right now, infectious disease and malnutrition are still the major killers on a global basis. But as countries develop, the importance of non-communicable diseases such as heart disease and depression increases. In 2020, depression could be the second most important cause of disability (after heart disease) in the population as a whole and the leading cause among women.[34]

In the UK, anxiety and depression contribute to more than 90 million working days lost due to mental health problems, costing the country £22 billion a year (there must be some overlap here with the number of days lost to stress-related illness).[35] The true figures for depression could be hard to measure, because a significant number of those affected may never report to a doctor.

Another way of getting an idea of the prevailing level of despair is to take a look at the suicide figures (likely to be an underestimate, because of the tactful coroner, as explained above). The WHO estimates that 786,000 people around the world commit suicide each year, giving a rate of 10.7 per 100,000 per year. This means that someone, somewhere, commits suicide every 40 seconds.[36]

The WHO average conceals some disturbing variations in the suicide figures. Only around a quarter to a fifth of the member states of the United Nations report national suicide figures to the WHO. So we have, at best, an incomplete picture of what is really going on around the world. In most countries for which there are data, suicide ranks among the top 10 causes of death for people of all ages. For younger people, in the 15–34 age group, suicide is among the top three most common causes of death.

In Europe, suicide claims; on average, about as many lives as road traffic accidents (some of which may be unrecorded suicides). Incidence varies across the European Community from 35 per 100,000 (male) and 19 per 100,000 (female) in Denmark, to 6.0 per 100,000 (male) and 2.0 per 100,000 (female) in Greece. The UK figures are close to the European average, at 12.4 per 100,000 (male) and 4.5 per 100,000 (female).[37]

In general, the countries of southern Europe have the lowest suicide rates, followed by the countries in the northwest. The Nordic countries and central Europe have the highest rates of suicide in Europe, and this pattern has been characteristic of Europe for the whole of the 20th century.[38] The reasons for these variations are unclear. It could have something to do with climate (lack of sunlight in the north could trigger seasonal depression), the availability of suicide prevention facilities, or cultural and religious constraints on either carrying out the act itself, or reporting it.

Recently, some disturbing suicide figures have emerged from China and other parts of Asia. Since 1990, two million Chinese people are believed to have killed themselves.[39] In fact, the Chinese population accounts for nearly half of the world's suicides, even though they are less than a quarter of the world's population, with a suicide rate of 30.3 per 100,000 population. Moreover, the female suicide rate is higher than the male rate in China – the only (known) country in the world where this is true. Among Chinese women aged 15 to 44, one death in four is due to suicide. Another turnabout is that suicide rates are three times higher in rural than in urban areas. Similarly high figures are found in the whole of Asia, from Sri Lanka to China via Hong Kong and Taiwan. The worst-hit country is Sri Lanka, with 36 suicides per 100,000. The reasons for the high suicide rates in Asia are not yet understood. It may be that rates of depression are higher (although as we said above, neurasthenia may sometimes be diagnosed instead). Or, it has been argued, there is easier access to the means: one of the most common methods of suicide in these countries is by swallowing weedkiller. In the UK, suicide rates fell when North Sea gas replaced toxic coal gas (and may fall again now sales of large quantities of paracetamol have been restricted). Maybe many of the Asian suicides are actually parasuicides (attempted suicides) without access to prompt treatment? Possibly banning toxic weedkillers would cut the suicide rate.

We do not have the data to know whether China's suicide rate has always been so high. But an analysis of European data shows that there has been a real increase in suicide risk in many countries (as well as in other highly industrialized countries around the world) over the past two decades.[40] The age distribution of suicide in both the Netherlands and the United States, for instance, shifted sharply from the older to the younger age groups between 1970 and 1987. Much of the increase has been borne by young men, rather than young women, particularly in Canada, the United States, Germany, Italy, Sweden, and Australia. The increases have been linked with a number of factors, such as a rise in unemployment, family breakdown, substance abuse and gender-role confusion. In England and Wales, there has been a rise of 172 per cent in suicide among young men since 1985[41] while, as elsewhere, there has been a decrease among older age groups. In other groups it has gone down.

One of the most tragic trends is seen in Northern Ireland, where suicides among males aged 16 to 24 are now greater than the number of deaths from road accidents. All this comes just as the Troubles subside, and peace is within sight – which vindicates what was said above about differing suicide rates in war and peace time. Suicide rates did in fact fall in Northern Ireland in 1969, when the conflict began, and they are still below those in the rest of the UK, where rates also fell in both World Wars and the Falklands War.[42]

If being young and male is a risk factor for suicide then so, too, are certain occupations. The England and Wales data show that people engaged in the medical professions and farming seem to be very vulnerable to suicide. Male and female doctors, nurses, vets, and male dentists all have a higher than average risk of killing themselves, probably because of a combination of job-related stress and easy access to means of suicide. The numbers of farming suicides are very high, accounting for 1.35 per cent of all male suicides (between 1991 and 1996, there were 190 suicides among farmers, one every 11 days). Unemployment is associated with a doubling of the suicide rate.[43]

There has also been a rise in attempted suicide – usually by drug overdose – throughout the Western world, with the UK now having one of the highest rates in Europe. For each completed suicide, there are around 10 times as many failed attempts. This is ominous, for 10–14 per cent of people who make a suicide attempt go on to die, sooner or later, by suicide. Their suicide risk is over 100 times that of the general population. So an epidemic of parasuicide now may foretell many extra suicides in years to come. Deliberate self-harm is concentrated in females in the 15–19 age group. However, there has been a trebling of figures for attempted suicide among young men aged 15–24 between 1985 and 1996. According to a survey carried out by the Samaritans, relationship difficulties are said to be the prime factor in attempted suicide, cited by 74 per cent of those questioned.

The signs are that some countries, at least, have woken up to the terrible costs of suicide and attempted suicide and are trying harder to prevent it. In Britain, the government aims to cut the death rate from suicide by at least one-fifth by 2010, which would save around 4000 lives a year.[44] Meanwhile, the WHO has pledged itself to at least reverse the upward trend in suicide.

A criminal waste

Crime is an enormously complex issue, most aspects of which lie outside the realms of pure science. Searching for trends over time, and between different countries, is tricky because of difficulties in obtaining and interpreting the necessary data. Moreover, not everyone who indulges in antisocial behaviour gets caught or is even, necessarily, committing a crime. And to some extent antisocial behaviour is part of the spectrum of normal human behaviour. In a recent survey 96 per cent of all inner London young men questioned admitted to committing one or more common offences such as theft, violence, vandalism, and drug taking.[45]

But there is a general perception that crime – and violent crime in particular – is on the increase. This is partly due, in Britain at least, to colourful media coverage of various kinds of 'rage': a form of casual violence, apparently fuelled by stress. For instance, the Automobile Association says that 90 per cent of drivers have experienced some degree of 'road rage' – threatening behaviour from another driver.[46] Fear of becoming a victim of road rage is now placed second on the list of drivers' concerns, after traffic congestion (which must be a contributing factor).[47] Next came 'air rage' with several well-publicized incidents on planes involving drunken passengers fighting or threatening cabin staff and passengers alike. Now there is 'train rage' (fury over cancelled or late trains being directed at railway staff) and 'trolley rage' in supermarkets, while traffic wardens are increasingly the target of 'ticket rage'.

Even more disturbing is a recent survey showing that attacks by patients on doctors and nurses in accident and emergency departments in the UK and Ireland are widespread, and generally precipitated by alcohol.[48]

Medical staff suffer fractures, lacerations, and soft tissue injuries – plus verbal abuse – at the hands of their patients. Only one in 200 of the perpetrators was convicted of a violent offence.

This kind of publicity creates a climate of fear. Three per cent of women (and one per cent of men) in the UK are imprisoned in their own homes, fearing to venture out after dark for fear of crime.[49] These figures are much higher among the over-60s, and in inner city areas.

Are these fears justified, though? In fact, crime has actually taken a downturn in the UK, for the first time since 1950. Official crime statistics (that is, crime recorded by the police) showed a decrease of 8 per cent, in all crime, between 1993 and 1995. During this period, the British Crime Survey, which collects data direct from crime victims, still recorded an increase – but of only two per cent, the lowest increase since the Survey was begun in 1981.[50] This apparent discrepancy in the figures arises because the Survey always records higher levels of crime than official figures, but at least the trends are in the same direction, suggesting the beginnings of a decrease. The following (and most recent), Survey, covering 1995–1997, recorded a 14 per cent fall in all crime, and a 17 per cent fall in violence. This is the first *decrease* that has ever been observed by the Survey.

Data from two separate sources suggest that this fall in crime, including violent crime, is real. Generally, the figures collected by the Survey run at around four times the official police figures; this is because not all crimes are reported to the police, and because the police do not record all the incidents that are reported. Because the Survey has always been carried out in the same way, it is a good source of information about the true level of crime and violence in our society (save that it does not record homicide, because it relies on questioning direct victims).

We still do not know whether this welcome decrease will be sustained, for it occurs against a backdrop of a massive increase in crime in England and Wales since 1950. Recorded crime quadrupled between the early 1950s and the late 1970s, and had doubled again by the early 1990s, reaching a peak in 1993.[51] Despite the fall in violent crime shown in the most recent British Crime Survey, levels of violence are still 54 per cent above those in 1981 (the first year of the Survey).

England and Wales are not alone; there has been a similar dramatic increase in the crime rate since World War II in most industrialized nations, according to an analysis of Interpol figures carried out by David Smith of the University of Edinburgh.[52] These increases have been steepest in Spain, Norway, Sweden and Canada, where crime rates have increased by factors of 29, 27, 14 and 13 respectively. There have been smaller but still significant increases in Australia, France, Germany, the Netherlands, and the United States. Only in Japan have crime rates stayed more or less the same over the last 50 years.

However, as in England and Wales, the crime rate has begun to decrease in more recent years in Canada, Australia and in the United States. Indeed, in the United States the crime rate began to level off as early as 1975. But the United States is still a very violent country; the homicide rate is ten times that of the UK, at 6.8 per 100,000, according to the US Bureau of Justice. Moreover, the arrest rate for violent juvenile crime increased by more than 50 per cent between 1988 and 1994. There may also be an increase in juvenile violence in the UK and elsewhere, although, to keep it in perspective, crimes of violence still form a small minority of all juvenile crimes.[53]

There has been a steady rise in crime in the former Soviet Union, since it split into its independent states. In Russia, there was a doubling in the murder rate between 1989 and 1993, while the rate of assault almost trebled.[54] Immediately prior to the downfall of communism, car crime and casual violence were almost unknown in the Eastern bloc. This surely tells us something about the links between capitalism and the thwarting of newly awoken aspirations.

But we cannot blame the growth in crime just on frustrated consumerism. The reasons are social, economic, cultural and, as we are becoming increasingly aware, genetic and biological. Even the experts cannot give a full account of the underlying reasons for the complex picture of crime worldwide. (Nevertheless, we will give it our best shot in chapter 6.)

Now that we have a broad-brush picture of stress, depression and violence, it is time to move on to a more considered study of each, in turn, and reveal what we now know of the underlying brain science.

PART II

Into the Mood Spectrum

CHAPTER FOUR

White-out: Blinded by Stress

The way people (even doctors) talk about stress, you would think it was an illness in its own right. Several years ago I had a temporary job standing in for Mr X, a chemistry teacher who, when not in the classroom, had a heavy load of admininstrative and pastoral work. He was on sick leave for many months, and eventually retired on ill-health grounds. I was told, and it was generally understood, that he was suffering from 'stress'.

At this point, you are nodding your head in agreement, because you know exactly what this is all about. Either you have a colleague who has been similarly afflicted, or perhaps you yourself are the 'stressed-out' one. Just as well. Because if your life was free from stress, you would be dead. Stress is not an illness, it is perfectly normal. But the widespread misunderstanding of what stress is, and what it is not, has polarized both public and medical opinion. On the one hand you have the 'stiff upper lip' school, typified by former British Prime Minister John Major, who claims not to 'believe' in stress. On the other hand, you have psychiatrists supporting claims of PTSD for trivial injuries, such as tripping over an uneven pavement.

Neither attitude is at all helpful to people like Mr X (who did appear to have a genuine stress-related illness) and those with similar problems. In this chapter we will look at the science of stress and see if we can create from it some kind of 'Third Way'.

Staying tuned through stress

Survival depends on adapting to change. This is true for all living things, from bacteria to humans. Safety, and a steady supply of the basics necessary for survival (food, water, energy, warmth), cannot be relied on in a constantly changing environment. So every organism *must* respond to changes that threaten its state of well-being – or die.

If a culture of *Escherichia coli* bacteria suddenly has its food supply switched from glucose (the universal biochemical fuel) to lactose (milk sugar) it responds in an astoundingly smart fashion. Before the switch it does not expend energy making the enzymes that would break down lactose (a clever survival tactic in itself) to release glucose. But as soon as lactose molecules are around, the genes that can make these particular lactose enzymes are suddenly switched on. What is more, lactose itself acts as the chemical signal which switches the gene 'on'. When there is no lactose around, the gene remains dormant. Jacques Monod and François Jacob were rewarded with the Nobel Prize in 1965 for the discovery of this supreme form of chemical intelligence.

Bacteria do not have brains, they do not 'know' that their food supply has been altered, but they can respond appropriately – at the molecular level. This response is stress at its most primitive. In more complex organisms, the response acquires a more obvious physiological dimension: a cat's fur standing on end when it is threatened, or you breaking out into a sweat on a hot day in an attempt to keep cool. But it always starts with molecules.

Stress is the sum of the biological responses to any challenge to an organism's state of well-being. It is universal, and it is a thoroughly good thing.

But people use the word *stress* in a very loose way, so that it sometimes sounds as if stress is something from outside which may cause us to feel bad ('dealing with stress', 'stressed-out' etc.). This use of language can create harmful attitudes, suggesting that stress is something that can – and should – be avoided. In fact it is impossible to avoid stress, and live.

To avoid confusion, we will use the word *stressor* for all the various challenges that induce a stress response. As we shall see, the problem is not stress *per se*, or stressors, but the nature and duration of the stress response which can lead to ill health.

Tigers, everywhere

For stress *can* lead to both mental and physical illness. There are two main reasons why stress-related disorders have had such a high profile in the last 20 years or so. First, the array of stressors facing a modern human is very wide ranging. Other mammals, whose brains, nervous systems and stress responses are very similar to our own, only have to deal with a limited range of stressors: mainly hunger, thirst, pain, and the attentions of various predators.

We face these big stressors too. Just ask the refugees from any war-torn region or victims of crime, accidents or natural disasters. But far more common are the day-to-day stressors like bills you cannot pay, traffic congestion, office politics, crime, ill health, relationships, the state of the world, and, above all, worry. Our primate cousins are, as we shall see, a good model for studying some human stressors, like low status in society, but it is debatable whether they have the capacity for worry (lucky them) and they *never* get red reminders for their phone bills.

Because the stress response starts at the molecular level, it is blind to the nature of the stressor. It goes through a broadly similar routine, whether you are facing a man-eating tiger or waiting impatiently in the queue for the office photocopier. The biology of the stress response has not evolved to keep pace with the more subtle demands of modern life. Too often we respond to situations which offer no obvious threat to life or limb in a manner which would be more appropriate to Stone Age man being chased by a large animal. The stress circuits in the brain do not know the difference.

The second reason why we seem to be suffering an epidemic of stress-related problems is historical. We (most of us in the West, anyway) live vastly more comfortable lives now than we ever did in past times. Many of our ancestors were subjected to lots of big stressors – the loss of their children, hunger, disease, and long hours of hard physical work – that we just would not accept. There is no reason to believe they felt it any less than we would have. It is just that they were not around long enough to complain about it. And if they had, who would have listened and understood?

Infectious disease used to be the main threat to health (and it still is on a worldwide basis). Now heart disease and cancer are the major killers in industrialized countries and are on the increase elsewhere. As we shall see, there is evidence that both may, to some extent, be stress-related. Now that we live longer, we have more time for stress-related disorders to reveal themselves. Moreover, advances in psychology and neuroscience have led to a better understanding of the mind and the brain in ill health.

The science of stress

The human response to a stressor – *any* stressor – is still not completely understood. Briefly, it arises from a complex interplay between hormones and neurotransmitters, orchestrated by the brain, the main aim being to gear up the body's resources for dealing with the perceived threat.

In simple terms, this means 'flight or fight': running away from the threat or staying to confront it. You need energy, diverted from its usual roles towards the muscles that help flee or confront. To get the energy, increased delivery of both glucose and oxygen to the muscles is required. So, in response to a stressor, heart rate goes up (more blood out to deliver the goods – in fact, output during stress can be five times that in a resting state), breathing rate goes up, and so does blood pressure. To achieve the necessary rise in blood pressure, blood vessels to the muscles constrict, through contraction of the muscles which surround their outer walls. In effect the circulatory system shifts up several notches.

The normal pattern of circulation alters too. Blood is diverted away from the digestive system, kidneys, and skin, and channelled instead towards the muscles. This has the effect of turning down functions like digestion, immunity, and reproduction temporarily. All these require biochemical energy, so it makes sense to have them merely ticking over while the crisis is underway.

BOX 12   *Stress and a hole in the stomach*

Much of what we know of the digestive process comes from the study of an accidental gunshot wound. A young French-Canadian, Alexis St Martin, working for the American Fur Company in the 1830s, was the victim, and the shooting left him with a hole in his stomach, much to the delight of researcher William Beaumont.[1] St Martin's digestive system was clearly visible, thanks to the unclosed wound, and Beaumont took the opportunity of watching the gastric juices go to work on various meals. Normally, the lining of the stomach and the rest of the digestive system were pink because they were suffused with the blood that would carry digested food around the body. But if St Martin was worried or upset, the linings became distinctly pale, as blood was diverted to the muscles by the sympathetic nervous system. Not that Beaumont understood why this was happening; but his careful notes were seized on by stress researchers more than a century later. Like Phineas Gage, Alexis St Martin unwittingly advanced our knowledge of emotion and the brain.

So, stress involves a profound shift in the body's biochemistry and physiology. How does it happen? And so quickly? (your heart begins to race instantaneously when you think someone might be following you). The physiologist Walter Cannon was the first to coin the term 'flight or fight', in the 1920s, to describe the actions of adrenaline and nor-adrenaline, the key players of the sympathetic nervous system (SNS). As mentioned in chapter 1, the SNS is the alerting arm of the autonomic nervous system, while the parasympathetic nervous system (PNS) has an opposing effect.

What happens is that stimuli from outside (and, in the case of worry, presumably from inside) pass through the thalamus, the brain's relay station, and are directed to various parts of the brain for processing, including the amygdala which is known to alert the autonomic nervous system. The adrenal glands get an 'alert' message via the nervous system (remember, all organs in the body are connected to the brain via nerves, forming a fast-track communication system). In response they pour out adrenaline, which acts as a neurotransmitter in the peripheral nervous system, connecting to all the relevant organs – the stomach, blood vessels, skin and so on.

Noradrenaline (a neurotransmitter in the brain which plays a role in depression, of which more in the next chapter) supports the action of adrenaline in the stress response; it is the main neurotransmitter in sympathetic nerve endings. And of course nothing physiological could happen if there were not noradrenaline (known as *noradrenergic*) receptors on most organs to receive the message from the neurotransmitter.

Meanwhile, the actions of the PNS are turned down. This is rather like accelerating your car while keeping the foot off the brake (but knowing that, when necessary, the situation could be reversed).

The SNS can kick organs into a response within seconds: that is why you feel your heart racing when someone is standing in the shadows. Noradrenaline constricts the blood vessels, so blood pressure is increased, it releases glucose into the bloodstream, and generally revs up the body to respond to a crisis.

All this, remember, is happening through the nervous system via the neurotransmitters adrenaline and noradrenaline. But there is also a second, slower, wave of response based upon hormones travelling through the circulation. This too starts in the brain, with the perception of a stressor; it culminates in the release of the stress hormone cortisol from the adrenal glands into the blood stream. The cortisol system relies upon co-ordinated teamwork between two brain structures, the hypothalamus and the pituitary, and the adrenal glands. For this reason, the system is known as the HPA (hypothalamus–pituitary–adrenal) axis.

Information, in the form of hormone released, flows in the direction H→P→A, but it also flows in the opposite direction, for the very presence of cortisol in the bloodstream is enough for the system to turn itself off.

BOX 13   *The HPA axis – stress on a seesaw*

If a stressor comes along, the brain rushes a message – via neurotransmitters – to the hypothalamus which, as we saw in the last chapter, works to keep you in tune with your environment. It responds to the alarm signal by releasing a pulse of the hormone, *corticotropin releasing factor* (CRF), which travels to the nearby pituitary gland. CRF homes in on specialized neurons in the pituitary, triggering production of a second hormone, *corticotropin*. This, in turn, travels through the bloodstream, reaching the adrenals within a few minutes. They respond by releasing cortisol into the circulation. The whole action is like tipping a seesaw, where the hypothalamus and the adrenals are the two ends, and the pituitary the pivot in the middle (see Figure 6).

The actions of cortisol on the body back up those of adrenaline, boosting emergency supplies of glucose fuel and so on. But cortisol can also turn off its own production, via a powerful negative feedback mechanism. It homes in on receptors in the hypothalamus and pituitary. They respond by closing down CRF and corticotropin production, which stops cortisol output. There is also powerful feedback from the nearby hippocampus, which is very rich in cortisol receptors. Think of the feedback as being a powerful sensor, feeding information about the current level of cortisol back to the HPA axis. The sensitivity of the hippocampus to cortisol depends upon the number of receptors it has – and this can be affected by various factors. The feedback is the equivalent of tipping the HPA seesaw in the opposite direction and setting it back in its original balanced position.

Meanwhile, other things are happening during the stress response. The pituitary gland releases endorphins and encephalins, the body's natural painkillers. This accounts for the fact that soldiers in battle, and footballers in mid-game, sometimes do not feel the pain of their wounds and injuries until after the action. The pituitary also releases vasopressin, a hormone which blocks urine formation; this helps the body conserve water.

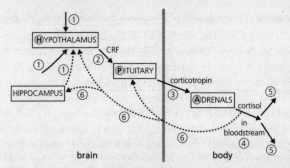

(Figure 6: The HPA axis) Stressor and stress response are linked through chemical information flow through the HPA axis. Neurotransmitters convey information about the stressor via various brain areas to the Hypothalamus (1), which produces corticotrophin-releasing factor (CRF) (2). CRF docks onto receptors in the Pituitary gland which, in turn, releases a pulse of corticotrophin (3). This travels to the Adrenal glands, above the kidneys, and results in the release of cortisol into the general circulation (4). Cortisol then travels through the body to target cells (5). Some also reaches sensor cells in the pituitary and hypothalamus which turn down the production of CRF and corticotrophin respectively, as well as affecting other brain areas, like the hippocampus (6), which form part of the feedback loop.

Selye's stress theory

Hans Selye, a physiologist working in Montreal from the 1930s, was the first to demonstrate that stress could lead to physical damage.[2] As so often happens in scientific research, Selye's discovery came about by accident. He began by looking at the effect of a hormonal extract from ovaries on rats. By his own account, he did not find the animals easy to handle: they were always running off, or nipping him when he tried to inject them. But he persevered. Naturally, he was delighted to discover a number of physiological effects in the rats after his injections: ulcers, enlarged adrenal glands, and shrinkage of the thymus in the chest, the master gland of the immune system. It looked as if he had discovered something pretty interesting about the ovarian extract. He sought to confirm his findings by running control experiments, where he injected the rats with saline solution. To his surprise, they showed the same changes: ulcers, and so on. This should not have happened, if the effect had been due to the ovarian extract. Soon he puzzled it out, though. The rats were responding to his own clumsy handling; they found it very stressful and, as he later argued, the constant outpouring of cortisol caused the physiological effects he observed. He confirmed his thoughts by deliberately stressing the animals: cramming them into small cages and forcing them to exercise. The same stress-related changes occurred.

Selye went on to describe a three-stage development of the stress response, which ended in illness, like ulcers and impaired immunity. The whole process became known as the *general adaptation syndrome*. In Selye's view, it began with the alarm reaction, where cortisol flooded the bloodstream (as we described above). This formed the initial response to the challenge, and was followed by the resistance stage, where the body attempted to return to normal. If this did not succeed, there followed the third and final stage of exhaustion where the system may have appeared to have returned to normal, but in fact was less able to respond to a further challenge.

It is now known that many of the details of Selye's model were wrong (although you will still see it copied in many psychology and self-help books). Perhaps his biggest mistake was assuming that the exhaustion stage occurred because the adrenals somehow 'ran out' of cortisol. Generally this cannot happen. The organs of the body carry on producing hormones, neurotransmitters, and other molecules, as required, through activation of the relevant genes, although of course they may produce more or less of these molecules, depending on circumstances.

The value of Selye's work is that he was the first to discover that stress could lead to physical damage (at least in rats) and to highlight the importance of cortisol in this process. In fact dissection of the HPA axis and its disturbances, particularly in depression, is now one of the hottest topics in brain science. We now know that cortisol can indeed act as a slow poison on the brain and the body: more of this later.

The anatomy of stress

One man's stress is another man's challenge

Stop reading for a moment, and make a quick list of the main stressors in your life at this moment. It is not usually difficult to identify the main causes of day-to-day stress, but if you were to compare your list with that made by a work colleague, or your partner, you would probably differ in how you rated various common stressors and how you handle them.

It is the way people interact with their stressors which is important, not the nature of the stressors themselves. For instance, being put on hold for several minutes when you make a phone call may make your blood pressure soar – or you may take a relaxing mini-break and look out of the window for a bit.

The subjective nature of stressors makes stress research quite difficult. Nevertheless, we will distinguish two main classes of stressors. First there are traumas: dramatic life-changing events such as war, physical abuse, serious road accidents, terrorist attacks, and natural disasters. These massive stressors can overwhelm the defences of the most phlegmatic person and, as we will see in later discussion of PTSD, can lead to long-lasting effects. Then there are the everyday stressors, ranging in severity from a run-in with your boss to the inability to find a parking space. How would you rate these two? Is the row twice as stressful as the parking problem? Or ten times?

In the 1960s, researchers at the University of Washington noted that people who had been through a lot of change in their lives over a short period of time – getting divorced, moving house, that sort of thing – had a more than average chance of falling ill in the next year or so. Two psychologists, Richard Rahe and Thomas Holmes, used this work as a basis for constructing a scale of stressors, each of which was given a value known as a *life change unit* (LCU).[3] This scale became well known and now appears in nearly every popular book on stress, and it has recently been updated to cope with current concerns.[4] Over the years it has been made into a questionnaire, known as the Recent Life Changes Questionnaire (RLCQ), which is used to help people calculate their stress burden over a period of time. Traumatic events like the death of a spouse or a child get an LCU of over 100, being fired from your job gets 79, while a less radical change like going on a diet rates 27. Even positive events like pregnancy, birth of a child, reconciliation with a spouse, and going on holiday are included. Christmas (which can be positive or negative depending on your point of view) gets a score of 30. A score of over 150 in a 12-month period is thought to increase the chances of becoming ill.

A comparison with the original scale reflected changes in society: unmarried parenthood, once a social stigma, is now rated as less of a stressor. This is the study, by the way, which concluded that there has been a 45 per cent increase in the impact of various stressors over the past 30 years (as we saw in the last chapter).

What is interesting about the scale is its emphasis on change, rather than the nature of the stressor itself. This is in line with what we know of the physiology of stress – response to change in the environment; at the molecular level of the response, the brain does not 'know' that a stressor is positive or negative, just that something is changing. Another scale which is often used by stress researchers is the 'hassles' scale of minor stressors (that have a drip effect over time on your mental and physical well-being) created by Richard Lazarus.

Holmes and Rahe's values are averages, compiled from asking hundreds of people about the impact of the stressors in their lives. And people vary enormously in the way they respond to change. The size of the response depends on both the context of the stressor and the individual.

Stressors which come out of the blue are often harder to handle than those which are predictable. A sense of being out of control seems to make our stress circuits work especially hard. Work based on the Selye model – stress a rat and see if it gets ulcers – shows that if you give rats an electric shock they get ulcers (naturally). But the interesting thing is that if you sound a warning bell before giving the shock, the number of ulcers the rats get goes down. In World War II, the Nazis bombed London night after night. Very stress-provoking. But oddly enough the ulcer rate in London, where the bombing was regular as clockwork, was lower than it was in the surburbs, where no-one knew when and where a bomb would drop. Psychologist Martin Seligman of the University of Pennsylvania calls this the safety-signal hypothesis. When you do not hear a warning bell you can relax; that is, the lack of warning bell acts as a safety signal,[5] because a stressor always comes with a warning.

More recently, as part of the Whitehall II study which is monitoring the health of thousands of civil servants, it has been shown that lack of control on the job front is linked to an increased risk of heart disease.[6] If this describes your job – no say in decision making, no idea what will be on your desk to deal with tomorrow morning – it might be worth trying to make some changes now.

Equally, if you *know* something nasty and stressful is going to happen, you can prepare yourself and so turn down the intensity of your response to it. This can cover the whole range of human experience, from leaving early when you know the traffic will be especially bad to getting as much hard information as possible if you are diagnosed with a serious medical condition.

The social side

Social support – a shoulder to cry on, a friend to phone to share good news or bad – can soften the stress response too. Stress expert Robert Sapolsky has shown, from studying primate tribes, that male baboons with lots of friends have lower cortisol levels than low-status lone males, for instance. In humans, experiments where students were asked to go through the stressful experience of giving a speech underlined the importance of friends and supporters.[7] One group gave the presentation alone, another in the presence of a supporter, and the third in the presence of a critic. All had their blood pressure monitored before and during the speech; those who brought a friend along had the smallest increase in blood pressure of the three groups, while those with the critic had the biggest increase.

Now imagine this effect magnified throughout a lifetime. A review of all the studies that have been done on the impact of social support on coronary heart disease incidence and mortality agreed broadly with the experimental study.[8] Social isolation really is bad for your health – perhaps you can never have too many friends?

A linked factor, social status, also moderates the way stressors are experienced. Back to Sapolsky's primate studies: low-ranking baboons have higher cortisol levels than those with a higher rank.[9] What is more, Sapolsky found that rank drives the biology rather than the other way round. Baboons born with an overactive HPA axis do not automatically end up at the bottom of the social pile.

What Sapolsky suggests is that low status is intrinsically stressful, because of lack of control, unpredictability and aggression from those of higher rank. This, in turn, causes changes in brain chemistry and, in particular, impairs the balance in the HPA axis. What seems to happen is that the number of cortisol receptors in the hippocampus is reduced by chronic stress. This has the effect of making it less sensitive to the amount of circulating cortisol. But the hippocampus is a major sensor in the feedback loop of the HPA axis; if it is less sensitive, then the feedback is less good, and the axis tips slightly out of balance.

Similar changes, incidentally, have been noted in serotonin levels: high-ranking vervet monkeys (who, like baboons, form societies with at least superficial resemblances to human society) have higher serotonin levels than their lower-ranking colleagues.[10] Maybe this is yet another parallel between stress and depression, although the nature of the link has not yet been identified.

The relevance of these animal studies for human society is not clear, for these variations in the HPA axis do not occur in all species. And no-one, yet, has measured cortisol or serotonin among human populations as a function of socio-economic class (the results could be fascinating). What we do have hard evidence for, however, is for a strong link between low socio-economic status and physical ill health which seems to operate through the chronic stressor of being poor.[11] An interesting historical note is the report that destitute people in 19th-century England who ended up on the mortuary slab were found to have enlarged adrenal glands (just like Selye's stressed-out rats).

Maybe this gives a clue as to how those of very high status in our society – Prime Ministers, royalty, business tycoons, and Presidents – cope with the burdens of office. For they are often faced with huge responsibilities, criticism from all quarters, relentless media attention and an enormous workload. Maybe they survive from the protective effect which high status has on their stress circuits? They may have risen to the top (if they were not born there, that is) through developing strategies for handling stress well (delegating work, or dumping frustration on their subordinates). They may also draw great strength from a supportive family. Or is resilience to stress ingrained in the personalities of high fliers – maybe even from birth?

Born to be stressed?

Whatever your circumstances, the way you handle what life throws at you depends ultimately on your personality type. We all know people who are habitually laid back, who 'take life as it comes'. And equally, we all know someone else who gets worked up and agitated over the slightest setback. Where do these individual differences come from? Maybe people are just born this way.

It is likely that genes will soon be found which influence how individuals respond to stress, either by having an obvious effect on the HPA axis, or by contributing to the creation of personality. Some people will have gene variants which make them secrete cortisol more rapidly than others, for example. These stress genes will probably be found to interact strongly with early childhood influences, shaping a child's future response to life's stressors. There is already evidence of how early life experiences can adjust the controls on the brain's stress circuits. Rats who are handled by humans for 15 minutes a day for the first few weeks of life produce less cortisol than rats who are left alone. This change persists into adult life.

The handling produces various hormonal responses, which end up by increasing the number of cortisol receptors in the hippocampus.[12] As we have already seen, this up-regulation increases the feedback sensitivity of the HPA axis (Box 13). To recap, the cortisol receptors act as molecular sensors for cortisol in the bloodstream (because they bind to it chemically) and so the more of them there are, the better they are at detecting it and signalling to the hypothalamus to stop secreting CRF. So cortisol production gets shut down long before any damage is done.

These handled rats do really well; further experiments showed that their nervous systems, protected from the toxic effects of cortisol, remained in good shape even into old age.[13] Control rats, who had not been handled, suffered a number of cognitive defects, like memory loss, as brain damage from excess cortisol exposure accumulated.

Now work by a team at McGill University in Montreal has added a new twist to the rat-handling story; it turns out that it is not the human handling of the rats that is important, but the behaviour of the mother towards her rodent offspring.[14] For what was *really* happening with the handled rats was that their mothers gave them more attention (in rat terms this means more licking and grooming) and that was the deciding factor (the human handling was a bit of a red herring). We know this because the control rats whose mothers gave them lots of licking and grooming (even though they got no human handling) also showed the same good changes in their brain chemistry.

What is more, the rats whose mothers doted on them acted more confidently (in rat terms, they explored their cages more) and had more receptors in their brains for benzodiazepines. This final observation needs a word of explanation. Benzodiazepines are tranquillizer drugs, like Valium and Librium, and the brain has receptors for them. What happens if someone is not actually on tranquillizers, though? It seems that the benzodiazepine receptors are probably part of a general circuit in the brain which calms anxiety. So the rats with the good mothers were just generally laid back and confident. Not only had their mothering shaped their HPA axis, it had also had a beneficial effect on other aspects of their brain chemistry.

This sounds as if it has extremely important implications for human society. Could lots of hugs and cuddles prevent babies from not just stress-related problems in adult life, but even dementia in old age? We just do not know, but there is new evidence that good parenting can certainly protect children from the potent stressor of low socio-economic status.

A team at the University of Rochester, New York, looked at a group of 159 youngsters in the 7- to 9-year-old age bracket living in a deprived inner city area. They asked parents and teachers to rate the children, and 85 of the group were classed as resilient and well adjusted, even though they had had more of their fair share of stressors (experience of violence, or death of a family member). The others were thought to be poorly adjusted and headed for problems in later life. The parents of the first group were found to be more responsive and nurturing, more consistent in applying discipline and, in general, just more positive about their children (the kind of parents who always turn up to parents' evening at school). They themselves had better mental health, more social support, and higher self-esteem, than the parents of the second group, who showed poorer parenting skills.[15]

It may seem obvious – good parents produce good kids. In fact, the contradiction here was that the good parents had not necessarily had a good upbringing themselves: many had histories of neglect or abuse, but had somehow managed to survive intact. Maybe some genetic factor is at work here? We do not know the state of the HPA axis in these children, of course, but drawing a parallel with the well-groomed rats, it might be fair to say that a similar neurochemical adaptation has occurred. Good parenting can shape the brain and, what is more, it can be learned – a sign of hope for the future.

In adult life, different personality types respond differently to stress. Work by Sapolsky and others has identified personality types in primates which have distinctly different biochemical stress profiles. Bullies, surprisingly perhaps, have low cortisol levels – maybe because they take out their frustration on others. However, macaque monkeys known as 'hot reactors' whose lives are one big stressor, and who over-react to the slightest provocation, have high cortisol levels, and are at increased risk of heart disease.[16] The third personality type is the 'high reactor' rhesus monkey, discovered by Stephen Suomi at the US National Institute for Health.[17] This sad creature is prone to overwhelming anxiety and depression when anything goes wrong in its life – and its system is flooded with cortisol. Although it may offend some people's idea of human dignity, there is a lot we can learn about ourselves from studying primate personality.

But there has also been research into how human personality influences the individual stress response. You may be familiar with the idea of the Type A and Type B personality. In brief, Type As, who are more prone to heart disease, are driven, impatient, ambitious and energetic. Type Bs, on the other hand, take life more slowly, and are less at risk of developing heart problems.

This link between mind and body was another of these important discoveries that was made by chance. In the 1950s, American cardiologists Meyer Friedman and Ray Rosenman were running a busy practice and wondered why the seats in their waiting room wore out so quickly. One day an upholsterer came in to fix yet more seating and commented that it was odd the way the two doctors' patients always sat on the edge of their seats, clutching at the armrests. No wonder the covers kept wearing down in the same place. It was just a short step from this shrewd comment to Friedman and Rosenman uncovering the link between the patients' fidgety behaviour and the state of their cardiovascular systems.[18]

Obviously the Type A personality profile is composed of several different traits. Which of them is associated with the poor stress-coping skills? There is no general agreement, but some interesting studies have been done in recent years. A group of 56 men and 56 women were given a frustrating anagram puzzle to solve. Those who had admitted, via a questionnaire, to being more hostile and suspicious showed markedly higher blood pressure rises in response to the task than their more trusting peers.[19]

Another study, carried out by Meyer Friedman himself, suggests that an important component of Type A behaviour is insecurity, which drives the aggression.[20] And social dominance (defined by behaviours like fast talking, interrupting, and argumentativeness) can be fatal. Psychologists from the University of Kansas discovered this in a follow-up study of 750 men and found that the trait, along with hostility, seemed to be linked with a risk of death from all causes.[21] Being placid – defined here as neither hostile nor socially dominant – was associated with a lower risk of mortality. Just a further word here about dominance, though: above we said that low social status was stressful, and now we seem to be saying that *high* social status is bad. This apparent contradiction comes about because there are different styles of dominance, and different meanings of dominance in different types of society: some are good for the stress circuits, some bad. According to Sapolsky's baboon studies, the best stress profiles were found in those animals who handled power well; they had good social skills, picked only the fights they were likely to win (to enhance their standing) and took out their frustrations on those below them.

Box 14   *The 25-hour day*

Certain groups in society are finding it increasingly difficult to cope with the stressors placed upon them. We now have some hard evidence that, as you might imagine, women who juggle a demanding job with family life are letting themselves be run ragged by stress. A sample of nearly 200 women in white-collar jobs with and without children wore a 24-hour blood pressure monitor. Women with a university education holding down a demanding job experienced increases in blood pressure while at work which did not return to normal when they came home.[22] This worrying trend was not seen in women without children or those with less demanding jobs. This will not surprise the millions of women in this position, but perhaps having the hard evidence to support the adverse effect of stress on their health may persuade employers and families to offer them a bit more support (help round the house from husbands, for instance, or flexible working hours).

Trauma and its aftermath

Noisy neighbours, queues, being late and all of life's small and medium-sized stressors can certainly lower quality of life in the short term and take their toll on your health over a period of years. But these pale into insignificance beside traumas – huge stressors where people's life and liberty are put at risk. War, assault, kidnap, being taken hostage, rape, childhood sexual abuse, accidents, natural disasters like earthquakes and tornadoes, are just a few of the traumas which may evoke intense fear, helplessness, and horror in those involved.

When exposed to trauma, the stress circuits in the body and brain are pushed to their limits in an attempt to cope. No wonder some people are left with long-lasting, and maybe even permanent, psychological damage.

A single act of violence, like the massacre at Dunblane in 1996, can affect hundreds of people directly, not just those who are hurt physically, but their families and friends, and those who deal with them professionally, such as ambulance staff and police. A recent report from RoadPeace, the charity for road accident victims, suggests that levels of psychological distress among the families of the injured and bereaved are comparable to those of the victims.[23] A disaster like a fire, earthquake, or an explosion brings many other stressors in its wake – loss of a home, maybe, or of treasured possessions, unemployment and financial strain; all these delay recovery from the trauma. And more and more people are being swept along on the tide of trauma, with increasing coverage of disaster in the media (just open today's newspaper).

In most cases, people's responses to trauma – revulsion, grief, fear, numbness and disbelief – are perfectly normal and understandable. Over time, they can expect to regain their pre-trauma mental state; they may even feel they have grown emotionally and benefited from the experience. But around 10 per cent of those who experience trauma will go on to develop a serious mental health problem.

In PTSD a characteristic pattern of symptoms arises. First, the person affected relives the experience through nightmares, intrusive thoughts and flashbacks. At the same time, they will avoid any reminders of the trauma and often report feeling emotionally numb. Especially characteristic is a radically altered sense of the future: the affected person may feel that they will never marry or have children, or will not live a normal lifespan. And people with PTSD show signs of increased arousal – they are tense, edgy, and likely to have angry outbursts and maybe an exaggerated startle response (the shock you feel when something makes you 'jump').

Obviously it is quite difficult to distinguish some of these symptoms from normal responses to trauma (especially when the trauma has been very severe) and from other mental disorders such as depression (emotional numbing and sleep problems are very characteristic here). An experienced psychiatrist will diagnose PTSD only if the above *pattern* of symptoms has been present for more than a month, and if the person is obviously distressed and not functioning normally.

Recent research, based upon survivors of bush fires in Australia, suggests that you can identify over 90 per cent of those who will go on to develop the disorder by using a specific questionnaire shortly after the disaster.[24] PTSD affects people at any age (including children) and, although symptoms usually appear within the first three months of the event, the onset is sometimes delayed by months, or even years. A study of Dutch resistance veterans from World War II showed that only 30 per cent first experienced symptoms within five years of the end of the war. In the rest, onset occurred up to 25 years afterwards.[25] Moreover, PTSD can be lifelong. Studies of prisoners of war from World War II, half a century later show that some people have never got over the conflict.[26]

But why do nine out of ten people *not* develop PTSD? We do not really know. As you might expect, the figures go up if the trauma is particularly horrific. There is also some evidence that pre-existing mental health problems, previous experience of trauma (the repeat victim syndrome), lower income and increasing age may be risk factors for PTSD.

It also appears that those who empathize and identify with victims are more vulnerable. In 1989, the US ship *Iowa* exploded north of Puerto Rico, killing 47 soldiers. The number of dead was too great for the professional mortuary staff to work with, so a number of volunteers (all members of the military) came in to help. A month after the event, they were questioned about whether they had identified with the victim, as either self ('it could have been me'), a family member, or a friend. Now we know why wise nurses, doctors and police officers tell their younger colleagues 'don't get involved' – because 33 per cent of those who identified with the dead as a friend developed PTSD over the following months (compared to only 3.4 per cent of those who did not identify at all). There was a smaller, but still significant effect associated with identification as a family member but, oddly enough, no effect for self-identification. These findings require further investigation, but they do point to one way in which the incidence of PTSD could be reduced among disaster workers: by emphasizing the importance of staying detached.

More recently, a related problem known as *acute stress disorder* has been described. In acute stress, the symptoms begin within the first month of exposure to trauma and last for at least two days (but not more than a month – then it becomes PTSD). Although the symptoms are similar to those of PTSD, the hallmark of acute stress is being dazed and disoriented: those affected often report feeling distanced from the event, numb, and unreal.

We should also briefly mention two related conditions: *adjustment disorder* and *panic disorder*. It is sometimes rather difficult to draw a strict dividing line between stressors which are traumas and those which are not. For some people, having their partner leave or being fired could be far more devastating than being in a road accident. When people react with the symptoms of PTSD to a non-traumatic stressor, psychiatrists diagnose *adjustment disorder*. The hallmark of panic disorder is intermittent (and sometimes very frequent) attacks of extreme anxiety, discomfort, often related to feelings of suffocation, which occur for no obvious reason.

In both PTSD and panic disorder, the stress circuits in the brain have become overwrought and unbalanced, primed by trauma or, in the case of panic, some kind of initial internal stimulus. Recent studies of the brain have revealed how the system may get out of balance in these distressing conditions.[27] First the SNS appears to become overactive. People with PTSD have been shown to have more noradrenaline in their urine than healthy people, a sign that there is too much of this neurotransmitter flooding the system. What is more, if a so-called challenge experiment (injecting something that stimulates the SNS) is done, individuals with PTSD and panic disorder both respond with a panic attack: a sure sign of over-sensitivity.

Second, the HPA axis is disturbed. You might expect increased cortisol production – actually it is lower than normal in PTSD. Receptors for cortisol, which have been measured on white blood cells (they are in many parts of the body and brain of course, but it is easier to measure them in blood) are increased. This up-regulation is to be expected: receptors increase in number in a desperate attempt to capture what little cortisol there is. What all this means is currently unclear, but hopefully one day a biochemical test for PTSD can be based on these findings. This would be useful in compensation cases, helping to sort out malingerers from those who have a genuine claim. It would raise the credibility of the PTSD diagnosis in the eyes of the general public and the medical profession.

BOX 15   *Indelible memories*

The role of memory in PTSD and panic disorder is crucial and here we turn again to the work of Joseph LeDoux and his associates.[28] The trauma appears to involve fear conditioning; the traumatic event, and its associated sights and sounds, create a powerful emotional memory at the level of the amygdala. Later, the associated stimuli (which may be innocuous in themselves: like a tune that was playing on the radio on the day of a murder, or a door slamming that sounds like a gunshot) will awake the memories, via LeDoux's 'quick and dirty' amygdala circuits. All this happens before the rational cortex has a chance to work out what is actually going on.

Recently it has been shown that noradrenaline and dopamine released in the amygdala during mild to moderate stress enhance memory consolidation in both rats and humans.[29] The intense emotion which is experienced with the memory makes it hard to extinguish – indeed, the memories laid down during trauma may be burnt into the brain forever. Flashbacks and nightmares may merely serve to strengthen them.

This mechanism also drives the creation of 'flashbulb' memories – the ability to remember *exactly* what you were doing on the day of a significant event, such as when President Kennedy was shot, or when Princess Diana died. But can you remember the preceding day in such detail? No, because there was no 'hook' for your attention; it was just another day. The analogy between PTSD and flashbulb memories must, incidentally, be quite subtle. Despite the national outpouring of grief, significant numbers of the British population were (secretly) emotionally unmoved by the events of 31 August 1997. Yet they still experienced the flashbulb effect.

Where panic disorder is concerned, the initial unconditioned stimulus comes from inside the body, not from some outside trauma. One plausible theory is that it starts with the activation of an evolutionarily old suffocation alarm.[30] Neurons in the brain stem are very sensitive to blood levels of carbon dioxide – these go up during suffocation. And the amygdala receives input from the brain stem. If it gets the message that carbon dioxide is low, symptoms of panic may develop – fast heart beat, increased blood pressure, and the urge to flee. On a future occasion, the stimulus of, say, a missed or fast heart beat, could be enough to trigger the full panic response in a sensitized person.

Box 16   *The chemistry of Gulf War syndrome*

In a further twist, it now looks as if another neurotransmitter, *acetylcholine* (ACh), may be implicated in PTSD. ACh is involved in memory and learning; deficiencies in ACh are specifically linked with the mental decline of Alzheimer's disease. In fact, the drugs which boost cognitive function in Alzheimer's, like tacrine, work by increasing ACh levels. On exposure to a stressor, mice experience changes in gene expression which cause a transient increase in ACh; this is then followed by a longer-lasting decrease. The same shift in brain chemistry also happens on exposure to toxins called ACh inhibitors.[31]

As we have seen, neurotransmitters are normally cleared away after they have done their job; ACh is cleared by a specific enzyme, which is blocked by the inhibitors. This leads ACh neurons to fire uncontrollably. Now ACh is involved not only in memory and learning but also in nerve circuits that control the muscles. Continual firing in these circuits soon leads to paralysis – which is why the inhibitors are used as insecticides and nerve gases.

A major group of inhibitors is the organophosphates (OPs), which have been implicated in a number of diseases. Most important, in the current context, Gulf War syndrome has been attributed to OP exposure by military personnel during the Gulf War in 1991.

There has long been controversy over the very existence of Gulf War syndrome; in some cases it has been described as a form of PTSD. Now we see that the symptoms could arise from either PTSD or OP poisoning[32] (or perhaps a combination of both). This latest research certainly seems to suggest that there is a genuine biochemical basis to the condition.

Stress and ill health – elusive links

There is a general awareness that stress can damage physical health, and an increasing acceptance of the idea that the mind can affect the body. However, the role stress actually plays in illness is really not at all well understood. Yes, we can demonstrate a link between exposure to various stressors and heart disease, infection, skin and gastrointestinal disorders, and (more controversially) perhaps even cancer. However, the demonstration of an association between stress and an illness does not mean that stress is the cause. You can argue, for example, for an indirect link. Too much stress could lead people to adopt an unhealthy lifestyle: they might smoke or be too busy to exercise. These factors might have a more direct bearing on ill health.

BOX 17   *Stress and ulcers – a change of outlook*

When people think of stress and disease, normally the image of a burnt-out executive with an ulcer comes to mind (though a middle manager would actually be nearer the mark – it is pressure from above and below which creates the most stress). Selye's stressed rats certainly developed ulcers from their chronic exposure to cortisol.

However, ulcers are no longer a major health problem, thanks to a major advance in medical science. Put simply, an ulcer is caused by stomach acid eating away at the lining of the stomach or duodenum. Whereas previously this painful condition was most often treated by major surgery, there is now a drug – ranitidine – which heals the ulcer without an operation. Ranitidine (Zantac) has been the world's top-selling drug for the last few years. It has also become apparent that infection of the stomach by the bacterium *Helicobacter pylori* plays an important role in ulcer formation, so antibiotics now form an important part of the treatment. So even if stress does lead to an ulcer, it is more easily treatable than ever before.

Heartbreaking stress

During the first few days of Scud missile bombardment of Tel Aviv by Iraq during the Gulf War, fatal heart attacks in the population increased by a factor of three, compared with figures for the corresponding days in the previous year.[33] In January 1994 the Los Angeles earthquake exacted a similar toll. On the day of the disaster the number of cardiac deaths in people with pre-existing disease shot to 24, from a normal daily average of around five.[34] This is proof of the widely held belief that the overwhelming stress produced by a sudden shock can be fatal.

There is also mounting evidence that the molecules of stress have a long-term effect on the heart and circulation. For instance, it is now known that even minor, everyday stressors have an adverse effect on the cardiac function of people with angina. In this disorder, the coronary arteries fail to deliver an adequate supply of blood, and therefore oxygen, to the heart. The oxygen deprivation causes chest pain, particularly on exertion. The underlying pathology in angina is usually diseased coronary blood vessels, narrowed by fatty deposits called *plaque*.

In one experiment, angina patients were fitted with a 24-hour cardiac monitor and asked to keep a diary noting feelings of tension, frustration, sadness, happiness and being in control throughout the day. From this study, it was found that negative emotions were linked with oxygen deprivation to the heart (cardiac ischaemia) – below the level that causes pain, but clinically significant none the less.[35]

What is happening here is paradoxical. In a healthy circulation, adrenaline should dilate the coronary vessels (via a chain of biochemical reactions occuring in the walls of the vessel), allowing more blood and oxygen to reach the heart, so it can pump it out to the rest of the body to meet the increased demands on it during stress.

But the chemistry of diseased vessels is different; for reasons that are not yet completely understood, adrenaline triggers the release of hormones including serotonin which make the vessels constrict instead of dilating. So people with pre-existing heart disease may need to learn to handle the stressors in their life better.

But how did their blood vessels get into such a state in the first place? Coronary heart disease (CHD) is still the leading cause of death in the Western world and developing countries are catching us up fast. We know quite a bit about the pathology of CHD (although there is still much to be learned). Put simply, over the years a process known as *atherosclerosis* leads to the build-up of plaque on the inner walls of the arteries, making them narrow. This can affect arteries anywhere in the body, but is most significant in those that serve the heart and brain.

Blood flows more slowly through narrowed arteries and may clot, blocking the blood supply to heart or brain and leading to a heart attack or stroke. Atherosclerosis may also lead to angina, as we saw above. Over time, heart attack survivors and those with angina (there is considerable overlap as angina increases the risk of a heart attack) may suffer heart failure, where the heart is no longer up to the job of pumping sufficient blood around the body.

We know plenty about the causes of CHD: a high-fat diet, smoking (above all), lack of exercise, obesity and so on. We also know, from the famous Whitehall study which is following the health of thousands of civil servants, that people in lower socio-economic classes are more likely to suffer from CHD.[36]

Further, low socio-economic status in childhood is linked to higher levels of the protein fibrinogen in the blood. Fibrinogen plays a role in blood clotting and high levels are linked with a risk of heart disease. In this study, three measures of childhood environment (adult height, father's social class, and the subject's education) were found to be inversely associated with levels of fibrinogen and, through this biological marker, with the risk of heart disease in later life.[37]

Yes, you can argue that the poor cannot afford to eat as well as the better off, but diet does not explain all the variation of CHD with social class. Cholesterol levels and saturated fat intakes are actually similar across the classes. What differs is the level of high-density lipoprotein (HDL) which removes cholesterol from the artery wall, decreasing the risk of atherosclerosis; HDL levels actually rise with social class.[38]

Research on primates (who, after all, do not smoke or have bad diets) are very revealing here, suggesting a direct causal link between stress and atherosclerosis. In Sapolsky's baboons the same total cholesterol and low-density lipoprotein (LDL) cholesterol (which does the opposite job to HDL and is sometimes known as 'bad' cholesterol) are the same across the rankings. But HDL levels were higher in the dominant than in the subordinate males.[39] The diminished HDL was also associated with elevated cortisol. This gives us a (probable) direct biochemical link between stress and heart disease through cortisol and HDL.

Moreover, work in macaque monkeys shows that animals whose ranks were switched from dominant to subordinate had coronary artery plaque levels five times higher than those who remained dominant.[40] This points to a similar link between stress and heart disease, via cortisol and HDL.

All this evidence is highly suggestive of a direct causal link between stress and heart disease, but we are not quite there yet. The final plank in the cortisol and atherosclerosis theory needs to be nailed into place, through experiments showing a molecular interaction between the stress hormones and the cholesterol transport mechanism in the blood.

We must not forget the effect of the acute phase of the stress response on the heart. As we have seen, blood pressure goes up, mediated by the actions of noradrenaline and adrenaline. High blood pressure is a known risk factor for CHD. It is not hard to imagine how this happens – blood coursing through the vessels with an abnormally high force will inevitably increase wear and tear on the arteries, roughening the inner walls and contributing to plaque formation in the long term. There is some evidence in animals that heightened cardiac response to stress through the SNS leads to plaque and that this can be reduced by using beta blockers (drugs which damp down the SNS and are often used to treat high blood pressure).[41]

BOX 18   *Homocysteine – a new player in the stress game*

Research over the last 20 years has pointed to the importance of elevated levels of the amino acid *homocysteine* as a risk factor in CHD. People whose diets are deficient in folic acid and B vitamins are particularly at risk. It is thought that homocysteine can damage the walls of the arteries and so exacerbate plaque development.

In a recent study 34 middle-aged women were given two stress-inducing tests. They had to rapidly subtract 17s from a four-figure number and were shown an anger-provoking video. Blood pressure and heart rate went up, but there was also a sharp rise in homocysteine levels. Though these were still within normal ranges, it may be that over the long term stress-linked accumulation of homocysteine could damage the arteries.[42] It will be interesting to see just where homocysteine fits in with the cortisol–HDL story outlined above.

It is also important to try to understand how the various factors affecting the stress experience (which we have discussed above) influence heart disease risk. One important report from the Whitehall study showed that lack of control at work is a potent risk factor. Male and female subjects with low job control had nearly twice the risk of heart disease compared with those with high job control.[43] The results could not be explained by other factors, such as workload, social support at work, or classic coronary risk factors such as smoking. What is fascinating about this study is that if the control aspect of the job changed (from low to high or vice versa), the heart disease risk changed in response to the new situation. Giving people a stronger say in decision making at work, or increasing the variety of the work could make a positive contribution to the nation's cardiovascular health. Even small, subtle changes, like inviting people to meetings or allowing flexible lunch breaks, could make a lot of difference.

A psychologically healthy workplace

We have seen that low job control and lack of social support lead to dangerous levels of stress, via hormonal and neurotransmitter action. Overactive stress circuits raise the risk of depression and heart disease. So, often, all this distress can be traced back to poor management in the workplace. Stress reduction and good management practices go hand in hand (while a stress policy may be merely a cosmetic exercise). People are not machines, and they are also the company's biggest asset. So it is not being unduly wimpish to take good care of them, and make them proud to be employees. In a caring company, everyone will say 'hi' to anyone else in the corridor or the lift (the MD who walks along with his nose snootily in the air is a health hazard). Little things like exchanging birthday cards, sending flowers when someone is ill, and having the odd meal out together foster that all-important social support.

Undue stress comes not only from being overstretched, but from not being stretched enough; staff development may mean time out from the job in the short term, but will repay in the long term in terms of better morale.

The good manager gets the balance right – work demands, yes, but plenty of support too. Personal space, yes, but shared responsibility for the office too. The emphasis should be on communication, rather than information overload. One of the most potent factors leading to feelings of low control and helplessness is being left out of the communications loop. Company loyalty and morale decline, and stress levels rise. It may require just one memo or circular email once a fortnight, or including people in more meetings, to turn this situation around.

One of the trickiest and most important areas of management is team building and group dynamics. A bully (let us hope it is not the boss himself) or perhaps even an antisocial person (all organizations have them) needs to be dealt with very firmly before he exerts his toxic influence and multiplies the stress level of the whole organization.

However employee-friendly the workplace, it is still having to cope with tremendous change. The future of work probably lies with short-term, part-time freelance working, perhaps with people having a portfolio of jobs.[44] This will, inevitably, have a profound effect upon team bonding and company loyalty as more and more people are thrown back on their own resources. The future office may look very different. Most organizations will have a small core of full-time permanent employees working out of a conventional office. All other skills will be bought on a contract basis, either from self-employed freelances, or from people on short-term contracts working in the office.

Where does this leave the 'psychological contract' between employee and employer? We will have to do without the security and protection of the big organization, who once looked after someone materially and psychologically from school leaving to retirement. The organization is becoming 'virtual', with people shifting loyalties many times throughout their careers.

The new freelance culture could either increase, or decrease, stress levels. Men may get more depressed, if they see women embracing the new workplace at their expense. People may work even longer hours, and children may lose out. But at least people will have more freedom, and more control over their destiny.

Run properly, the workplace can be a good source of social support. This, in turn, can be protective against heart disease, for lack of a social network appears to be a potent stressor. In Japan, for instance, rates of heart disease are very low. Some of this can be attributed to a low-fat diet, but it has also been suggested that the nature of Japanese culture, which involves a high degree of social support, may be a factor.[45]

More recently it has been shown, among a group of Swedish women, that social isolation is linked to heart-rate variability. It is well known that the more the heart rate varies throughout the day the healthier it is. Low variability seems to increase the risk of early death, especially from heart disease. One way of understanding this is to think of variable heart rate as a sign that the cardiac system is flexible and more able to cope with the demands put upon it. When heart rate does not vary much, the system is more rigid and vulnerable to damage. In the Swedish study, the lonely women were more likely than the gregarious ones to have low heart-rate variability.[46]

BOX 19   *A tale of two cities*

There is a large, and widening, gap in life expectancy and incidence of cardiovascular disease between the countries of Western and Eastern Europe.[47] In all the countries of the European Union, life expectancy is well over 70 years, while it is up to ten years less in the countries of the former Soviet Union and its neighbours. There are many reasons for the relative ill health of the Eastern Europeans. Smoking is more common, while diets are lower in fresh fruits and vegetables. Environmental pollution also makes a contribution. But the major cause of the big health divide could be the socio-economic problems coming in the wake of the collapse of the communist system in the 1980s. Shortages of food and other daily needs, feelings of deprivation, unfulfilling work and lack of control over events create chronic stress.

A recent Swedish study has assessed the contribution of psychosocial factors in the East–West divide by comparing men in two cities, Linköping in southern Sweden and Vilnius, the capital of Lithuania. The Lithuanian men reported more social isolation, job strain and depression than the Swedes – all signs that stress was getting to them. Then, all the men did a standardized laboratory stress test; the results varied depending on nationality and income group. All the Swedish men showed a normal rise and fall in cortisol in response to the test. The high-income group from Vilnius had low baseline cortisol, like the Swedes, but a relatively slow return to baseline after the test. The low-income group were very different: they had high baseline cortisol which did not respond to the challenge at all.[48] This parallels all we have already said about low social status and high cortisol and an unbalanced HPA axis. Put these findings together with the mortality data, and the social and political implications are profound, and deserving of urgent investigation.

Stress and immunity

It is well known that there are physical connections between the CNS and the immune system. Like all the other organs in the body, the components of the immune system, like the thymus which produces infection-fighting T cells, are surrounded by nerve endings. And some of the chemical messengers of the immune systems, like the *cytokines* which are key players in inflammation, can cross the blood–brain barrier and influence the CNS.

There could also be indirect links between them: the CNS drives behaviour which, in turn, affects susceptibility to disease. To take a simple example, a poor diet, which may be one consequence of depression, can result in lowered vitamin C levels and so increased susceptibility to infection. Psychoneuroimmunology (PNI) – as the study of the interaction between the CNS and the immune system is called – is a relatively new branch of research. It has only really taken off in recent years as techniques for measuring the cells and molecules of the immune system have become available.

Many changes in immunity with exposure to stressors have indeed been noted. What is currently missing, however, is an understanding of how these affect our susceptibility to disease, for the immune system is fearsomely complex, and is in a constant state of flux. Put simply, it is the body's defence system which is mobilized against disease. There are three main areas where it plays an important role. First, it fights infection; invading organisms are recognized as being 'foreign' because they bear 'foreign' protein molecules, like flags, on their surfaces. The presence of these protein flags – known as antigens – alerts the immune system in two ways. Both are based on the action of lymphocytes, a type of white blood cell produced by the bone marrow or thymus gland. T lymphocytes attack the invader directly, perhaps even engulfing it, while B lymphocytes produce molecules called antibodies which lock on to the antigen and neutralize the invader.

Second, cancer cells also bear foreign antigens on the surface and these are attacked by the immune system in a similar way. Finally, an overactive immune system may give rise to auto-immune disease such as rheumatoid arthritis where it mistakenly attacks the body's own tissue. It may also attack harmless invaders like house dust mite or pollen, leading to allergic disease. And it will reject transplanted tissue, which means that people with organ transplants need to take drugs to suppress the response of their immune system.

Research to date does show that the various components of the immune system alter on exposure to stressors. There are a number of tests which are carried out on blood samples; for instance, you might look at how well lymphocytes proliferate (they need to multiply in order to mount an effective response) or how many of the various immune cells there are in the sample.

Another method of investigating the effect of stress on immunity is to inject volunteers with an antigen and measure how much antibody is produced in response: this can be measured either in a blood sample or, more easily, in saliva. Medical students studied during exams showed decreased immunity on all the above markers, compared with when they were relaxed during vacation.[49]

A further study monitored salivary antibodies in a group of people keeping a daily stress diary over a period of 12 weeks,[50] after swallowing a harmless protein capsule which produced an antibody response. The reporting of positive events was related to greater salivary antibody production while that of negative events was related to lowered production. Like the angina and stress study mentioned earlier, this provided evidence for an immune response to everyday ups and downs.

The reality now appears to be somewhat more complicated. More sensitive analysis suggests that the immune system is probably initially boosted in response to a stressor, and *then* either returns to baseline or overshoots the mark and is depressed. A study of a group of students undergoing academic assessment showed that cortisol, salivary antibodies, and arousal were all higher on the day of assessment than in the week before the test (and highest immediately after assessment).[51] Cortisol, however, is well known to depress immunity by halting the formation of new lymphocytes; it can even kill lymphocytes. It also inhibits the release of immune system molecules like interferon. What probably happens is that cortisol is involved in the return of the immune system to baseline and, in the case of a chronic or major stressor, in its long-term depression. Meanwhile, the SNS can depress the immune system, too. But administration of a beta blocker, which damps down the action of adrenaline and noradrenaline, has been found to counteract this effect.[52]

But does all this translate into measurable effects upon health? There is some evidence that stress may increase the number of upper respiratory tract infections (such as colds and flu). Carers for people with Alzheimer's disease – a job which most people would agree involves chronic and severe stress – had significantly more colds and flu than control subjects, particularly if they suffered from a lack of social support (a key stressor in heart disease too, as we saw above).[53]

Experimental work at the former Common Cold Research Unit in Salisbury, England, first revealed a link between stress and getting a cold in an experimental setting.[54] Further research showed that acute stressful life events (duration under a month) were not associated with a higher risk of getting a cold, but chronic stress was. Most of these stressors derived from unemployment and interpersonal difficulties.[55] It looks as if a molecule called interleukin-6 (IL-6) may link stress and the symptoms of upper respiratory tract infection. IL-6 is a cytokine, one of a group of molecules involved in producing an inflammatory response (symptoms like red nose, sneezing and fever in the case of colds and flu). Stressed volunteers had worse flu symptoms and produced more IL-6 than their unstressed counterparts, when both groups were deliberately infected with the flu virus after taking a stress questionnaire.[56] Meanwhile among monkeys, animals with lower social status were more likely to catch cold than their dominant peers.[57]

Finally, wounds heal more slowly in patients who are under stress. In a recent experiment, a small group of female volunteers took a stress questionnaire and were given a small blister wound. The researchers looked for two cytokines, IL-1 and IL-8 (chemical relations of IL-6 mentioned above), known to be involved in wound healing. They also looked for *neutrophils*, immune cells which help repair damaged tissue. Meanwhile, the women's cortisol levels were also checked. There was no decrease in the number of neutrophils which had migrated to the wound site in any of the women. But the women with high cortisol had much lower levels of cytokines at the wound site: a clear demonstration that stress can impair the wound-healing process.[58] This is a major worry when it comes to surgery – for the very prospect of having an operation is a potent stressor, yet that stress means that the surgical wound will not heal as fast as it could. Slow-healing wounds can become infected and prolong a stay in hospital (occasionally they may even be fatal). It is therefore important for the patient and the surgical team to do all they can to reduce cortisol levels prior to surgery.

BOX 20   *Does stress cause cancer?*

There is a popular belief that there must be a link between stress and cancer. In fact there is little hard evidence that this is the case, although there have been many research studies. Most of these, unfortunately, have been of indifferent quality and difficult to interpret.[59] Too often they have relied on asking people about stressful events before they developed the disease. There are problems with the retrospective approach, though. First, people have selective (and sometimes poor) memories for life events. And, as we have seen, it is hard to measure stress by self-report (it is better if these data are backed up with cortisol measurements, say). Also, the patients will probably be looking for a cause for their disease and so may tend to attribute too much significance to life events.

But, even with the best-quality research, firm answers on a stress–cancer link would be hard to come by because of the nature of the disease. The development of cancer takes place in many stages over many years; it may be almost impossible to determine when and where exposure to stressors had an effect.

Stress hurts the brain

Finally, we return to stress and the brain. Evidence is mounting (as we also saw in chapter 1) that cortisol can act as a slow toxin, which causes damage to the brain over a number of years. The site where most damage occurs is at the hippocampus, which has numerous cortisol receptors.

Injecting cortisol into rats[60] or subjecting them to chronic stress[61] has profound effects on hippocampal neurons. First, it causes the dendrites to shrivel. The good news is that this damage is reversible. Second, cortisol makes neurons more vulnerable to damage from ischaemia (oxygen deprivation) or injury, according to work done in Sapolsky's lab.[62] And finally, the damaged neurons just die off, leading to shrinkage of the hippocampus.[63]

Similar neuronal loss has been seen in primates and, recently, even in humans. The first human study concerns people who have Cushing's disease, where a tumour somewhere in the HPA axis causes excess production of cortisol. MRI scans showed that the hippocampus, but not the rest of the brain, was smaller than average in these patients, and they also had memory problems.[64] The greater the excess cortisol secretion, the more the hippocampus shrank. If the tumour was removed, and hormonal levels went back to normal, the hippocampus and the memory recovered. This strongly implicates cortisol in the death of human hippocampal neurons.

Hippocampal shrinkage has also been seen in cases of PTSD in Vietnam veterans[65] and in adults who had suffered childhood abuse.[66] However, in these cases we cannot be sure whether cortisol is causing the hippocampal shrinkage, or whether it is related to trauma exposure or to PTSD, or, indeed, whether the small hippocampus preceded either the trauma or the cortisol exposure.

However, the PTSD findings look more significant next to a study which shows hippocampal shrinkage in people who had recovered from major depression (see also Box 1, p.10). Although their cortisol levels were normal at the time of the study, their hippocampal volume was still significantly reduced, suggesting that damage could have occurred during the bout of depression. What is more, the longer they had been depressed, the smaller the hippocampus.[67] But, tantalizingly, we *still* cannot prove that cortisol caused this shrinkage, because we do not know what the cortisol status of the patients was when they were depressed, or at what stage the hippocampus damage took place. Cortisol is guilty merely by association. Is this enough to make a firm theory about cortisol and depression? No, but it is powerful evidence that cortisol may be a brain toxin. And that is the cue for going deeper into depression – in the next chapter.

CHAPTER FIVE

Blue Mood, Grey World:
The Problem of Depression

It seems strange that the most common human diseases are also the least well understood by science. We can explore the solar system, sequence the human genome, even (perhaps) clone humans – but we cannot cure the common cold and we do not do all that well in treating cancer.

It is the same with mental illness. Depression is often called the 'common cold' of psychiatry precisely because it *is* so common: up to 20 per cent of us can expect to suffer a major, disabling, bout of the illness during our lifetime, while the prevalence of depression among the general population is around 5 per cent. As we saw in chapter 3, depression is universal (although it manifests itself in different ways in different cultures) and, indeed, is on the increase.

Where the analogy between depression and the common cold breaks down is that there are successful treatments for depression (and no prospect whatsoever of a cure for the common cold). The tragedy is that so many people with depression do not get the help and treatment they need.

The bare bones of depression

The tip of the iceberg

Depression is still a vastly under-recognized problem. First, those who are depressed often do not realize what is wrong with them, or know that their illness is treatable. Even if they do, they may not feel motivated to do anything, because negative thinking is so bound up with the condition. The depressed person convinces himself either that he is unworthy of treatment, or that the treatment could not possibly work.

Another contributing factor is the social stigma that is attached to mental illness, including depression. People with mental illness are thought of as being unstable, violent, unpredictable and just – well – different. Naturally, these attitudes are hardened every time a mentally ill person being cared for (or, more usually, *not* being cared for) in the community commits a random act of violence. So someone with depression may be reluctant to see a doctor because they do not want to be labelled as 'mad' or 'mental'.

It is rather difficult to count depressed people who have never sought help, but the surveys that have been done in the community do suggest that the majority go undiagnosed and untreated – even the most severe cases.[1]

Although a good psychiatrist should be able to spot depression in all its guises, the family doctor is usually the first port of call. If he or she is not well educated in mental health matters, the patient stands little chance of receiving the help they need – even though a typical general practice will probably see one case of depression on most days. In fact, up to 10 per cent of patients visiting the doctor are probably suffering from some form of depression (although they may focus on a physical complaint, like backache).

Research shows that doctors miss around half of the cases of depression on the first consultation. Second time round, though, the doctor will spot depression in a further 10 per cent of the total. Given that around half of the unrecognized cases (say, 20 per cent of the total) get better by themselves, this still leaves 20 per cent whose illness is never diagnosed and who may be set on a course of chronic, untreated depression.[2] Just imagine if these figures applied to the diagnosis of cancer or heart disease.

However, public understanding and awareness of depression has certainly increased in recent years thanks, in part, to initiatives like the Defeat Depression Campaign run by the Royal College of Psychiatrists in the UK. Moreover, eminent figures such as the biologist Lewis Wolpert and the Pulitzer Prize winner William Styron have done much to reduce the stigma by writing openly of their own experience of depression. Indeed in *Darkness Visible* Styron notes receiving thousands of letters after a magazine piece he wrote about the book. A BBC programme on depression brought a similar response.[3]

Meanwhile, brain science is really beginning to illuminate the mystery of depression. The subtle, yet profound changes in brain chemistry in depression, and the areas of the brain involved, are becoming increasingly well understood as (albeit more slowly) is the role played by genetics. All this suggests that, although there is still a long way to go, people with depression may look forward to a brighter future.

A darker shade of blue – the experience of depression

Each person's experience of depression is different although, as we will see, there are some common features. Here is one man's account. Glyn Jones, now 71, is a successful TV producer. He is the creator of the acclaimed science and technology magazine programme *Tomorrow's World* and has produced numerous thought-provoking documentaries. Depression struck, he says, at the height of his most prolific period, in the 1960s.

> *I can never remember a time in my life when I felt really cheerful and happy. Daphne, my wife, says she always thought of me as being tense, nervous and moody. But my first experience in the foothills of real mental illness came in 1962 when I was researching the Moon landing programme in the United States. On this journey, I had a severe panic attack in my hotel room. I suddenly had this feeling of utter terror and I began to shake. I felt as if I was dying.*

As work pressures grew, there were further panic attacks and Glyn's mental health deteriorated, exacerbated by a working environment where no-one knew anything about depression. He developed agoraphobia and was unable to go out or see people.

> *I would drive to a certain roundabout near the M4 and be unable to get past it and would have to return home. I got to the stage where I couldn't even get out of bed. I was treated with tranquillizers for two years, which made things worse.*

In fact it was not until the late 1980s that Glyn received a correct diagnosis and treatment. Until then, there were extended periods of blackness and inertia.

> *The experience of depression is hard to describe unless you have experienced it. It is like being in a pitch-black cave, with the darkness pressing in on you with an almost physical force. You can see the entrance of the cave not far away, and outside it the world, sometimes bright and sunny, sometimes dull or stormy, but always full of human activity; it does not matter because it has no relevance or meaning to you. You cannot touch the world outside your own dark sphere of misery, terror and wracking anxiety. You wake in the morning and at once fear floods into your mind as water must flood into a sinking ship. You are not going to be able to get up, you are not going to be able to deal with the day: the postman will only bring more terror: it is all unrelieved and underneath there is a deep fear. Fear of what? I can't*

tell you. Your wife may be lying alongside you but she is no longer part of a relationship with you. Nor are the rest of the family. They would not possibly understand why you shrink from them or what you are feeling even if you could describe it to them: one of the things you can't distinguish is whether they are the exclusion zone or you. Only later will you realize that it is you that is insulated against human contact.

I simply don't believe that anyone untouched by serious depression can understand the horror within which depressives are cocooned. I cannot recall understanding that I was in any way desperately ill, which is another penalty in the sense that the disease does not allow you to understand your problems.

When depressives look back over their lives, there are often many regrets, even if they have recovered, as Glyn has.

Depression played havoc with the family; it's a miracle we're still together and without them I would certainly be dead by now. It also ruined me financially because I couldn't work. The real pain is the failure of aspirations. I was a good television producer and doing extremely well. I just wanted to make programmes for people, but I wasn't able to do all I had in me to do.

Still, we were in North Wales the other day, and it gave me such great pleasure to look at the scenery – the landscape there is just wild enough to please me – and the sunlight on the Menai Straits. If you are clinically depressed you couldn't experience any of that – and that is the utter tragedy.

Perhaps depression is really not the right word to describe these experiences. Like the word stress, it has become debased by over-use. Life is full of minor setbacks that produce feelings of disappointment, sadness, and frustration which are all lumped together as the experience of depression. Now think of the worst thing that could possibly happen to you. For many of us, it would be the death of a loved one or a life-threatening illness. This is how Kay Redfield Jamison describes the way she felt after the sudden death of her husband.

But grief, fortunately, is very different from depression: it is sad, it is awful, but it is not without hope. David's death did not plunge me into unendurable darkness.[4]

Her experience is echoed by Lewis Wolpert in his account of a serious bout of depression:

> *It was the worst experience of my life. More terrible even than watching my wife*
> *die of cancer. I am ashamed to admit that my depression felt worse than her death*
> *but it is true.*[5]

Sufferers also rate depression as worse than physical illness. Dr John Horder, former President of the Royal College of General Practitioners, has suffered from renal colic (an excruciatingly painful condition), a heart attack, and depression. He says, reflecting on the pain of the three different illnesses.

> *If I had to choose again I would prefer to avoid the pain of depression.*[6]

Glyn Jones echoes this view:

> *I had to have a difficult heart operation in 1988 – I had an artificial aortic valve*
> *implanted – and coming out of the anaesthetic I thought that I would even go*
> *through this operation again rather than endure another bout of depression.*

Not all depression is as severe, or as devastating, as this. It can take the form of a mild, persistent gloom which, for some people, has been the way they have been for as long as they can remember. Should we call this pathological?

Some depression appears to be merely an exaggeration of a normal response to an event, such as grief following bereavement or job loss, or the natural low mood that comes with physical illness. Sometimes, as in post-natal depression, the response seems paradoxical, but at least there is a link to some external event.

Other depressions follow a pattern; in manic depression, as we shall see, low moods are interspersed with high ones, and in seasonal affective disorder, mood waxes and wanes with the calendar: depression in winter, elevated mood in summer. But some depressions strike for no apparent reason.

So how can we make clinical and scientific sense of this wide spectrum of experience? What is just part of the range of human expression – and what is abnormal, destructive, and ill?

There is, as yet, no physical diagnostic test for depression. The formal diagnosis of the condition depends on a questionnaire administered by a psychiatrist. The two most common tests are known as the Hamilton Rating Scale for Depression and the Beck Depression Inventory, and they have been designed to tease out the pattern of characteristic symptoms. A family doctor can give these tests, and of course you can test yourself: there are many versions available on the Internet, and in self-help books and literature.

There are also two systems for describing mood (or affective) disorders, the name given to the broad diagnostic category which includes depression. One is the DSM-IV system of the American Psychiatric Association (which we mentioned in the previous chapter), and the other is the WHO ICD-10 system (ICD stands for International Classification of Disease). In broad terms, the diagnostic check lists offered by the two systems are very similar. They are also quite complex in the number of subtypes of depression they describe. To simpify matters we will look at just two of the major categories: first, major depression, and then bipolar disorder, often also known as manic depression.

Depression by degrees

There are two main dimensions to depression. First, there is the time dimension: the person concerned will have been in a depressed mood or experienced a loss of interest or pleasure in life for a period of at least two weeks and for most of the day. For adolescents and children with suspected depression, being in an unusually irritable mood over this period of time is the usual criterion (although irritability can be a marked feature of depression in adults too). In addition, the depressed individual will find their condition is interfering with their life: they may not be able to concentrate on work, say, or they may not be able to get out of bed or carry on their usual social activities. Second, there is a specific check list of mental and physical symptoms which form a typical pattern; depression is diagnosed only if five or more of these are ticked off. In brief, these symptoms are:

- depressed mood
- loss of interest and pleasure
- disturbance in appetite
- changes in sleep and activity level
- fatigue
- inappropriate feelings of guilt
- difficulty in concentration
- thoughts or plans of suicide.

The wide spectrum of symptoms reveals how depression is a problem of both the mind and the body, underlining its fundamental biological nature. It is worth looking at these symptoms in more detail, to try to capture more fully the nature of depression.

The daily variation of mood is interesting: most people with depression feel at their very worst first thing in the morning and may feel more or less normal by bedtime. This is perhaps not surprising, for the body goes through daily physiological cycles (known popularly as biorhythms) and one of the many chemicals which varies is cortisol, which is at its highest in the early morning. There may be a link, although it has not been proved.

A sure sign that depression is worsening is when the 'good' period in each day gets shorter and shorter, until it dwindles to nothing. This pattern is superimposed upon the person's natural energy cycles. For someone who is normally alert and does his best work first thing, the onset of depression will be particularly noticeable. For 'night owls', depression may not feel much different from their normal dopey morning mood – only it takes longer and longer for energy to build up as the day progresses.

Now let us look at the language used to describe the depressed mood: 'low', 'fed up' or 'empty'. This obviously overlaps considerably with loss of pleasure or interest, but for some people this will be the predominant feature. So, if you have many interests and are normally an enthusiastic type of person, the first sign of depression could be when you do not particularly want to watch your favourite TV programme, have a drink with a friend or see a new film or play. In short, you have nothing to look forward to. This is devastating, for it robs you of motivation: life will become progressively more difficult from now on. Without motivation, the simplest action becomes a chore.

There is a scientific term for this loss of interest in life: it is called *anhedonia* (the opposite of hedonism). Anhedonia is not peculiar to depression; it occurs in other mental illnesses like schizophrenia and is thought to arise from imbalances in specific brain regions. These are now under active investigation through brain-scanning techniques.

Now for those physical symptoms. Depressed people lose their appetite; there may be some overlap here with anhedonia because food loses its taste and interest, which is a major driving force in appetite. Loss of weight might be quite noticeable (but typically cannot be appreciated by depressed people who would have loved to have lost a few pounds when they were well; nor should it be, for it is a sign of illness). In some forms of depression – particularly seasonal affective disorder – there is overeating, which leads to weight gain. For some people, the appetite problem will be a major feature. In fact, many people with eating disorders (anorexia and bulimia) go on to develop major depression, so it can be rather hard to disentangle the two.

The nature of the sleep disturbance in depression is quite characteristic. You may not have any problem getting off to sleep but, typically, you will wake early – a couple of hours, or more, before your usual time – and be unable to get back to sleep.

Sleep disturbance contributes to another physical symptom of depression, which is profound fatigue. This is a feeling of exhaustion that comes on after the slightest exertion and is not relieved by rest. Some people are so disabled by this fatigue that they will be completely unable to get out of bed in the morning – a disastrous development. The final physical symptom of depression is a *change* in level of activity; either you feel sluggish and lacking in energy, or you may feel restless, agitated, 'hyper' or 'wired-up'.

Hand in hand with these physical symptoms go the typical thought processes of a depressed person. Low self-esteem and guilt are very common, along with a generally negative attitude to the world around them (typically, they blame themselves when things go wrong, and generalize this into a feeling that everything is bad). Intellectual performance suffers too. Concentration, memory, and attention are all impaired; this plunges self-esteem to new lows, and magnifies feelings of guilt and failure.

An obvious outcome of all this distress is thoughts, or even plans, of suicide. While non-depressed people think about suicide too (and even attempt it), in depression suicidal ideas may dominate a person's thinking and the person may become obsessed with plans to carry out the act. You only need to look at William Styron or Lewis Wolpert's accounts to see how the world suddenly becomes full of suicide opportunities. And here is the great novelist Leo Tolstoy describing his preoccupation with suicide during a period of depression in the midst of a happy and fulfilled life:

> *The thought of suicide came to me as naturally then as the thought of improving life had come to me before . . . . And there I was, a fortunate man, carrying a rope from my room, where I was alone every night as I undressed, so that I would not hang myself from the beam between the closets. And I quit going hunting with a gun, so that I would not be too easily tempted to rid myself of life.*[7]

At its worst, depression includes psychotic features: that is, people lose touch with reality. They might imagine they are responsible for some terrible, distant catastrophe, like an earthquake, or believe their body is rotting; these false beliefs are known as delusions. Another psychotic feature is hallucinations: hearing or, less commonly, seeing things which are not really there. Voices in the head can prompt suicidal acts.

But there are degrees of depression. As discussed above, anyone with five or more of the above symptoms would be diagnosed with major depression (note, the term clinical depression is also used sometimes). Anyone with fewer symptoms, or a lesser impairment in quality of life, will be said to have moderate or mild depression. Mild variants are sometimes called *dysthymia* and, in fact, it can be hard to separate this condition from having a generally negative and gloomy outlook on life, while still functioning in a normal way.

One of the complications with depression is that it often co-exists with other mental and physical illnesses – such as schizophrenia or heart disease. This makes it hard to know where the depression ends and the other illness starts, for there can be a huge degree of overlap. Do the symptoms of depression actually arise from the other condition, or are *those* symptoms a 'masked' form of depression? Or is the patient just unfortunate enough to have two (or more) distinct illnesses, one of which is depression?

All this is important, because it affects the treatment that should be given. Maybe it is better to solve a chronic pain problem than treat the ensuing depression. But maybe that stomach pain will clear up with antidepressants and they should be tried instead of yet another exploratory operation?

Incidentally, when depression presents mainly in the form of physical symptoms, it can be a real headache (if you will excuse the pun) for the family doctor, because he or she will have to run tests, which will turn out to be negative. This leaves them with the problem of discussing a diagnosis of depression with the patient, who may be unwilling to accept it. The masking of depressive symptoms with physical problems is known as somatization and is most common in cultures, like China, where pure mental illness carries even more of a stigma than it does in the West. A related problem is hypochondria, which is a preoccupation with bodily symptoms in the absence of organic disease. The relationship between depression and hypochondria is complex, but it is probably safe to say that most hypochondriacs are probably suffering from depression.

Up to 90 per cent of people with depression also suffer from anxiety, while about a third also have formal anxiety disorders like panic disorder or obsessive compulsive disorder. This has led some psychiatrists to suggest a unitary theory – that is, depression and anxiety are two different forms of the same illness.

You often see alcohol and drug abuse in the context of depression. But again, as with physical illness, it is not clear where the causal link lies. As we saw in chapter 1, there is evidence that depressed people often use alcohol and drugs as a form of self-medication, to raise the levels of serotonin and other brain chemicals. But these drugs can also cause depression (hardly surprising, as they act on the brain).

A gloomy outlook

Suppose, then, despite all these complications, a diagnosis of depression has been given. Now what? Here is another difference between the common cold and depression. A cold lasts, at most, up to ten days. On average, an episode of depression lasts for several months. Plenty of time to wreck your job, your relationships, and your finances. Untreated – which most depression is – many people will recover spontaneously. But a minority may continue to be affected for years, and some may never fully recover.

The really sad thing about depression is that it is probably a chronic condition: something you have to live with, like diabetes. Because once you have been through one bout of major depression, the chances of recurrence are as high as 60 per cent. And after two episodes, the chance of having a third is around 70 per cent. After three or more episodes of depression, a chronic course is more or less set.

It is crucially important to understand the chronic course of depression, especially if left untreated. To keep well, some people might need to take antidepressants for the rest of their lives (in much the same way as people with high blood pressure may have to be on tablets long term). And while the first few episodes may be triggered by some obvious stressor or event, later episodes may occur for no apparent reason. There is some evidence that a first experience of depression can actually remodel the brain, sensitizing it to further episodes – a phenomenon known as *kindling*. We will look at the kindling theory below.

There are great variations in the patterns of depressive episodes in someone's life. They may be separated by many months or even years, or they may begin to increase in frequency. Although most bouts last for months, briefer – yet equally intense – episodes lasting weeks or even days may occur.

Box 21   *Dire consequences*

The most obvious negative outcome to depression is suicide, and 15 per cent of those who are most severely affected by major depression die in this way (and of all those affected by any degree of depression around 20 per cent make at least one suicide attempt).

But that is not all. Depression also leads to an increase in physical illness. According to the DSM, it is associated with a fourfold increase in overall mortality in the over-55s. One of the main risks is of coronary heart disease. A recent American study reports on the progress of 1190 male medical students who had been monitored for between 30 and 50 years. Those who developed clinical depression in this time period (12 per cent of the total) were more than twice as likely either to develop coronary heart disease or to have a heart attack than their non-depressed peers.[8] In some cases, the heart attacks occurred ten years after the episode of depression.

Another study, based on patients in British general practice, showed that men with depression in the preceding ten years were three times more likely to develop heart disease than men without depression. Once they had a heart problem, they were about twice as likely to get depressed than men with healthy hearts.[9] Curiously, no such link could be found in women patients.

A recent study also suggests that depression makes the blood vessels of heart patients less able to respond to changes in blood pressure, possibly through moderating the effects of the autonomic nervous system.[10] However, although the depressed heart patients may have less flexible and efficient cardiac response to circulatory change, it is not yet known if this leads to any increased risk of heart attack.

We do not know exactly how depression gives rise to heart problems, although it is tempting to say that stress must play a role, perhaps through the effects of cortisol (as discussed in the last chapter). Remember too, that serotonin is found in blood as well. If dysfunctional serotonin in the brain is linked to depression, then maybe there is a problem with blood serotonin also – perhaps making it more likely to clot. But this is speculation: only further research will reveal how a (psychological) broken heart can become a physical reality.

Meanwhile, depression has also been found to increase the risk of hip fracture in elderly people. Nearly 19,000 Norwegian women over the age of 50 were monitored for three years. Of these, 329 had a hip fracture.

> The researchers found that the 10 per cent of women who were the most depressed (as measured by levels of loneliness, life dissatisfaction, sleep disorders, anxiety and mood) had twice the risk of hip fractures than the lowest 10 per cent of the women.[11] However, we do not know if the depressed women increased their risk indirectly via poor diet or smoking, or if it was some direct effect of increased cortisol on the bones.

Swings and roundabouts – the puzzle of bipolar disorder

Who would not want to be bubbly, optimistic, sociable, creative, charismatic, and confident – and all this on only a few hours' sleep a night? Surely this must be the pinnacle of mental health – the kind of psychological drive that makes for successful businesses and great parties. Yes, it can be all that, but sometimes this state – known clinically as hypomania – is the prelude to something far more frightening and destructive.

We use the word *mania* casually, usually to describe an obsession (remember Beatlemania?) or a state of excitement ('I'm a bit manic at the moment') but there is nothing casual about a state of full-blown mania. Put very simply, mania is the reverse of depression. The best way to describe it is as an excessively good mood: in other words, a mood of optimism and expansion which is hardly justified by the circumstances. The symptoms of a manic episode are overactivity, incessant talking (Virginia Woolf, during a manic phase, talked non-stop for three days, brooking no interruptions and becoming increasingly incoherent), decreased sleep, racing thoughts, maybe hyperacusis (heightened sensory awareness) and increasingly indiscreet behaviour, whether sexual promiscuity or running wild with a credit card (possibly both).

Sometimes mania is marked by irritability and violent outbursts, which can lead to fights, injuries, and involvement with the law. Delusions of grandeur are not uncommon (he has a plan to save the world, she can make a million if she cashes in her pension now) and nor are terrifying hallucinations. Left untreated, someone in a manic episode could even die from exhaustion or dehydration. (An acute attack of mania is considered to be a serious psychiatric emergency.)

But mania rarely occurs in isolation. Most often it is as part of the picture of bipolar disorder (so-called because the affected person swings between two opposite poles – mania and depression). Sometimes major depression is known as unipolar disorder, but this is probably a bit misleading because although there are some similarities between bipolar disorder and depression, the differences are actually quite significant. We should probably think of them as separate disorders, rather than depression being a form of bipolar disorder, but without the mania.

As with depression, there is currently no biochemical test for bipolar disorder. A psychological questionnaire is used to uncover a pattern of mood swings over time. Having three or more of the symptoms described above will usually prompt a diagnosis of mania and, usually, it is interspersed with periods of depression. Typically, a manic episode will last between a fortnight and perhaps four or five months, while the depression is longer, lasting up to six months. But the person concerned will be completely normal between episodes of both mania and depression (which may make it harder for them and their associates to accept the illness and the need for treatment). Sometimes, episodes happen at a higher frequency, say several times a year, and this is known as rapid cycling. Recurrence is key to bipolar disorder: having a one-off episode is virtually unknown (unlike major depression, where a single episode is relatively common).

Bipolar disorder affects about one per cent of the population, and so it is less common than depression (which affects between five and nine per cent of women, at any one time, and two to three per cent of men). There is also no sex difference in its incidence and, as we will see, there is also a stronger genetic factor than in depression.

Bipolar disorder can have very serious consequences if left untreated. Up to one half of those affected attempt suicide at some time in their lives (compared with one per cent of the general population) and around one in five actually commit suicide (note too that around two-thirds of all suicides are linked to bipolar disorder or depression)

Substance abuse often occurs along with bipolar disorder,[12] as it does in depression, complicating what is already a difficult condition. Like depression, bipolar disorder also occurs in a milder form, known as *cyclothymia*. This is the clinical description for someone you or I might just call moody or volatile; they are subject to periods of gloominess alternating with bouts of mild elation, giving a long-term impression of emotional instability. It is arguable whether cyclothymia really constitutes a clinical condition (surely we are all entitled to our emotional ups and downs without their being labelled pathological?). Perhaps where cyclothymia poses a problem is that the mood swings are not seen as being related to external events, or under the control of the person affected. Cyclothymia often occurs in families affected by bipolar disorder, suggesting a biological relationship between the two conditions. And, of course, there is always a risk that cyclothymia will develop into full-blown bipolar disorder.

At this point it is worth reviewing the similarities and differences between major depression and bipolar disorder. Depression is far more common than bipolar disorder, affecting up to ten times as many people. It affects more women than men, whereas bipolar disorder affects men and women equally. Bipolar illness, on the other hand, is more likely to run in families than is pure depression. It also shows itself at a younger age than depression. Both these observations point to a stronger influence of genetic factors in bipolar disorder; depression is, as we will see, more influenced by environmental factors. Bipolar disorder is nearly always recurrent and chronic, while major depression is a one-off event in a significant number of cases. The suicide rate tends to be higher in bipolar disorder. All this points to important differences in the genes, brain chemicals, and brain circuits involved in the two disorders – more about this later. Finally, the drug treatments for bipolar disorders and depression are quite different too.

BOX 22   *In good company?*

It is not tactful to suggest to someone whose life is falling apart that there could be a good side to bipolar disorder or depression. But the link between mental illness and high achievement goes back to the ancient Greeks and (controversial though it is) has persisted. Hundreds of great men and women have suffered from mood disorders and we can only list a few of them here just to give a broad-brush impression.

The extensive diaries and letters of Virginia Woolf give a frank picture of her sufferings with manic depression; she eventually committed suicide by drowning in 1941. William Styron we have already mentioned, but from the world of literature we could also add William Blake, Charles Dickens, Lord Byron, John Keats, the poets Gerard Manley Hopkins, Sylvia Plath and Anne Sexton and many others who were known to suffer from either depression or bipolar disorder.

Several famous composers, including Tchaikovsky, Mussorgsky, and Rachmaninoff were similarly affected. Particularly interesting is an analysis of the life and work of Robert Schumann in the context of the highs and lows of his bipolar disorder.[13] Peaks of creativity (measured in numbers of compositions) occurred in 1840 and 1849, coinciding with periods of what we would now call hypomania. In contrast, a severe depression in 1844 coincided with zero output, as did 1854, the year when he attempted suicide (he died in an asylum in 1856).

Everyone knows Vincent Van Gogh suffered from mental illness – in fact, the experts have been wrangling over the exact nature of his disease for years (was it schizophrenia, epilepsy, too much absinthe or a form of early dementia?) – but so too did artists like Munch, Landseer and Gauguin.

Joseph Schildkraut of Harvard Medical School has found a high prevalence of mood disorders, often compounded by alcohol abuse, among 15 of the mid-20th century Abstract Expressionist artists of the New York School. Mark Rothko and Arshile Gorky committed suicide, while Jackson Pollock and David Smith died in single-vehicle car crashes in circumstances that may have reflected suicidal intent. Four (possibly) out of 15 gives a suicide rate far higher than the general US population (around 12 per 100,000). Schildkraut argues that depression, inevitably, involves turning inward, confronting existential questions ('to be or not to be'); these artists used techniques based on free association to express their inner struggles on canvas.[14] The works of genius they left behind reveal much about the experience of depression, which is so hard to put into words.

The occurrence of depression alongside great achievement is found in science too. Isaac Newton probably suffered from bipolar disorder while the Austrian physicist Ludwig Boltzmann (1844–1906) had a lifelong history of depression. Boltzmann's great advance was to apply the laws of statistics to the behaviour of atoms, and so predict the properties of matter – a huge and fundamental advance in both physics and chemistry. But his work was controversial and, stung by his critics, he committed suicide. Equally shocking was the suicide of Wallace Carothers (1896–1937), the inventor of nylon. Depression defeated him as he stood on the brink of huge commercial success, and he killed himself just after his marriage at the age of 41.

Meanwhile, a survey of 291 world-famous men including scientists and inventors, thinkers and scholars, statesman and national leaders, painters and sculptors, composers and writers concluded that the mood disorders are most prevalent among writers and artists.[15] However, we know of at least one great leader who suffered from depression, for Winston Churchill's struggle with his 'black dog' was no secret. And a survey of 100 male British and American writers shows that no fewer than 93 per cent suffered from some form of mood disorder, frequently complicated by drug and alcohol abuse.[16] For a fuller list consult Kay Redfield

Jamison's *Touched With Fire* (indeed, she could have included herself – she has bipolar disorder, and has risen to become one of the world's leading experts in the field).

But is there more to this than just historical interest? Are mood disorders really any more prevalent among the famous and talented – or does it just seem that way because we know more about their lives?

We may be able to gain more insight by looking at living people. Jamison has studied 47 living eminent Britsh writers and artists[17] and found that 38 per cent had been treated for mood disorders (far more than the general population). One-third of the total reported a history of cyclothymia, and nearly all had intense productive periods, marked by many of the characteristics of hypomania: energy, decreased need for sleep, flow of ideas, and so on. Incidentally, although the research suggests that writers and artists have the lion's share of mood disorders, it is rumoured that many of our leading captains of industry and politicians have bipolar disorder or, at the very least, prolonged periods of hypomania (but are not as open about their history as Professor Jamison is about hers – perhaps understandably).

Note the link between hypomania and creativity, which is just what you might expect. Another interesting pointer comes from an analysis by Ruth Richards and her team at Harvard University which shows that creative talent and bipolar disorder (and its milder variant, cyclothymia) seem to congregate in the same families.[18] They found a higher degree of creativity among people with these mood disorders *and* their first-degree relatives than among families either with no mental illness, or with other types of psychiatric disorders.

This suggests that the same genes could influence both mood disorder and creativity, but even if this is so, we know very little about the brain science involved. And of course, the majority of high achievers do not have a mood disorder.

Yes, but why?

You may be surprised to learn how little is known of the actual causes of disease. The great Greek physician Hippocrates, who lived around 450 BC, argued that illness arose from within the body, although he did not know how or why. But it was also widely believed that disease was a punishment from God, at least until the 17th century, when medicine started to become a science in its own right.

The germ theory of disease, which was developed by Louis Pasteur in the 19th century, was a great advance. Now doctors knew they needed to fight the invading bacterium *Mycobacterium tuberculosis*, not the devils inside the patient (whereas the Great Plague of London in 1665 brought calls for repentance as the bodies piled up). But there are still huge gaps in our understanding of the causes of disease. For instance, we do not know the origin of most cases of high blood pressure, and the causes of coronary artery disease, heart disease, and Alzheimer's disease are not all that well understood either.

In contrast, the pathogenesis of disease – what happens in the body as the disease progresses – is better understood. That is probably why most treatments act on symptoms, rather than the causes of disease. So while antibiotics tackle the root cause of an infection, by eradicating bacteria, the use of anti-cancer drugs is mainly a damage limitation exercise.

This distinction is important in depression. We do not really understand what causes it, but the pathogenesis – specific patterns of brain activity and disordered brain chemistry – has been observed. Antidepressant drugs mainly balance the brain chemistry, but they relieve the symptoms of depression rather than curing it. An analogy would be the use of an over-the-counter cold remedy: it clears up the symptoms, but does not cure the cold (whereas an antibiotic should cure an ear infection).

The cause of blue moods cannot easily be pinpointed because depression is a very complex disorder, in which many different factors are at play. In one person, genetic factors may be so influential that they seem almost destined to develop a mood disorder even if they have a relatively carefree life. In another, one bad life experience after another eventually triggers a major depression, and cause and effect look very clear-cut. And in a third, a mood disorder seems to be an almost random event, occuring for no apparent reason, but if you look carefully it might then become evident that there is a combination of factors: a slight genetic predisposition, a chronic stressor (like a difficult relationship), and a bout of illness or change of medication that pushes the person over the edge into clinical depression.

Now we will look at some of the factors underlying mood disorders, starting with what you are born with (family history), then moving to childhood experience, and finally factors in adult life.

Family fortunes

Mood disorders often run in families for many generations. The pattern of inheritance is complex because, from the little we know of the genetics of mood disorders, it looks as if many *susceptibility* genes, each exerting a small effect, are involved (as we saw in chapter 2). This is in sharp contrast with a single gene disorder, like the brain disease Huntington's chorea, or familial hypercholesterolaemia (a serious disorder of cholesterol metabolism) where genetics are destiny – if you have the gene, you get the disease. In mood disorders, the possession of several of the predisposing genes is probably necessary. Moreover, we cannot be sure how these genes interact with other factors. So mood disorders are familial, rather than genetic. That is, genes make a contribution, but are not the whole story.

If a first-degree relative (parent or sibling) suffers from major depression, you have a greater risk of developing the disorder than the rest of the population: studies to date suggest 1.5 to three times the risk. Where the onset of the depression was at a young age (less than 20) the relative risk is even higher. This reflects what is seen in other diseases, including breast cancer, Alzheimer's disease and heart disease: the younger the age of the person affected, the more important the role of genetic factors. Put simply, the longer you live before a disease affects you, the more likely it is that environmental, rather than genetic, factors are the underlying cause.

As we discussed in chapter 2, twin studies are one way of discovering the relative contribution genetics makes to a disease. In major depression, the concordance between monozygotic twins in one recent study was found to be 46 per cent, while that between dizygotic twins was only 20 per cent.[19] In other words, if one of the monozygotic twins had major depression, then the chances of the other developing it were nearly 50-50.

If you put these figures together with rates of depression among the general population, then the role played by heredity comes out to between half and three-quarters, depending on which figures you use. Very roughly then, we could say that around half of an individual's vulnerability to major depression is governed by genes. In other words, some of us are born more susceptible to depression than others, and being aware of one's vulnerability is no bad thing.

When it comes to bipolar disorder the familial factor is far more pronounced. People with a first-degree relative who has bipolar disorder run a ten times greater risk of developing it than the rest of the population, and they also run twice the risk of developing major depression. In families with many affected members, the risks may run even higher. Twin studies have revealed striking differences in concordance between monozygotic and dizygotic twins. For monozygotic twins, the concordance is 63 per cent and for dizygotic twins it is 20 per cent, according to a study of a very large sample of Danish twins.[20]

Childhood factors and psychological theories

It may seem obvious that early childhood influences can lead to depression. Early development and psychology is a huge topic, much of which is outside the scope of this book, but we will review a few of the ideas which seem to have a bearing upon mood disorders.

One of the most influential figures in this area was John Bowlby, who developed the concept of maternal deprivation in the 1950s. His studies on children demonstrated the importance of emotional attachment and he noted that separation caused anxiety and sadness.[21] There is a crucial need, he argued, for adequate early parenting, for the experience of relating to the mother is internalized and will affect future relationships. Bowlby's studies also showed that a secure attachment created self-confidence and high self-esteem (the opposite of depression): secure infants were more likely to explore their environment, for example.

However, the evidence that severe childhood difficulties lead to adult depression is conflicting and complicated. Even an obvious risk factor, like the death of a parent, need not necessarily mark a child for life[22] and does not necessarily lead to adult depression.

It is very difficult to separate out these early parental influences from the temperament a child has at birth. Temperament can be defined as the biological underpinnings of personality – the set of innate responses to stimuli we are born with. Any parent knows that, even though their children may be treated equally, they are very different in personality, and these differences can become apparent very soon after birth – surely before parental influences have moulded the personality to any great extent?

This is not quite the same thing as being born with genes that predispose to depression, although the two will probably turn out to be closely related. Temperament does appear to be quite strongly linked to later development of mood disorders. Hagop Akiskal, of the National Insitute for Mental Health, has found two specific temperaments linked with the development of mood disorders in later life. The main features of the dysthymic temperament are introversion, gloom and lethargy. Dysthymics are more prone to major depression, while cyclothymics are vulnerable to bipolar disorder.[23] Temperament, according to Akiskal's model, can be seen as a stepping stone between genes and mood disorder; the temperament is set (at least partly) by genes, and temperament detemines the risk of later mood disorder.

Another long-term study, carried out on children in New Zealand, revealed that you can pick out future depressives as early as age *three* on the basis of temperament. Inhibited three-year-olds were more than twice as likely to have been diagnosed with depression by age 21, compared with other children.[24] Meanwhile, the work of Stephen Suomi in rhesus monkeys (which we discussed in the last chapter) is quite revealing on the relationship between temperament and early childhood experience. Within a group of monkeys, two specific temperamental types could be identified. The so-called high reactors, which typically would account for around 20 per cent of the group, were nervy, anxious individuals from birth; they left their mothers later, and explored their surroundings less. Another 5–10 per cent were impulsive – they tended to be aggressive, were often expelled from the troop and usually had low social status. Both temperaments proved to be highly heritable and, you have to admit, the parallels with human behaviour are indeed striking.

Maternal deprivation (separating infant monkeys from their mothers at birth and hand-rearing them, before returning them to live with other infants) could turn normal rhesus monkeys into high reactors or, particularly with males, impulsive types. It also makes them into poorer parents in their turn. Furthermore, if the group was stressed by varying the amount of food available, so that parents had to go and forage and so neglect their offspring, similar effects were seen.[25]

But if the early environment was enhanced, the opposite happened. Suomi picked out a number of especially nurturing mothers and employed them as foster mothers. This had a wonderful effect on the high reactors: when fostered by a 'supermum' they became even more confident than normal monkeys and later on acquired higher social status. What is more, when they became mothers themselves, they showed the same nurturing style as the foster mothers. This strongly indicates that temperament can be modified by early experience while, conversely, long-term effects of early experience are controlled by temperament.

You will remember similar studies, of the handled rat pups and the children who coped with stressful environments well after exceptional parenting, in the last chapter. True, we looked at those from the point of view of stress but, as is becoming increasingly apparent, there is a huge overlap between stress and depression.

We have been talking about loss and deprivation, which leads into a closely related idea about the psychology of depression which was put forward by Martin Seligman in the 1970s.[26] Classic experiments show that if you yoke two rats together and give one of them predictable shocks, while the other is exposed to the same shock only in an unpredictable pattern, then the second one develops a state which Seligman called learned helplessness: it loses the ability to cope with everyday life. The same state can easily be induced in humans by exposing them to experimental stressors. We saw in the last chapter that under these conditions, a stressor is less easy to bear: here we look at it from a slightly different perspective, showing it can be a factor in depression.

Learned helplessness is very closely related to negative thinking. We saw in chapter 1 that depressed people see the world through darkly tinted spectacles. Aaron Beck of the University of Pennsylvania has fruitfully developed this idea, viewing depression as a cognitive problem, where those affected tend to overgeneralize or catastrophize from one negative event to everything: this is the source of most of the gloomy self-talk and rumination that churns around the mind of someone during a bout of depression ('It'll never work out', 'I'm no good', etc.). The good news is that Beck has shown that negative thinking in depression can be turned round; this is the basis of cognitive therapy, which will be discussed in chapter 8.

Stress and depression revisited

We have already seen in chapter 1 that stress can lead to depression and, indeed, the childhood factors discussed above are all major stressors. In adult life a similar pattern is seen, although, of course, we do not all get depressed after a run of stressful events. Again, we saw in the last chapter the kind of factors which modulate individual responses to stressors. In fact, although most doctors 'know' that a patient handling stress badly is headed for either a heart attack or a major depression, concrete evidence of the link is hard to come by.

A useful study, which we have already discussed, is that of people living with the chronic stress of physical disability. You will remember that they ran a significantly higher risk of depression than the general population.

But what about other everyday stresses? Well, if you ask depressed people about life events in the months preceding the depression, they do seem to report a higher than average number of stressors. Of course, this kind of retrospective research has its drawbacks: for a start, memory is selective, and the memory in depression may be even more selective (more negative events are recalled, and people may be looking for a 'cause' for the depression). Nevertheless, an analysis of studies of this kind suggested that stressful life events raised the risk of subsequent depression by a factor of five or six, and the more serious the stressor, the higher the risk.[27]

Let us look in some more detail at some of these stressors. A classic study from the 1970s of 539 women in Camberwell underlined the crucial importance of social factors.[27] Women with three or more children at home, reporting low self-esteem and lack of a close confidant, and who had lost their mothers before age 11, were most prone to depression. Depression was also found to be four times more common among working-class people. Of course, the driving factors here are poverty coupled with the lack of social support which, as we saw in the last chapter, are potent stressors which can precipitate depression. (However, it is worth noting that Redfield Jamison says that bipolar disorder appears to be concentrated in the higher socio-economic classes.)[28]

And of course, as the study of depression and disability showed, illness can be a source of depression, In fact according to the DSM notes, around five per cent of all major depressions can be attributed to physical illness. This is something worth remembering if you, or someone close to you, is ill. Around a quarter of all those with a chronic medical illness, such as cardiovascular disease, diabetes, and cancer – especially pancreatic or stomach cancer – develop major depression. Ten per cent of people on kidney dialysis get depressed too. Of course, this is hardly surprising, but the presence of depression will just complicate the condition and severely impair quality of life if left undiagnosed and untreated. And, as expected, those with hormonal abnormalities are vulnerable to depression (Cushing's disease, obviously, as we have mentioned, for it is associated with high secretion of stress hormones, but also thyroid problems: often correcting thyroid imbalance can clear up depression too). Ten per cent of people with AIDS have severe depression (again, hardly surprising) and 20 per cent of those with rheumatoid arthritis (pain is a potent stressor). Neurological diseases, such as multiple sclerosis and Alzheimer's disease, also increase the risk of depression: in Alzheimer's this is particularly important because it can be confused with depression. But chronic depression alone is different from Alzheimer's plus depression.

Many drugs cause depression as a side effect. The list includes (but is by no means limited to) beta blockers, steroids, oral contraceptives and some antibiotics (even, ironically, some antidepressants, as we will see in chapter 7). It is interesting that Lewis Wolpert traces back the origins of his own life-threatening depression to a change of heart drug. Since there is nearly always an alternative medication that can be prescribed, no-one should ever put up with depression as the side effect of a drug.

Another cause of depression which may be overlooked is minor head injury. According to a recent report over half of those who had had a bang on the head severe enough to warrant hospital treatment (but followed by apparently complete recovery) were suffering from various psychiatric problems a year later. They were suffering from mood swings, depression, irritability and verbal outbursts, and difficulty in planning and making decisions.[29]

It looks as if you can even catch depression. Borna virus is an animal pathogen and antibodies to it have been found in the blood of psychiatric patients, suggesting infection. Now the virus itself has been isolated from the blood of two patients with bipolar illness and one with obsessive compulsive disorder, although further studies are needed to assess the significance of the infection as a causal factor.[31]

Even the place where you live can affect whether you get depressed or not. Seasonal affective disorder (SAD) is linked with lack of sunlight, with those affected becoming depressed as the nights draw in. Their mood only lightens when the days lengthen again in spring and early summer. Some cases of SAD are like bipolar disorder, with a period of hypomania or even full-blown mania occurring in the summer months. Others have depression only. The symptoms of SAD are not like those of a typical depression: there is overeating, particularly of carbohydrates, and subsequent weight gain, and over-sleeping. In fact, the SAD profile is not unlike the hibernation of animals. Often people find their depression improves if they can move to a sunnier climate, or even take a winter holiday in the sun.

We have left until last a consideration of one of the most important risk factors for depression: gender. On average, three times as many women as men suffer from major depression (although rates are equal in bipolar disorder). Surprisingly, no-one knows quite why this is. It is tempting to blame female hormones (certainly they seem to play a part in post-natal depression and maybe in pre-menstrual tension) but no mechanism for this has yet been verified. It could be that women are less ashamed of depression and more likely to seek help, but this, too, cannot be the whole story: community-based samples also suggest an excess of depression in women.

Maybe, then, it is women's relatively low socio-economic status in society and the stress of sexism? Again, this is hard to prove, but what is interesting is that the shift in the balance of power towards women seems to have made men – particularly young men – more depressed and anxious. According to a recent article in a Sunday newspaper, boys are confused over the mixed messages they get from society and by the academic ascendancy of girls.[32] Traditionally men have masked their emotional problems with alcohol, and some express their depression through violence and crime (of which more in the next chapter). But the rise in the suicide rate, especially in young men, is so worrying that the Royal College of Psychiatrists in Britain has now launched a campaign, 'Men Behaving Sadly', to help create awareness of the problem in men.

Mood disorders, then, are immensely complex and variable in their causes and the way they affect people. Understanding the biology of mood is one of the biggest challenges facing brain science: we will now look at the progress which has been made.

Depression and the brain

Blue genes

Genes must be involved in mood disorders, because they are familial. But we do not know the identity of the genes, how many there are, how they work, or how they interact with other factors. In fact, when it comes to investigating the science behind mood disorders, the genetics is probably the least advanced aspect: far more is known of the brain chemistry and the regions of the brain involved in depression.

That is likely to change, for the Human Genome Project is bound to uncover many genes involved with brain function. But for now, all we have is just a handful of genes that look as if they may have something to do with depression.

The search for genes involved in mood disorders began with the analysis of families with many cases of bipolar illness in the Old Amish religious community in the United States. This close-knit group appears to be ideal for such research. They are isolated from the general population and can trace their ancestry back to around 30 European founders; this makes them genetically simple to study. They have strict social rules, conforming to an old-fashioned, simple way of life, so diagnosis is not confounded by alcohol or drug use. They are also well educated, co-operative and have good records.

Imagine the excitement, then, when markers to bipolar disorder were found in the Old Amish in 1987.[33] But two years later, the research team from the US National Institute for Mental Health admitted that their discovery did not stand up to further analysis.[34] Bipolar disorder has also been linked to markers on chromosomes 18 and 21 and the X chromosome, but again the claims have not been substantiated.

The pattern of two steps forward and one step backwards in the search for mood genes has been compared, wryly, by some experts to the progress of the disease itself. More seriously, it has brought the already controversial field of psychiatric genetics into some disrepute. In fact, the difficulty in pinpointing mood genes is in itself quite illuminating, because it strongly suggests that there are several susceptibility genes involved (as we saw in chapter 2) and the disorder is probably far more complex than was previously thought.[35]

Larger studies may prove to be more informative, and so, too, could stratifying the disorder into various subtypes to simplify the genetics. For instance, it has been suggested that looking at the families of young people with very early onset of mood disorders could be especially productive; a study of 125 youths who became depressed in childhood showed an extremely strong family history of the depression.[36]

The hunt continues, and recently there have been reports linking mood disorders to specific genes with known brain functions. For instance, linkage with the dopamine transporter (DAT) gene has been found in several families affected by bipolar disorder, including some from the Old Amish order.[37] Transporters, as the name suggests, are molecules involved in ferrying neurotransmitters back to the pre-synaptic neuron (where they came from) for recycling after communication between the two neurons.

We should not speculate too much at this stage (the nature of the defect in DAT is not known) but one could imagine a defective transporter being involved in either increasing or decreasing neurotransmitter levels – and dopamine abnormalities have been found in mania. What is more, DAT is the site of action of amphetamine and cocaine, and there are marked similarities between the euphoria and energy of mania and the effects of these drugs. Meanwhile, several studies have now pinpointed polymorphisms within (rather than just linkage to) the serotonin transporter (SERT) gene in both bipolar disorder and major depression. This is interesting, because SERT is the place where certain types of antidepressants act so as to increase the low serotonin levels found in depression. However, it is not obvious what the nature of the defect is and some of these findings have not been replicated.

An analysis of the SERT work to date concluded that the defect in the SERT allele which is associated with increased risk of mood disorders occurs in the control region of the gene, known as the promoter.[38] These control regions are very important; they can instruct the gene to make more or less of its protein. So you might think that, in depression, the gene is making *more* SERT, rushing serotonin back into the neuron and leaving low levels within the synapse (thought to be the hallmark of depression). In fact it appears to work the other way round: the SERT allele linked to depression gives lower levels of SERT, which seems a bit odd. And indeed there is currently no easy explanation for this paradox; for now, it is best to stick to the idea that serotonin metabolism is disturbed in depression, and this could be at least partly driven by genetic factors. The latest (but surely not the last) word on this subject is that none of the serotonin system genes studied to date have any influence in bipolar disorder.[39]

Another candidate gene which is under active investigation for its link with manic depression, suicidal and possibly even violent behaviour is the *tryptophan hydroxylase* (TPH) gene. As we said above, most genes code for enzymes, which make important biological molecules. Tryptophan hydroxylase, in short, makes serotonin from *tryptophan*, an amino acid found in the diet (of which more in chapter 9). In one study, a definite association with a TPH gene polymorphism was found,[40] only to be refuted a year later by two other groups of researchers.[41]

Meanwhile, there have been reports that the human equivalent of a gene which turns the red eyes of the fruit fly white could be linked to both mood and panic disorder,[42] at least in men. The gene, which has been mapped to human chromosome 21, is involved in the transport of tryptophan in the cell, and so could be involved in serotonin metabolism.

A genetic marker of panic disorder has been discovered, in the region where the gene for a peptide (short protein) called *cholestocystokinin* (CCK) is located.[42] CCK is produced in the brain and in the gut (where it induces a feeling of fullness) and it it is already known that injecting it induces symptoms of panic.

No doubt the current confusion surrounding the genetic input into mood disorders will clear within the next decade. We now move on to look at brain chemistry and mood, where understanding is more advanced.

Mood molecules

The chemistry of depression involves (at least) two interacting brain systems – one neurotransmitter-based and one hormonal. We have already introduced these systems in previous chapters. To recap, in chapter 1 we saw how the hormone-based HPA system provides a vital link between the experience of stress and the onset of depression. Then in chapter 2, we looked at neurotransmitter action. In the last chapter, we revisited the HPA axis in the context of the stress mechanism. Here we look at how these systems operate in depression.

Box 23   *Building a model of depression*

The biogenic amine theory of depression arose from the discovery that the antidepressant drugs discovered in the 1950s exerted their effects by increasing the levels of the three neurotransmitters in the brain (exactly how this happens we will see in chapter 7). Later, it was noticed that some antidepressants did not have any effect on dopamine levels, although they still relieved depressive symptoms. So dopamine was dropped from the cast, and noradrenaline and serotonin became the key biochemical players in depression.

Then came the opposite observation: that a drug which *decreased* levels of the three neurotransmitters plunged some people into deep depression. The drug was reserpine, a medicine with a fascinating history. It is the active ingredient of the Indian snakeroot plant, *Rauwolfia serpentina,* which had long been used in folk medicine to treat mental illness. Reserpine was first developed as a treatment for schizophrenia, but had to be withdrawn because it lowered blood pressure. But sometimes, in pharmaceutical chemistry, a drawback can be turned into a bonus. Reserpine was reborn as a medicine for treating high blood pressure.

Meanwhile, it was already known from experiments with rats that reserpine depleted the brain of noradrenaline, serotonin, and dopamine. The rats must have been through hell, because it soon became evident that reserpine acted in the opposite way to an antidepressant; 15–20 per cent of patients on reserpine for high blood pressure became deeply depressed, and several even committed suicide. The frightening thing was that none had any previous history of depression. This was powerful evidence in favour of the biogenic amine theory. However, we would now say that this model of depression is too simple – for many reasons, some of which we will explore in chapter 7.

The earliest theory of depression suggested that the disorder arose from the deficiency of noradrenaline, serotonin and dopamine in the brain (just as anaemia arises from iron deficiency). They are all neurotransmitters, by function, but from their chemical structure they fall into a family called the amines. The theory became known, therefore, as the biogenic (i.e. biological) amine theory, and soon researchers were off searching for depletion of serotonin, and so on, in the brains of depressives to back it up.

A Swedish researcher, Marie Åsberg, was the first to show evidence of low serotonin levels in living patients, by demonstrating low levels of its breakdown product 5-HIAA in cerebrospinal fluid.[44] But it is not just serotonin itself which turns out to be important. We have to look at the components of the whole serotonin system. So, for instance, an increase in the number of serotonin receptors in various parts of the brain has also been seen.[45] Think of this as a desperate attempt of the neuron to scavenge what little serotonin there is in the synapse (and remember, the whole system is fluid and flexible: receptor numbers can go up or down, depending on what is going on in that particular brain circuit).

Since then, hundreds of other papers have shown the importance of brain serotonin dysfunction in depression, and in a number of related disorders such as panic disorder, obsessive compulsive disorder and anxiety.[46] The emphasis on serotonin has come from the runaway success of drugs like Prozac (fluoxetine) which acts specifically to inhibit serotonin reuptake by the synapse.

But the pendulum is swinging back to noradrenaline, with the discovery of drugs that act only upon this neurotransmitter. Since dopamine too acts in the parts of the brain which control emotion and mood, it too must play a part in mood disorders. As we will see in chapter 7, up-regulating one or other of these two neurotransmitters has some fascinating and subtle differences on behaviour.

We can look at the biogenic amine theory in another way. The American psychiatrist Robert Cloninger has developed a neurochemical theory of temperament, where levels of the three neurotransmitters are associated with different aspects of temperament. Serotonin is associated with harm avoidance (timidity and inhibited behaviour), noradrenaline with rejection sensitivity (shyness and worrying what people think of you).[47] It could even be possible to employ 'cosmetic pharmacology' to alter personality by using medications that altered the balance of the neurotransmitters: a fascinating, yet alarming prospect which is discussed further in chapter 7.

The hormonal connection

Depression can also be a hormonal problem, driven by imbalances in the HPA axis. Just to recap, when the brain perceives a stressor, the hypothalamus, in the middle of the brain, increases its production of CRF (corticotropin-releasing factor) and this, in turn, induces the nearby pituitary gland to release a second hormone, corticotropin, which kicks the adrenal glands into action, causing them to release the stress hormone cortisol (see also Box 13, p. 70). As a result, physiological changes occur in the body which prepare it for defence against the stressor (cortisol delivers extra fuel to the muscles). All very useful – in the short term.

And short-term is what the actions of the HPA axis are meant to be; cortisol sends messages back to the brain which are picked up by the hypothalamus and cause it to shut down secretion of CRF. In other words, the system can close itself down – a process known as negative feedback. This protects the body and brain from the damaging long-term effects of cortisol.

Around 50 per cent of those with depression seem to have an overactive HPA axis (the name of this stress system). They have abnormally high levels of cortisol in their blood, urine, and CSF, for instance. Their pituitary and adrenal glands are enlarged too. The problem seems to be a loss of negative feedback, as shown by an abnormal response to a test called the dexamethasone suppression test (DST).

Dexamethasone acts like cortisol: when exposed to it, the hypothalamus should turn down its production of CRF. In many depressed people this just does not happen. It is like a tap that you cannot turn off, and the brain and body get flooded with cortisol.

Recent studies have suggested that CRF neurons in the hypothalamus and elsewhere are just overactive;[48] like noisy neighbours, they are just insensitive to the pleas to 'turn it down' from neurons nearby. Elevated levels of CRF have been found in the CSF of depressed patients, and there is an increase in CRF-producing neurons in post-mortem brain tissue. What is more, CRF levels are decreased by successful treatment for depression, while injecting it into rats produces symptoms of depression such as insomnia, lack of appetite and anxiety.

But how does the HPA axis get this way? It may turn out that some people are born with a genetic predisposition to having an overactive hormonal response to stress – although none of the susceptibility genes studied so far involve the HPA system. However, Charles Nemeroff of Emory University, Atlanta, and his co-worker Paul Plotsky have recently shown, in an animal model, that early abuse or neglect causes permanent alteration in CRF production.[49] They separated new-born rats from their mothers for a short time on ten out of the first 21 days of life, then allowed them to grow up normally. As adults, they showed an increase in CRF in several areas of brain, and increased levels of corticosterone (the rat version of cortisol). The most intriguing discovery was that the neglected rats also had an *increase* in CRF-receptor density in several regions of the brain. Normally, this up-regulation is what you would expect if there had been *less* CRF around, not more. This would serve only to enhance the effects of CRF, revving up the HPA axis to an even higher level of activity. The researchers saw similar results in Bonnet macaque monkeys, a closer model to humans than rats. Here they exposed newborns and their mothers to three conditions of food supply: plentiful, scarce and variable. In the last group, mothers got very anxious and neglected their offspring. They, in turn, exhibited depressive symptoms as adults – they were less active, more anxious than the other two groups, and also showed increased CRF in their spinal fluid. Other experiments show that stressful stimuli can also alter the expression of genes that govern the multiplication of neurons.[50] Therefore stress, perhaps very early on in life, may have a permanent effect upon the chemistry and structure of the brain, predisposing it towards depression in later life. Earlier we said that there is not much hard evidence, at least from human studies, of a difficult childhood causing adult depression. But maybe here we have the beginnings of a biochemistry of depression linked to childhood stress.

BOX 24   *Can depression remodel the brain?*

Certainly these experiments linking childhood stress with alterations in the HPA axis shed light on one significant aspect of the natural history of depression and bipolar disorder. It has long been known that depressive and manic episodes tend to recur and become more frequent and more severe. Moreover, later episodes are more likely to arise spontaneously rather than being linked to an obvious cause, suggesting that the illness is somehow self-perpetuating. Over time, then, the person is more, rather than less, likely to become depressed (they grow into it, rather than growing out of it).

Robert Post, a psychiatrist at the US National Institute for Mental Health, has likened this to a phenomenon called kindling, which also occurs in an animal model of epilepsy. If an electric current is passed through a rat or monkey's brain, it will undergo a seizure. If the site is then stimulated again, the current needed to precipitate seizure is less. Eventually, with repeated stimulation, it takes less and less current to produce a seizure until, in the end, the fits occur spontaneously.[51]

While no-one is saying that mood disorders have anything to do with epilepsy (except that they both originate in the brain) this pattern of more frequent and more easily triggered attacks is very similar in the two conditions. The suggestion is that stress remodels the brain so as to make it more prone to depression. This is why there is now a trend for people to be given antidepressant drugs long-term, to prevent the brain changes which occur with repeated bouts of depression.

It could be possible to identify those at risk of adult depression after a difficult childhood by brain imaging to check for overactivity of CRF neurons. For it has been shown that Prozac-like drugs can, by raising serotonin levels, return CRF levels to normal. There must be a connection between the HPA axis and serotonin and the other neurotransmitters in depression – but as yet, the nature of the interaction is elusive. All we can say is that there are CRF neurons in the raphe nuclei and the locus coeruleus in the brain stem, which are also the source of the serotonin and noradrenaline pathways.

Inside the depressed brain

Given that there are chemical imbalances in the brain during mood disorders, it is hardly surprising that a depressed brain even *looks* different from a happy one. Many depressed people have a smaller than normal hippocampus, especially in hard-to-treat depression.[52] There were also the studies linked with stress and depression discussed in the last chapter, where recovered depressives still had a smaller than average hippocampus. More recently, the same team, from Washington University School of Medicine, have also found a reduction in amygdala core nucleus volumes in people with a history of depression. This was a small study in which 20 depressed patients were compared with 20 controls who were not depressed. The amygdala itself and the whole brain were not reduced in volume in either group; it was only the core nucleus that was reduced (on both sides of the brain) in the depressed patients.[53] MRI findings are easier to interpret when taken with other data. In this case, it was already known that people with depression have impaired functioning in emotional tasks involving the amygdala, and abnormal resting amygdala blood flow.

The amygdala and hippocampus are not the only brain structures to be affected in depression. Another study finds that the prefrontal lobe volume is decreased in late-onset minor and major depression.[54] This form of depression can be particularly tragic; after a lifetime of work and family, you finally put your feet up only to be visited (often for the first time) by a particularly debilitating form of the illness. Late-onset depression is known for its severity and high suicide risk. At best, it blights the retirement years; at worst it robs a family of a well-loved spouse, parent and grandparent. The researchers, based at the University of Philadelphia, find that the volume of the pre-frontal lobe decreases with the severity of the illness; they did MRI scans on 18 patients with late-onset minor depression and 35 with late-onset major depression. Compared with the 30 non-depressed controls, the depressed volunteers all had reduced pre-frontal lobe volumes. The volume of the whole brain, however, was normal in both depressed people and controls.

So depression really can shrink (parts of) your brain. There are also differences in blood flow and uptake of glucose in various regions of the brain between depressed and non-depressed people. In particular, blood flow to the pre-frontal lobes, which are associated with thinking, planning and decision making, is often reduced in depression, but increased again after successful treatment.[55]

It is all fairly complicated and we do have to be careful not to over-interpret the results. Still, it is interesting that one of the most recent discoveries finds a particular region of the pre-frontal cortex to be underactive in depression and overactive in mania. The region, which is called the *anterior cingulate gyrus*, lies underneath the corpus callosum, the band of tissue that joins the right to the left hemisphere. It lies at the interface between the emotional regions of the brain – being connected with the amygdala and the basal ganglia – and the higher association areas of the cortex. Probably the abnormal activity here is able to alter mood in the long term by shifting the balance between thought and emotional responses.[56] Lesions around this area are associated with emotional deadening and inability to plan ahead (remember Phineas Gage and Elliott in chapter 2?). Meanwhile, other areas of the brain actually become more active during depression: the amygdala and hypothalamus, which are probably involved in generating negative emotions and an overactive stress response. These changes can be reversed by successful treatment for depression.

Other areas of the pre-frontal cortex become active too: a recent study showed that when non-depressed women had to recall a sad event, PET scans showed increased activity in a number of regions which are quite close to the anterior cingulate gyrus. These changes were reversed when depressed *men* were treated successfully with Prozac. At the same time, sadness decreased activity in a region of the pre-frontal cortex concerned with attention – suggesting, perhaps, introspection. Again, a reciprocal relationship was seen, with the depressed men experiencing an increase in activity in this region on successful treatment and improvement of mood.[57]

Obviously we have to take care not to over-interpret these results.[58] There is still so much to be learnt about depression and the brain. But at least we have an increasingly firm basis for understanding it in biological terms. By contrast, our understanding of the neural underpinnings of aggression is rather less advanced; we will now try to get to grips with this controversial and intriguing subject.

CHAPTER SIX

Red Mist: Inside the Criminal Mind

On 17 February 1991, 25-year-old Stephen Mobley walked into a Domino's Pizza store in Oakwood, Georgia, cleaned out the till and then shot the store manager dead. It was the culmination of a long criminal career that had included at least six other armed robberies, credit card theft, forgery, fighting and, allegedly, sexual assault. A month after the murder he gave himself up. The bare facts of this crime are nothing unusual; it was just one of around 25,000 homicides committed in the United States that year.

But the Mobley case was different. Not in the depressing facts of the murder itself and the trail of destruction that led up to it, but in what happened when the case came to court. For Mobley's lawyers argued that Stephen's genetic background should be allowed as a mitigating factor during sentencing.[1] Evidence provided by a cousin revealed that the Mobley family were a difficult lot: several members, through four generations, showed a pattern of behavioural disturbance marked by extreme aggression (especially domestic violence), alcohol abuse and trouble with the law. But, on the other hand, others were marked out for their business acumen – indeed, Stephen's own father was a self-made multimillionaire and (according to the cousin) a good and kind man.

The argument put together by the defence was that a particular form of aggression ran in the Mobley family. In some members you only saw the good side of this aggression, in business success, whereas in others it turned ugly and came out as criminal violence. The legal team asked the court's permission to back up the theory with scientific evidence, and many experts offered to test Stephen's DNA and to check for abnormalities of serotonin and other neurotransmitters.

A brief look at Stephen's early history suggests that these tests would have been especially revealing. His behavioural problems began very early on in life, and could be summed up as a complete inability to control his impulses. So it is likely he would have low brain serotonin levels, as we discussed in chapter 1. Had his DNA been analysed, along with that of other family members, we might have seen mutations in one or more genes involved in serotonin metabolism.

However, the court refused to admit this type of evidence and it appears that Stephen Mobley has not, to this day, been subjected to any kind of genetic or biochemical testing. He was sentenced to death and his case is currently on appeal before the Georgia Supreme Court.

In the Mobley case the court took the view that not enough is known about how biochemical and genetic findings relate to behavioural abnormalities to justify the admission of this kind of evidence. But this will change. As more and more genes are discovered and, more importantly, understood, the biological processes driving behaviour will become clearer at the molecular level, as will their interaction with environmental and psychological factors. The courts will then *have* to admit genetic evidence. The question is – what will they make of it?

On the one hand, there are issues of personal responsibility and free will. Could you really absolve yourself of, say, 50 per cent of the responsibility for a crime because you had bad genes? Then there is the commonly held myth that genetics is destiny, which could lead to the assumption that nothing could be done to change a criminal's behaviour. There is also the danger that the criminal's whole family could be stigmatized, because several of them could be carrying the same gene or genes.

On the other hand, if the relevant biological factors became more prominent and widely accepted, crime could be seen more as a health issue than a legal one, with treatment taking priority over prison. This is unlikely to find much favour with public opinion, however, for there is a strong drive to exact retribution from those who have harmed us (or, as former British Prime Minister John Major put it, 'let us understand a little less and punish a little more'). Ironically, since prison does not seem to be particularly effective in preventing crime, the treatment option may, ultimately, serve society better.

Behaving badly

But we are getting ahead of the game. For, as we shall see, only one gene with a possible impact on criminal behaviour has been discovered to date and even this is likely to be extremely rare. Trying to understand the biology underlying criminal and antisocial behaviour poses far more of a challenge than it does even in depression (and, as we saw in the last chapter, that is surely hard enough). For these human behaviours are extremely complex and are shaped by many other influences. It is hard to disentangle the genetic and biochemical from the environmental and psychological factors. Did the Kray twins share genes predisposing them to organized crime, or did they just learn to be bad boys from absorbing the neighbourhood culture of the East End of London during the post-war years?

Moreover, the worlds of criminal justice and biological psychiatry are a long way apart, not just because their respective experts do not speak the same language, but also because the types of behaviour they deal with are not the same.

Crime is, to a great extent, a cultural construct which covers a vast range of human behaviour from the trivial to the grotesque and catastrophic. This means most of us have committed at least one crime: riding a bike on the pavement, 'borrowing' stationery or the use of the telephone from an employer, fiddling our income tax, smoking cannabis or drinking after hours in a pub. Some environmental activists consider the vandalism of pulling up a crop of genetically modified crops an honourable act which society will thank them for in years to come.

Again, many crimes are defined by an age limit: in the UK, having sex with a girl the day before her 16th birthday is a crime, the day after it is legal. On 26 July 1967, gay sex between consenting adults was a crime, and on the 27 July it was not, because the law had changed. And we probably disapprove more of drinking and driving and domestic violence now than we did, say, 20 years ago.

And what about war? Although many conflicts, such as the NATO involvement in the Balkans, have government and public backing, to many people these are moral crimes. They certainly involve killing and destruction of property which would be illegal in different circumstances.

In truth, although crimes involving physical violence such as murder, arson and rape are the ones that hit the headlines, these are relatively uncommon. There are many more ways in which violence can express itself. During the 1998 World Cup, for instance, the performance of a small number of English football hooligans made the nation cringe in shame as violent scenes were broadcast on TV. Meanwhile, a recent decision to keep the gates of my local park open all night resulted in a weekend orgy of vandalism, causing several thousand pounds worth of damage.

Why do people behave like this? Aggression – negative or hostile behaviour or feelings towards others – is probably an innate human drive and one which we share with other animals.[2] It has an obvious survival value – in defending family, territory, and property. In modern life it can fuel a positive drive towards success and achievement. It is only when it is expressed inappropriately and out of proportion to a perceived threat that aggression spills over into violence and, perhaps, a criminal act.

Even this is all relative. One person may consider an aggressive telling-off of someone who has offended them to be quite justified; to someone else, this may be over-reacting. And of course, direct aggression towards another person is not a feature of most crime: petty theft, for instance, or credit card fraud are commonly believed to be 'victimless' crimes (try telling that to someone who has just had their bag or wallet snatched).

So crime really is a very heterogeneous phenomenon. Many people who commit minor crimes are mentally normal. But buried within a group of football hooligans, or IRA terrorists, there are likely to be a few individuals with a history of mental disorder with its origins in early childhood, which predisposes them towards antisocial behaviour. Forget the high principles, the semi-accidental overstepping of the limits of behaviour fuelled by drink – these guys are just out to make trouble and they really do not know any other way to be. The same is probably true of persistent offenders, those invididuals who are usually well known to the police and courts from an early age. There is plenty of good evidence that suggests that a disproportionate amount of crime is committed by a small percentage of offenders. For instance, a classic study that followed 10,000 boys born in Philadelphia in 1945 for 27 years found that six per cent of offenders accounted for more than half of all the crime in the whole group.[3] Specifically, this hard core committed 71 per cent of the homicides, 73 per cent of the rapes and 69 per cent of the assaults attributed to the group. Several more recent surveys have confirmed this finding.

This small group of troublemakers, however they express themselves, may show a distinct pattern of personality traits and behaviours. They may also have disordered brain chemistry, abnormal genes, and subtle defects in brain anatomy. Equally, people with these behavioural disorders may not commit any crimes at all, although they may wreak all kinds of other havoc. It is this group which we will look at in this chapter.

Box 25   *Not just an English disease*

The English love their football – it is the nation's favourite sport – and the same can be said for many other countries around the world (apart from the North Americans, who remain curiously impervious to its attractions). A pity then that football fans so often put the nation to shame and force so many reasonable and law-abiding enthusiasts to watch the game on TV from the safety of their living room.

Bad behaviour at football matches first hit the headlines in the 1960s, but the problem goes back much further. At the end of the last century 'roughs', as they were known, regularly caused trouble in the early years of the professional game, particularly during local derby matches. The roughs not only attacked visiting fans, but also threw stones at the visiting team and even the referee. Between the wars, football fans quietened down and the game became respectable again.

When trouble erupted again, in the post-war years, it was linked to the rise of the 'teddy boy' movement and to racial tensions symbolized by the disturbance at Notting Hill in 1958. The football match was likened to a playground where disaffected youth let off steam – albeit in a more or less antisocial manner.

Analysis suggested that the mid-1960s showed the formation of alliances, on match days, between youths from local working-class estates and suburbs, who saw the goal-end terraces as their own territory from which they excluded older, and rival, fans. From this, a national network of gang rivalries, focused around football, developed. The action then shifted outside the ground, where rival fans may confront one another directly before and after the match.

It is often assumed that football hooliganism is an English 'disease'; in fact, England wanted to pull out of European club competitions in the 1960s, because they feared the bad behaviour of foreign fans. Hooliganism is a particular problem in The Netherlands, West Germany, Italy and Spain, although English football hooligans now tend to export their antisocial habits to foreign fixtures, where they are usually highly visible. The worst incident was the charge of Liverpool fans at the Heysel Stadium, Brussels, in 1985 before the European Cup Final which caused panic among the rival Juventus fans and led to a wall collapse that resulted in the deaths of 39 fans. This led to the (temporary) banning of English clubs from European competitions. Sobered by the experience, perhaps, the fans gave little trouble when English sides were readmitted to the European game in 1990. However, there have certainly been problems involving English fans since then, particularly during the 1998 World Cup in France, although the German fans were quite badly behaved too, with one being charged with murder.

So is bad behaviour at football matches just high spirits, or is it a sign of true antisocial behaviour? A recent phone-in on UK's Radio 5 about the often foul and aggressive language used by fans during matches was sharply divided. Some callers claimed it was a harmless way of letting off steam and defusing the stresses of the week, with white players as likely to be abused as black. Others were more concerned, sensing a genuine undercurrent of violence, often racist in tone. There is undoubtedly a hard core of known hooligans, with more interest in fighting and creating trouble than in the game itself. Alcohol undoubtedly fuels the aggression but does not cause bad behaviour, for people drink to excess during rugby and cricket matches too, and there is rarely the same kind of trouble. And in the 1998 World Cup Scottish fans drank (probably) as much as the English, but their behaviour was, on the whole, impeccable and won the affection and admiration of local residents.

It has also been claimed that football hooliganism is orchestrated by far-right political groups. While there is some evidence for the involvement of neo-fascist groups in football disorder, their input into the English game is less obvious. However, the nationalistic sentiments the game arouses do appear to serve as a focus for those with extreme views and certainly racism towards foreign players is still a problem, although attitudes may have improved over the last few years.[4]

Naughty children

Most criminals were naughty children. But most naughty children grow up to be respectable, well-adjusted adults. It is crucial to know who are the *real* problem kids, so that they can be helped before they start causing real harm to themselves, their families and society at large. We will return to this issue soon – but first we will pay a brief visit to the world of the child psychiatrist.

Put simply, there are three main classes of childhood behavioural disorder described by psychiatry: oppositional defiant disorder (ODD), conduct disorder (CD) and attention deficit hyperactivity disorder (ADHD).

ODD, as the name suggests, is characterized by severe disobedience and wilfulness, far outside the normal range of childhood tantrums and difficulty. Normally diagnosed in the under-10s, the child with ODD is negative, hostile and defiant, deliberately annoying and often spiteful and vindictive. But he or she generally stops short of violating the law or rights of others and so will not be involved in stealing, cruelty, bullying or other antisocial behaviours.

However, there will still be disturbances in normal functioning: inability to make friends, or learning difficulties, for example, which is why these children come to the attention of psychiatrists. ODD occurs with roughly the same frequency in girls and boys, although there is a tendency for it to become more common among boys in the older age groups.

The significance of ODD is that it may progress to CD, which is strongly associated with juvenile crime. The typical teenager with CD tends to be aggressive, dishonest, destructive and disobedient, to a degree which goes way beyond the ups and downs associated with normal adolescent rebellion. Their behaviour is often illegal, including theft, assault and vandalism. Even if they do not actually commit criminal acts, they may nevertheless indulge in markedly antisocial behaviours like bullying or cruelty to animals. Typically they will also cause concern by staying out all night, truanting and generally flouting any attempts to control them.

To be diagnosed with CD, the teenager will show at least three features of the behaviour described above and the problem will have been going on for more than six months; these criteria distinguish CD from the normal spectrum of behaviour in this age group.

Conduct disorder interferes with the young person's family, school and social life, often setting the scene for further problems. It is diagnosed, roughly, twice as often among boys as among girls, a pattern which is reflected in later criminal behaviour. Indeed, 40 per cent of boys with CD, and 25 per cent of girls, progress to adult crime and other difficulties.[5] Many teenagers who would be classified by the courts as delinquents have CD; indeed, a psychiatrist gave Stephen Mobley this diagnosis when he was 16.

More naughty children

When I was a science teacher I had a pupil, Tom, with two extremely annoying habits; firstly, if he was standing near the door, he would click the light switch on and off incessantly and secondly, if he was at the lab bench, he would do the same with the gas taps. He always arrived at the lesson without anything to write with and could not stay in his seat for more than a couple of minutes; I do not believe he ever completed a piece of homework in two years. I had a vague notion that Tom was hyperactive and attributed it to either lead poisoning (this was before unleaded petrol was the norm) or the artificial colourings from the junk foods the children consumed at break.

If a psychiatrist had interviewed Tom, he would probably have been diagnosed with ADHD. Actually, this diagnosis is quite controversial – not least because it seems to be on the increase and is often treated with the drug Ritalin (of which more in the next chapter). It has been suggested that children are being stigmatized with a psychiatric label when parental neglect, poor schooling and a lack of outlets for youthful energies in built-up urban environments should be blamed. However, more recent research seems to suggest a genuine biological basis for ADHD.

Known as hyperkinetic disorder in Europe, ADHD has two main characteristics. Attention deficit is very obvious in a school setting; the child does not listen when addressed directly, makes careless mistakes, is forgetful and disorganized, and does not care for sustained mental effort. Inevitably school work suffers, and reading and other learning problems are common.

The hyperactive–impulsive component involves fidgeting, fiddling with things, noisiness, an inability to wait in turn, and a tendency to interrrupt and intrude on others' conversations and activities. In some children, the attention-deficit component may predominate over the hyperactive–impulsive aspect, while in others, the reverse may be the case.

The first signs of ADHD usually appear between three and five years and it is at least three times more common in boys than in girls. Of course, very young children are naturally distractible, active and impulsive in comparison with older children and adults. To diagnose ADHD, the child must show the symptoms descibed above to a far higher degree than other children of the same age.

A psychiatrist will look for at least six symptoms in both attention-deficit and hyperactive–impulsive categories to make a diagnosis of ADHD. The frequency of the disorder varies between one and ten per cent, depending upon country. It is more commonly diagnosed in the United States and Canada than it is in Europe.

A study by Eric Taylor and colleagues of the UK Medical Research Council's Child Psychiatry Unit has revealed considerable cultural differences in diagnosis of the disorder.[6] They asked British and American clinicians to assess the same cases. The American doctors were more likely to diagnose biologically caused ADHD, while the British doctors opted for socially caused CD. There is indeed a high degree of overlap between the two conditions, but Taylor's research goes on to suggest that CD follows on from ADHD. The reasons are not hard to fathom, for the child with ADHD is often unpopular with his peers and gets into trouble at home and school (but generally for misdemeanours rooted more in carelessness than in outright defiance).

The social and academic difficulties that follow in the wake of ADHD set the scene for CD in adolescence. ADHD also leads to further problems in adult life and increases the risk of violence, antisocial behaviour,[7] drug abuse[8] and other psychiatric disorders, such as depression.[9] And the disorder itself does not go away: Russell Barkley and his team at the University of Massachusetts studied a group of 158 children with ADHD from the 1970s[10] and found that two-thirds were still affected in adulthood (although the persistence of ADHD to adult life remains controversial).[11]

BOX 26   *The biology of attention deficit hyperactivity disorder*

Barkley has developed a biological model of ADHD[12] in which he argues that there is a failure in the brain circuitry which drives self-control. He has identified four specific problems. First, there is a problem with working memory and therefore in the ability to hold information in mind while carrying out a mental task. Second, there is a failure to internalize the self-directed speech and questioning used to guide you in solving everyday problems ('Where do I keep my school bag? Oh, it's by the back door.') through a task. This means that the child gets hung up on tasks that should become routine and automatic. Then there is the inability to control emotions and to delay gratification. And finally, the child with ADHD appears to have a problem with integrating information and learning from experience.

More research is needed, of course, but the model could fit what is known of the biology of ADHD. Magnetic resonance imaging has been carried out on a group of 57 boys with ADHD.[13] Compared with 55 healthy controls, the ADHD boys had differences in three distinct brain areas: the right pre-frontal cortex, the basal ganglia, and the cerebellum (see Figure 7).

These deficits are highly suggestive of the symptoms of the condition. For the right pre-frontal cortex has a role in 'editing' behaviour, resisting distractions and being aware of both oneself and the passage of time. The *caudate nucleus* and the *globus pallidus* are the two of the five basal ganglia which are affected. These have a role in co-ordinating input from various parts of the cortex during mental activity. And the *cerebellar vermis* (the part of the cerebellum which is affected) may regulate motivation. Altogether, these data tend to support Barkley's biological theory of ADHD described above.

It looks as if there may be a problem with dopamine transmission in

---

the circuits linking these parts of the brain in ADHD. First, people with ADHD respond to Ritalin (methylphenidate), a stimulant drug which inhibits the dopamine transporter (the molecule that takes excess dopamine back to the pre-synaptic neuron to be recycled). Genetic studies also show that there may be alterations in genes for either the dopamine transporter[14] or the dopamine D4 receptor, which receives incoming dopamine signals at the post-synaptic neuron.[15]

A strong genetic influence on ADHD has been shown in many studies. An investigation of mono- and dizygotic twins, for instance, suggests a heritability of 80 per cent for the condition.[16] That is, 80 per cent of the difference in hyperactivity, attention and impulsivity between people with and without ADHD is explained by genetics. A large study of Australian families tended to confirm this, with the added proviso that ADHD should be looked at as a continuum of human behaviour, rather than as a disorder with a distinct cut-off point; such considerations also apply in depression, as we saw in the last chapter).[17]

The standard view of ADHD presents it as a distinct disadvantage. However, writer Thom Hartmann argues for a more positive perspective on the condition. He describes people with ADHD as 'hunters' who continually scan their environment, have insatiable curiosity and high energy levels. Some high achievers, like Winston Churchill, Benjamin Franklin, Thomas Carlyle and Ernest Hemingway, may have had ADHD, he says (note the parallel with the higher than average occurrence of bipolar disorder among creative individuals).[18] Hartmann's theory is controversial, though, and needs more testing. But if he is even partly right, it suggests that offering people with ADHD education and jobs which satisfy their restless curiosity could make a difference.

Biology – or rites of passage?

The above discussion may suggest that antisocial behaviour in young people is always pathological, requiring a psychiatric diagnosis. In fact, the above descriptions apply only to a minority. However, most teenagers will admit to indulging in at least one or more activities which incur adult disapproval, such as minor vandalism, or experimenting with drugs. This may escalate into illegal behaviour.

In one famous study of inner London boys, 96 per cent admitted committing at least one of ten common offences, including theft, violence

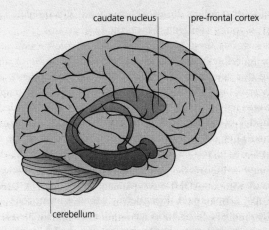

(Figure 7: Brain regions involved in ADHD)
The regions involved in ADHD (as shown by brain imaging) span the whole brain –
from the prefrontal cortex to the cerebellum at the base of the skull. Two of the five
basal ganglia are involved – the caudate nucleus and the globus pallidus (only the
caudate nucleus is shown here, for clarity). These regions – important in movement
and general co-ordination of brain activity – lie clustered together deep inside the
centre of the brain, in the vicinity of the limbic system.

and vandalism.[19] In fact, one of the most striking and universal facts about crime is the way rates rise steeply in adolescence, peaking around age 17 and then falling off into adult life. Terrie Moffitt, now at the Institute of Psychiatry in London, has developed the theory that there are two kinds of teenage delinquents. One, which she calls the life-course persistent (LCP) type, starts to indulge in antisocial behaviour in childhood and continues into adulthood, while the second, which she calls adolescence-limited (AL), goes through a period of such behaviour in their teens but settles down later on.[20]

The young people in the first group are those with the disorders, such as ADHD, which we described above, while the second group are essentially normal youngsters. Moffitt is involved in the Dunedin Multidisciplinary Health and Development Study, a long-term survey of 1037 New Zealand children born in 1972–73. The children were assessed at the age of three and at two-yearly intervals thereafter (indeed, some are now bringing their own children along to the assessment).

At three, around 5 per cent of the sample were diagnosed as 'difficult'; they carried on being difficult – getting into trouble with the police, being diagnosed with conduct disorder – and were still indulging in criminal behaviour in young adult life. This is the LCP group.

Moffitt suggests these young people act as role models for the other group during adolescence, causing a dramatic increase in antisocial behaviour in this age group. In other words, AL delinquency is a form of social mimicry, but LCP delinquency, of early onset, is pathological.

The reason why the persistently badly behaved child suddenly becomes a role model could be rooted in the social predicament of today's adolescents. They reach physical maturity earlier than in the past (thanks to better nutrition) and naturally want all the privileges of adult life. But these remain tantalizingly out of reach. Whereas their parents and grandparents could have been out earning real money in their mid-teens, young people now remain dependent on their parents for longer, as the period of compulsory education has lengthened. So the two key advances of 20th-century society – better health and better education – exert opposing forces on modern teenagers.

Perhaps we should be more sympathetic to their inner struggles? In most modern societies, there are no formal rites of passage or initiation into adulthood, yet the psychological need for such a transition remains. Suddenly, the difficult child – the one who had few friends in primary school because of his boisterous or mean behaviour – is to be envied. For he indulges in early sexual activities, acquires property and money by stealing, and experiments with forbidden activities like drugs. In other words, he seems adult and independent.

Moffitt suggests that the AL group go through a period when they imitate the behaviour of their LCP peers (who, by this time, are quite experienced in antisocial behaviour) until they enter into true independence and maturity – when they leave home for university, say, or marry. Then they are able to desist from antisocial acts because these acts no longer have any benefits. Thus, we could see AL antisocial behaviour as a healthy response to the psychological constraints of the teenage years. The sad thing is that this option does not seem to be open to the LCP group.

Lumping all teenage delinquents together is a big mistake, Moffitt thinks. While the AL group should not escape punishment if they offend, the realization that their behaviour is self-limiting should make the authorities think twice before labelling them and placing them formally in the criminal justice system. At the same time, the LCP group may need psychiatric help and, again, being put into the prison system without treatment will not help them either.

From bad to worse

Most people in the UK have heard of Michael Stone, the man who destroyed the Russell family. In July 1996, he killed 45-year-old Lin and her six-year-old daughter Megan with a hammer as they strolled home along a footpath in Chillenden, Kent. The other daughter Josie, then nine, was attacked too and left for dead, with severe head injuries (from which she made a remarkable recovery).

How could anyone do such a thing? Stone, now serving a life sentence, had a long history of serious mental illness and was described in the media as a 'dangerous psychopath'. It is hard to feel a shred of sympathy for Stone, naturally, but it is chilling to learn that he himself was brought up with great violence, his own stepfather beating him with a hammer.[21]

And surely the professionals who let him slip through the net and placed the public at risk must bear some of the responsibility for this dreadful crime? In their own defence, the psychiatrists complained that the system found it hard to deal with Stone because he was suffering from severe antisocial personality disorder, which is considered untreatable.

Fortunately for all of us, people as extreme in their behaviour as Michael Stone are rare. Antisocial personality disorder (ASP) is not. It affects around three per cent of males and one per cent of females. The term ASP is now preferred over the older terms of psychopathy and sociopathy. The behaviour of someone with ASP (we will use the word 'antisocial' as shorthand) is rooted in their utter indifference to the feelings and rights of others. Antisocials exist in a kind of moral vacuum, where empathy, affection, concern, or guilt have no meaning. Typically (but not invariably) they will be involved in criminal activity of one sort or another; the prevalence of ASP in the prison population is 30 per cent or higher. And even if they stay within the law, generally spend their lives swimming against the tide of normal human society (to a greater or lesser degree). They lie and deceive without conscience, they cannot tolerate frustration, are easily bored, and are irritable, impulsive and prone to outbursts of physical and/or verbal violence.

Yet the antisocial often has a superficial charm which enables him to form relationships easily – although these never last. Antisocials are often big talkers, with big ideas, and a huge tendency to blame others for their mistakes. When they come up in court, they are the ones who express no remorse for their crimes and will often continue to deny their guilt even when the evidence against them is overwhelming. (Michael Stone protested his innocence of the Russell murders; in fact there was no forensic evidence against him in the case, which turned on a confession he made in prison on remand.)

Antisocials show an appalling lack of psychological insight, worse, in its way, than that you encounter in psychotic people who are bound up with delusions and have lost touch with everyday reality. The lack of insight makes it very difficult for anyone to help them, for at the same time they are technically sane. This is the main reason why ASP is considered to be untreatable.

However, sometimes antisocial people do achieve a measure of success in life; in business, for instance, they may do well, by trampling on others to get at their goals, although commercial failure and fraud are far more likely to be the outcome, given their lack of responsibility and inability to plan ahead. If they do work, people with ASP tend to do best if they are self-employed or in jobs where there is little structure, few rules and minimal direct supervision for them to kick against. You might find them working as sales reps or truck drivers – anything that keeps them on the road may satisfy their restless urges. You probably have one or two antisocials among your friends, acquaintances and work colleagues and you will know the havoc they create: broken appointments, inability to hold down a job, money borrowed and not returned, unpaid bills, frequent grudges and quarrels, substance abuse, and brushes with the law.

As you might expect, people with ASP have little talent for parenthood or family life. Hard data are not available, but it seems more than likely that a high proportion of men who abandon, and then fail to support, their children have ASP.

ASP is usually diagnosed only in people over 18 and is far more common among men. It affects up to four per cent of men, but less than one per cent of women. In women, ASP often expresses itself in the form of vague physical complaints, such as unexplained stomach pains and chronic headache. This is known as *somatization disorder*, and is often found, too, in female relatives of males with ASP. Sometimes *factitious disorder* – feigning illness to get attention and hospital treatment – is associated with ASP, especially ·in women. Both these disorders can be quite difficult to distinguish from 'masked' forms of depression.

ASP has a strong link with CD in earlier life (although this does not mean that all children with CD will progress to ASP). Depression is a frequent complication, as are substance abuse, compulsive gambling, and other behaviours linked to lack of impulse control. Homelessness, unemployment and long stretches in prison are common consequences of ASP.

Antisocials often suffer from chronic ill health, through self-neglect and substance abuse. Their bodies are often covered with scars from fights and accidents (oddly, perhaps, they are also more likely than average to sport tattoos). Unsurprisingly, ASP is associated with a high risk of premature death by violent means, whether accident, murder, or suicide. The only ray of hope is that the disorder tends to get less severe over time; if circumstances are favourable, the person concerned may start to settle down in their 30s or 40s.

There is, as yet, no clear understanding of the biology of ASP, nor any proven treatment. The UK is about to become the first country in the world with the legal power to detain antisocials, without their having committed a crime, if they are thought to pose a risk to the public. Had such a law been in place in 1996, the Russell murders would probably not have happened. There are thought to be around 300 to 600 dangerous antisocials in the community in Britain. Under the new law, they could all be locked up, maybe without limit of time. Obviously, while this protects the public, it raises a very serious civil liberties issue for the men concerned who, remember, would be innocent of any crime (although they could have committed offences in the past).

For their sake and ours, let us hope that brain science can come to the rescue. As we shall see, certain abnormalities of the brain and nervous system have been associated with ASP. Maybe these discoveries are the first glimmerings of an understanding of this difficult disorder and, one day, they will lead to successful treatment and therapy.

Seeing red

Being bad-tempered is hardly an illness, but sudden, over-the-top out-bursts – maybe with accompanying violence – can be a symptom that all is not well mentally. Such tantrums are common in ASP. They are also the hallmark of a somewhat different condition called intermittent explosive disorder (which is exactly what it sounds like). The key difference between the two is that the person with IED knows the meaning of the word 'sorry' and will often confess, 'I don't know what came over me.'

And at the level of the brain, IED is a category in its own right, being linked with low serotonin levels. This is the kind of impulsive aggression which was discussed in chapter 1, and we will take a further look at it later. As a diagnostic category, IED is often used as a 'dustbin' when psychiatrists cannot quite pinpoint the pattern of symptoms which includes the out-burst; the person is not antisocial, they are not suffering from an obvious mental illness, but they do have problems. And they deserve to be recognized and helped, perhaps more than they are, for these are decent, usually high-achieving, individuals, whose lives are often wrecked by terrifying outbursts of anger which seem to be beyond their control.

Care in the community

The Michael Stone case highlights the risk which a small minority of mentally ill people pose to the community at large. The trend towards caring for people with mental health problems in the community – rather than locking them up for years in mental hospitals – has been driven, in the scientific sense, by the availability of effective drugs and a political desire to cut health care costs.

Unfortunately, mentally ill people with a propensity to violence have sometimes been left unsupervised and without support, setting the scene for a number of tragic incidents. In 1992, the National Confidential Inquiry into Suicide and Homicide by people with mental illness was set up at the University of Manchester, in response to public concern. The latest report reveals that 40 homicides a year (about eight per cent of the total) are committed by the mentally ill and people with schizophrenia account for fewer than ten of these cases (even though these are the ones that hit the headlines).[22] To put this into context, note that there are around 1000 suicides a year among the mentally ill, which represents about a quarter of the UK total.

Professor Louis Appleby, the Director of the Inquiry, has shown that there is a high proportion of untreated mental disorder among people convicted of homicide.[23] Starting with a total of 718 homicides, he noted a lifetime history of mental disorder, including ASP, depression or schizophrenia, in 44 per cent of the 500 cases for whom a psychiatric report was available. Of these, only one in five were actually in contact with mental health services in the year before the offence. And around the same proportion (though not necessarily the same people) were suffering from active symptoms of mental illness, such as delusions or acute depression, at the time of the offence.

Alcohol and drug abuse were also common, whether or not mental disorder was involved. In fact, alcohol was thought to have contributed to the offence in 85 per cent of all cases, and drugs in 27 per cent. Mental health professionals thought that maybe eight of the 40 homicides committed by the mentally ill could clearly have been prevented, although the risk could have been reduced in several other cases by better compliance with treatment.

Another British study has looked at whether schizophrenia raises the risk of being involved in crime.[24] This followed all the cases of schizophrenia recorded in Camberwell, South London, between 1964 and 1984: a group of 538 men and women. When all crime was considered, women with schizophrenia were three times more likely to have committed an offence than a control group. Men with schizophrenia were four times more likely to commit a violent offence than average, although their overall crime rate was actually no different from that in the rest of the population. People with schizophrenia were also more likely to acquire a criminal record than people with other disorders. The study concluded that schizophrenia was an independent risk factor for crime, but cautioned that it is small in comparison with other factors like substance abuse. The risk, however, is associated with symptoms such as delusions, rather than the disorder *per se*.

Furthermore, a recent study from the United States suggested that people discharged from a mental hospital, and monitored over the following year, were no more likely than a control group in the same neighbourhood to commit a violent act,[25] with the rate being around 18 per cent. However, the rate increased to around 30 per cent when substance abuse entered the picture. Although the rates were still no greater for the mentally ill than their control group neighbours, the mentally ill group were more prone to substance abuse, which inflated the figures. In general, however, the rates of violence tend to decrease over time, and most of it took place in the home, being directed towards family and friends. The fears of the American (and British) public about being attacked in the street by a mentally ill stranger are therefore largely unfounded.[26]

Although the risk of violence from the mentally ill can be reduced, it can never be eliminated. It is a matter of balancing the civil liberties of those with mental health problems with the safety of society at large. The figures also suggest that prevention programmes also need to take into account the role alcohol and drug abuse play in homicide.

BOX 27   *Predicting violence*

If only we could predict the individuals with mental illness who were most likely to be violent. This minority could be targeted for supervision and intensive treatment, while the stigma on the vast majority who pose no risk would be lessened. And we could all rest easier. Maybe brain imaging will soon provide this important diagnostic information. A new study used fMRI to image the brains of 60 men from four groups. Men in the first three groups had a history of violent behaviour and had been diagnosed with schizophrenia, personality disorder, or both. Men in the fourth group were healthy controls, with no history of violence. The scans revealed differences in several key regions; in particular, the hippocampus and the amygdala were smaller in the violent men than in the controls.[27] Why this should be is still under investigation. The take-home message from this study, though, is that violence is a behaviour in its own right – perhaps with a specific pattern of brain dysfunction – rather than being a symptom of a particular mental disorder.

Box 28   *Catch them early*

Only days after the killings at Columbine High School, the US National Academy of Sciences held the latest in a series of pre-planned meetings on child welfare: on this occasion, the subject was how to detect and respond to early childhood signs of antisocial behaviour. Many of the experts there agreed that such signs become apparent as early as three years old and that early intervention is essential to stop the seeds of future high school massacres from taking root.

But this is not just about preventing the violent catastrophes, like Columbine, that always hit the headlines; the sheer volume of petty crime undertaken by these individuals and its attendant social, economic and psychological costs also need to be reduced.

The Dunedin study, mentioned earlier, gave the first concrete evidence of a link between the observed behaviour of three-year-old children and psychopathology in adult life.[28] Undercontrolled children, i.e. those toddlers who are impulsive, restless and distractible, were more likely than average to have antisocial personality disorder or to be involved in crime at age 21. Specifically, they were nearly three times more likely to have ASP, twice as likely to be on the way to becoming chronic offenders, and nearly five times more likely to have a conviction for violence. They were also *17* times more likely to have attempted suicide. The boys in this group were twice as likely to have become dependent on alcohol. (Incidentally, this is the study which uncovered the link between inhibited behaviour at age three and depression at age 21, which was discussed in the last chapter.) Another study, from Oregon, showed that boys from a high-crime neighbourhood who had been arrested by age 14 were 18 times more likely to become chronic offenders than those who had not (and the chronic offenders were 14 times more likely to commit violent offences).[29]

Meanwhile, Donald Lynam of the University of Kentucky has developed the theory of the 'fledgling psychopath' which could enable those most at risk of chronic offending to be identified and helped at the earliest possible stage.[30] He suggests that within the population with ADHD there is a subtype who display symptoms more towards the impulsive end of this behaviour spectrum and also show signs of conduct disorder. This group also appears to share certain brain and nervous system deficits with adult psychopaths (which will be discussed in further detail later).

The essence of this subtype is a failure to inhibit behaviour with respect to social and environmental signals and, Lynam suggests, it may originate in a serotonin deficit (remember our description of the 'policing' function of serotonin on behaviour, in chapter 2). In behavioural terms it translates into lack of planning and forethought, and poor self-discipline. The corresponding personality trait is often called constraint and those who are low on constraint are impulsive, adventurous and uninhibited.

Of course, this fearless attitude can be very positive: mountaineers and great creative artists alike often show this personality trait. But lack of constraint can also evolve in a pathological manner. In early childhood, it will look like ADHD, and the affected child will be restless, inattentive and impulsive. Later, as he becomes more mobile and verbal – and adult restraints on behaviour become more marked – the constraint deficit looks more like CD. The child becomes verbally aggressive, destructive and antisocial. Over time, this evolves into fully fledged adult psychopathy – fuelled by a range of negative environmental, social and psychological factors such as rejection by others, failure at school and so on.

It is arguable, however, that the child with this deficit born into favourable circumstances or with a slightly different genetic make-up could turn it to positive advantage and become an adventurer or an original creative artist: one of Thom Hartmann's 'hunters', in other words. Maybe Winston Churchill and Thomas Carlyle had a surprising amount in common with the persistent offender who spends most of his life sleeping rough or in jail.

Above we suggested that ADHD is often a stepping stone or a risk factor for later CD. In other words, the negative consequences of ADHD set the scene for the development of CD. Lynam suggests something a bit different: the deficit is there from the start, and ADHD and CD are just two consecutive stages in its relentless evolution towards psychopathy.

The relative importance of the theories has not been fully investigated, so we must keep an open mind. If Lynam is right and we *can* pick out a subtype in the ADHD group by blood tests, brain scans, psychological tests or whatever, this is potentially very significant – although it obviously raises important ethical issues as well as questions about what would be appropriate treatment. What would you do if you were told that your difficult toddler had a 90 per cent chance of becoming a violent criminal without, say, serotonin-lowering medication or a behavioural programme? Have him stigmatized when he is still an innocent child, when there is a one in ten chance the prediction is wrong? Or would you try to save him from destroying his own life, your family's, and those of who knows how many innocent victims?

The vicious circle – looking at the causes of crime and antisocial behaviour

If only there *were* a gene for crime – a single gene that would out whatever the circumstances. Those with it would be criminals, those without would be law-abiding. It would make what is to follow a whole lot simpler. But it is no use looking to genetics alone to illuminate the causes of bad behaviour; it plays a role, but only along with other, more important, factors, such as the psychology of the family and socio-economic status.

Disentangling the complex relationships between the root causes of bad behaviour is a major challenge; there is still much to be learned and the arguments that follow will, necessarily, be brief and simplified.

We all have various notions about the causes of bad behaviour. The lad who vandalizes the park benches hangs round with a couple of older brothers who have been up in court a few times, and their father has been inside: that must be 'bad blood'. We feel a certain foreboding if we have to go to certain districts in our home city (and want to know which ones to avoid when we are abroad) because they are 'bad areas'. And ten to one the guy who snatched your wallet did it to finance a drug habit.

Genetic, environmental, social and psychological factors are all important in crime. They interact with one another, and the weighting to be placed on each one may be different in each individual case. It is also important to note that often it is not clear whether a particular factor is a potential *cause* of bad behaviour or a correlate – something linked, but not causal. To impose some kind of order on our discussion, we will try a 'bottom-up' approach: genetics, then family, immediate environment, and then society at large.

Bad blood

Yes, crime does tend to be familial. It has long been known that if the father has been convicted, the son is more likely to follow in his footsteps than if his father was law-abiding. But what does this mean? A criminal parent is more likely to be a poor parent; if he is not actually in prison – and therefore absent – harsh, erratic discipline (of the kind he himself was probably subjected to) is likely to be the order of the day. And unless the father has done extraordinarily well in his criminal career (villa in Marbella, Swiss bank account and so on), poverty is likely to be part of the picture too. Another factor is that if you have a criminal parent, they are not exactly likely to bring you up to make sure you pay for your TV licence. The parental message will surely be that criminal behaviour is acceptable. And if elder siblings follow in father's footsteps, the criminal role model is promoted even more strongly.

That might sound like a complete explanation: no genes needed. And yet, many children of criminal parents grow up to be decent and honest, despite the adverse psychological and social factors they are exposed to. Genes must be part of the picture, to account for these individual differences (since each child inherits a unique combination of genes from its parents, except for identical twins).

Several twin and adoption studies have been done in an attempt to uncover the genetic influences on bad behaviour. The bottom line is that the genetic association is strongest in ADHD, particularly when it persists into adult life; it is strong for property crime and, surprisingly perhaps, weak for violence. Now we will look at the research in more detail.

First, there is an ongoing study on male twins who served in the Vietnam War (for whom there are good records) covering 3226 pairs of monozygotic and dizygotic twins.[31] Here, the subjects were asked about arrests and criminal behaviour. The analysis suggested that the twins were most alike when it came to early arrests (before age 15) and this effect had more to do with their shared environment than with genes. The genetic effect was more important in those twins who were arrested after age 15, had multiple arrests and for behaviour that persisted into adult life.

This is an interesting and important study – with two weaknesses.

Firstly, we have already seen how heterogeneous crime is, so from a scientific point of view, we cannot be sure what kind of behaviours and underlying potential brain dysfunctions we might be measuring, if only criminal records are studied. The justification for doing it this way, though, is that crime is a concrete thing which can be recalled and recorded, whereas acts of antisocial behaviour are more difficult to define.

Secondly, although the researchers did their best to check for this, can you really rely on people giving their own accounts of criminal offences? And you would expect the worst offenders (who may have the most marked genetic influences) to have been rejected as unfit for military service and so not to have contributed to the study. In fact, that is a criticism we could make of any study into the genetics of antisocial behaviour: why would such people want to help researchers for the benefit of others?

In the Stockholm Adoption Study, the effect of genes on criminal behaviour is compared with that of the environment by looking at whether the adoptees are more like their biological parents (genes) or their adoptive parents (environment).[32] The researchers found the genetic factor to be stronger in petty criminals, where alcohol abuse was not a complicating factor. But among those dependent on alcohol, crime was more likely to be violent in nature, and seemed to be linked more with level of alcohol abuse than with criminality in either set of parents. It looked as if the alcohol abuse, rather than the tendency to crime, was the inherited behaviour.

Other studies have looked at how far aggressive and antisocial behaviours are heritable. For instance, a team from the University of Iowa has investigated a group of 95 males and 102 female adoptees who were separated at birth from parents with either antisocial personality disorder and/or alcohol abuse and compared with a control group; the subjects were aged between 18 and 47 at the time of the study. Briefly, those adoptees with a genetic risk were more likely to develop childhood and adolescent aggression, CD, and ASP disorder.[33]

If there were problems in the adoptive family, such as marital discord, the risk was increased for all these problems, except – strangely perhaps – for ASP disorder. The control group appeared to be unaffected by stress in their adoptive homes, which underlines the way genetic factors can render those affected more vulnerable to their environment.

A recent meta-analysis (an 'analysis of analyses', drawing together all the significant research) suggests that there is a strong genetic effect on aggression, which becomes more pronounced as the subjects get older.[34] This makes sense: as children become adult and move away from the

immediate family environment, new influences may shape their behaviour. But where there is an inbuilt genetic vulnerability to aggression,
positive influences may make less of an impact: put crudely, 'genes will out'
in these cases.

Is testosterone the world's most dangerous substance?

The most obvious feature about crime and antisocial behaviour is also one
of the least well understood: most bad behaviour can be attributed to
males. The male–female ratio for conviction, for instance, is currently
around four to one in England and Wales – though it varies somewhat with
time and place. The trend in the ratio over previous years has been
downwards – that is, there has been an increase in the female conviction
rate. Males tend to commit more violent and more serious crimes, and
account for most of the chronic offenders. Also, as we have seen, they are
more likely to have CD, ADHD, and ASP disorder.

It is tempting to think that the male hormone testosterone accounts for
the male propensity for violence, but there is no good evidence that this is
so (incidentally, females have testosterone too, only at a lower level than
the male). There is also no evidence that genes on the Y chromosome
(which confers genetic maleness) account for criminal behaviour. Several
years ago, it was suggested that men with an extra Y chromosome were
more likely than average to be criminal and violent, but this has not been
borne out by subsequent research. It may be that females are just less
exposed to situations where crime can develop, or they experience and
respond to social and environmental risk factors differently. We just do not
know, and we should.

What does seem likely is that girls make an indirect contribution to
antisocial behaviour by becoming mothers; girls with ASP are more likely
than average to become teenage mothers, and to associate with antisocial
men (who are often violent to them),[35] thereby creating an adverse family
environment which fosters antisocial behaviour in their children. This
does not mean, of course, that all teenagers make bad mothers; but girls
with ASP are unlikely to have adequate parenting skills. Moreover, depressed mothers raise the risk of antisocial behaviour in their children (one
of Oliver James' arguments in *Juvenile Violence in a Winner–Loser Culture*, see
the Further Reading section).

A question of temperament?

As every parent knows, a baby becomes its own person very early on in life. You can have two or more siblings brought up in roughly the same environment, loved equally by their parents, yet they can have very different personalities – even when they are only a few months old.

It is tempting to think that genes must, surely, have some influence on personality (or, rather, on temperament, the biological underpinning of personality) because at this age, the baby's life experience is limited. Remember, we have already looked at this issue in the context of depression in the last chapter.

The Dunedin study, mentioned above, has also looked at how the temperament of a very young child affects later behaviour.[36] Avshalom Caspi of the University of Wisconsin, and his team, analysed the behaviour of the children in the study in terms of 22 different characteristics, such as restlessness, impulsiveness, self-confidence and so on, at ages three, five, seven and nine.

They defined three different 'dimensions' of behaviour which began to emerge from age three. The first, *lack of control*, covered emotional instability, restlessness, limited attention span, and generally reacting in a negative, hostile way (what child development experts call the 'difficult' child). The second dimension was *approach*, which described friendly, confident and self-reliant children who were always ready to explore. Finally, *sluggishness* was the term used to cover passivity, malleability, shyness and fearfulness.

It looks as if temperament could become fixed very early on in life, for temperament dimensions measured for each child tended to remain stable from ages three through to nine. What is more, these correlated well with behaviour problems reported by parents and teachers at ages nine, 11, 13 and 15. At nine and 11, four main dimensions were assessed: anxiety, inattention, hyperactivity and antisocial behaviour. Then at 13 and 15, the researchers looked at anxiety, inattention and CD. They also asked parents to rate their childrens' strengths, such as popularity, maturity and so on at ages 13 and 15.

They found that lack of control at ages three and five was strongly linked with inattention, hyperactivity and antisocial behaviour at ages nine and 11 and, later, with conduct problems and inattention. Even their own parents tended to admit that these children were neither popular, determined, well-behaved nor confident.

Therefore, temperament at age three is linked to specific behaviour problems in adolescence and, as we saw in the previous section, to further problems in adult life. Maybe we can begin to see how genes *could* lead to antisocial behaviour. Genes determine temperament, at least in part, and then, in turn, temperament drives behaviour.

Difficult births

Congenital disorders – conditions which are present at birth – may be caused by a genetic problem, or by damage that occurred to the baby either during pregnancy or during the birth itself. There is some evidence that birth complications may increase the risk of violent criminal behaviour in later life.

In a study of over 4000 boys born in Copenhagen between 1959 and 1961, 4.5 per cent were found to have suffered from both birth complications and rejection by their mother. This group accounted for 18 per cent of all violent crime committed by the total sample.[37] It is not known how this comes about: possibly these boys suffered from minor brain damage (perhaps even too subtle to be picked up in the usual way). It also seems hard to separate out the physical and the emotional damage. Birth complications are more likely to arise with teenage mothers and those whose lives are too chaotic to attend antenatal care classes. So the birth complications could be a sign of more potent underlying risk factors to the child. We also do not know if the maternal rejection was a response of the mother to the difficult birth, or whether it was a further sign of her being antisocial or depressed (that is, the birth complications and the rejection were both related to the same kind of predisposing characteristics in the mother).

This study was followed up with an in-depth investigation of ten per cent of the original group.[38] Four different groups were identified: biosocial (with birth complications and social problems, similar to those identified in the original study), those with just birth complications (the obstetric group), those with just social problems (mainly linked to poverty), and normal controls.

The biosocial group had far higher rates of offending than the normal controls: 33 per cent compared with two per cent for all crime, 30 per cent versus 0 per cent for theft and 13 per cent versus two per cent for violence. Within the three disadvantaged groups, the biosocial group had twice the rate of total offending, 2.5 times the level of theft and 2.3 times the level of violence compared with the other two groups. Overall, they accounted for 70 per cent of the total crime committed by the three disadvantaged groups, even though they only represented 44 per cent of the sample. The poverty group actually had lower rates of crime than the other two groups – especially when the boys had good parenting. This shows that although, as we shall see, poverty is a potent factor in crime, it is far from being the whole story.

Smoking during pregnancy – a criminal habit?

It is well established that maternal smoking during pregnancy increases the risk of miscarriage, low birth weight, low intelligence, and other perinatal health problems. Now there is another good reason for not smoking when you are pregnant: it may increase the chance of your son becoming a violent and persistent offender in adult life.

A recent study on the group of Danish boys described above checked their criminal records at age 34 with their mothers' smoking history.[39] Those whose mothers smoked more than 20 cigarettes a day during the third trimester were 1.6 times more likely to have been arrested for a non-violent crime, twice as likely to be arrested for a violent crime, and 1.8 times as likely to have become a life-course persistent offender, when compared with those whose mothers did not smoke during pregnancy.

You may think that mothers who smoke during pregnancy are quite likely to be loaded with risk factors such as poverty, depression and bad genes which would account for these results. However, this study controlled for many of these factors and the association with smoking remained robust. Only when there were also birth complications did the two factors interact.

Twenty-five per cent of males with the highest levels of both maternal smoking and birth complications had been arrested for a violent criminal offence. The investigation did not control for a direct genetic effect, however. antisocial behaviour and smoking tend to go hand in hand and it is possible that both types of behaviour are influenced by the same genes. To check for this genetic influence, we need studies of twin offspring of smoking mothers. That aside, this research seems to suggest that there could be a causal relationship between maternal smoking and antisocial behaviour, although the actual mechanism needs to be worked out.[40]

We do know that nicotine affects the brain, which is replete with receptors for it (nicotinic receptors, which normally interact with the neurotransmitter acetylcholine). Maybe maternal smoking alters serotonin or dopamine circuitry in the developing brain, or deprives it of oxygen, so the child is born with a subtle brain dysfunction that predisposes towards bad behaviour.

Inside the toxic family

So far we have implied, several times, that bad parenting is a major risk factor for bad behaviour in later life. Now let us try to confront this issue head on – albeit briefly. For a detailed dissection of the masses of social science and psychology research on this aspect of crime and antisocial behaviour is outside the scope of this book (please look at the books by Michael Rutter and colleagues and by Oliver James in the Further Reading section if you wish to take this further).

What seems fairly obvious is that childhood abuse and neglect stand out as the key features of the toxic home, sending a child down the road to antisocial behaviour. The problem with much of the research is that it has not separated out other confounding factors, like poverty or demographic factors.

One respected investigation, by Cathy Spatz Widom of Indiana University, addressed this issue by looking at a group of abused and neglected children, comparing their subsequent criminal records with those of a matched control group.[41] The results suggested that abuse and neglect do raise the risk of bad behaviour in later life, independent of socio-economic factors. Twenty-six per cent of the abused group had a juvenile crime record, compared with 17 per cent of the controls. For adult offending, the figures were 29 per cent and 21 per cent and for any violent offence, 11 per cent and eight per cent. Physical abuse was a more potent risk factor than neglect, but neither were as significant as sex (male versus female), race or age. This study relied on official figures for child abuse and neglect (where the parent had been prosecuted).

A more recent research project, based on 600 youths and their mothers in New York State, underlines these findings. The group were interviewed at regular intervals from 1975 through to 1993, and data collected on any cases of abuse or neglect recorded by the authorities. Those who had suffered abuse were four times more likely to be diagnosed with personality disorder.[42] These are just the worst cases. What about lesser degrees of maltreatment? Even witnessing violence (the father hitting the mother) may be as harmful as being the direct victim.

This brings us to a disturbing trend recently uncovered in the Dunedin study. At age 21, young mothers (ten per cent of the total group) were twice as likely to be abused by their partners as childless women. And young men who had become fathers were three times more likely to abuse their partners, compared with their peers who did not have children.[43] It is very likely that the children involved witness or, worse, are victims of the violence and abuse of their young parents. With such a start in life, it is hard to be optimistic about the future of these children.

It may also be that *any* degree of violence inflicted on a child – even a 'loving' smack – raises their criminal propensity (which is why there is such a strong campaign to outlaw smacking among those who believe this to be the case). The problem seems to be that violence escalates: a smack becomes a slap and physical punishments are administered even more frequently (usually for diminishing returns).

Aside from the obvious psychological damage caused by physical abuse, there is a strong risk of brain damage: a severe shaking of a very young child could, for instance, sever some of the white nerve fibres which link the prefrontal cortex to deeper brain structures. This is precisely the sort of damage that could lead to later problems with impulse control.

Stress again

Why do some parents act this way? Even if their negative behaviour is milder than outright abuse, many children still suffer the long-term effects of lack of affection and warmth, inconsistent or poor discipline, and lack of supervision.

Maybe this poor parenting arises from stress. The social stressors we discussed in chapter 4 – poverty, lack of social support and marital breakdown – may be particularly hard to deal with for some vulnerable adults. They may become depressed and it is probably this group of parents who give their children a raw deal. One study which suggests this could be so looked at two groups of 11- to 12-year-old boys, from rural Iowa and a medium-sized city in Oregon. They found that high stress among the parents, especially mothers, led to depression and this, in turn, impaired the quality of discipline that was meted out to their children.[44]

We should not forget one of the major stressors of all: the children themselves. The parent–child interaction is, of course, a two-way street. A hyperactive, difficult toddler will try the patience of his parents to the limits – and maybe this limit is reached quite quickly if they have other problems. So the child in a very real sense may contribute to his or her own difficult circumstances.

Therefore, while factors like poverty and unemployment are certainly linked with crime – as has long been believed – the association is indirect. Further evidence for this comes from studies of children who emerge unscathed from a poor background.

Lessons from the survivors

We already know from chapter 4 that a warm parental relationship helps children from tough neighbourhoods to weather the stresses of their environment. Another study, by psychiatrists in New Zealand, identifies two further factors in childhood resiliency: (relatively) high IQ and a particular temperament.[45]

The IQ factor is a tricky one to analyse. Low IQ has long been linked to crime but it is not really clear whether those of lower IQ are more likely to get caught and so feature more in the official crime figures. Furthermore, low IQ may not be a risk factor in its own right. Maybe it is merely a marker of educational failure, arising from hyperactivity and attention problems (which are therefore the true risk factor). It could also be a sign of brain damage occurring prenatally or as a birth complication (of the kind discussed above).

As far as temperament was concerned, the resilient youngsters were lower on novelty seeking than their delinquent peers and, as you might expect, were less likely to associate with them socially (they did not share their interest in breaking into cars, experimenting with drugs and other thrills). One could speculate that these well-balanced, intelligent teenagers just had the intellectual capacity to create more positive social and recreational options for themselves. So they were less likely to be exposed to situations where bad behaviour occurred.

Drink, drugs, and video tapes

So far we have concentrated mainly on individual risks for developing criminal behaviour: genes, the family, and so on. But we should also look at various influences which are society-wide. The first is alcohol. There has been a massive rise in alcohol consumption, particularly in Western societies, over the past 50 years or so. And, as we saw above, alcohol is a big factor in crime – especially violent crime. Alcohol seems to raise aggression by releasing inhibitions,[46] particularly when people get frustrated. However, most people drink but only a small proportion get into fights. As you might expect, the likelihood of getting into trouble with drink depends on context and pattern of drinking: public drinking and binge drinking pose the greatest risk.[47]

There has also been a huge increase in consumption of recreational drugs like cannabis, Ecstasy and heroin. Again some drugs will act on the brain so as to reduce inhibitions and so increase the likelihood of committing a crime. For addicts, theft to finance a habit is very common. But you cannot really consider alcohol and drug abuse to be separate risk factors for crime, for they are also linked with a poor work record and are often found among people with other problems, such as depression.

Advances in culture and technology have brought potential problems too. Yesterday's screen heroes were strong and silent and used minimal violence. But from the 1970s, a long line of film stars from Bruce Lee onwards have starred in roles that glorified violence. Having the good guy act like the villain sends out a message that validates all our worst impulses. Moreover, with video you can fragment the narrative and watch the violence out of context.

However, it is unlikely that violent films and videos will increase violent behaviour in the population at large. Research by Kevin Browne at the University of Birmingham for the UK Home Office looked at the effect of violent films on a group of young offenders. The films had a disproportionate effect on violent – as opposed to non-violent – offenders in that they preferred them, and remembered them for longer.[48] Most of these boys had experienced violence themselves in childhood and the films merely served to reinforce their experience.

The message from this and related research is that violent films and videos (and, although not much research has been done, computer games) do not create violent offenders. But they make a vulnerable minority, who are already violent, more likely to act out, by reinforcing their ideas. So, indirectly, we are all at risk from violence in the media.

The antisocial brain

If we find differences in brain structure and chemistry in depression, then surely similar biological markers will be there in crime and antisocial behaviour too. We can certainly point to characteristic brain differences in children with ADHD, low serotonin levels in people subject to impulsive aggression, and abnormalities in both the brain and the nervous system linked to antisocial behaviour. But it may be many years before these discoveries are fully understood and maybe even longer before they are applied.

One reason why we have just begun to use the tools of molecular biology and genetics on bad behaviour is that we are dealing with such a complex phenomenon. Why do some arsonists have low serotonin? Does this drive them to start fires – or does it occur after the act? Why – as described in

Box 31, – does a gene apparently linked with crime act in a paradoxical way?

We could go on, for each new discovery raises more questions. There is another reason why the biology of crime is a difficult area. This kind of research is controversial; many professionals who deal with criminals find it reductionist and stigmatizing, and fear it may be misused. For their part the scientists concerned are cautious in communicating their results and afraid of being misrepresented. So we have a polarization of views which does not help anyone interested in understanding the roots of bad behaviour – be they biological, psychological or social.

The serotonin saga

As we discussed in chapter 1, a low level of the neurotransmitter serotonin is often a biochemical marker of impulsive, violent behaviour, including suicide. Low serotonin levels have also been associated with depression, as we saw in the last chapter. However, it is likely that these two types of serotonin operate in different brain circuits (remember, there are at least 14 different subtypes of serotonin receptor known to date). Also, we cannot say whether the role serotonin plays in aggression is causal: it may be that people born with low serotonin are prone to bad behaviour and failure, or that adverse events trigger a fall (so far the evidence suggests that both can happen).

Box 29   *Serotonin and the social scene*

Implication of serotonin in aggressive behaviour has been found in both animals and humans. A classic study on the social life of vervet monkeys demonstrated the role serotonin plays in acquiring dominance.[49] Monkeys treated with drugs like Prozac became dominant in a group, while those treated with drugs that had the opposite effect became subordinate. This only happened, however, when the naturally dominant male had been removed. When he returned, he rapidly assumed his former position of authority, suggesting that altering serotonin does not really alter the status quo. Still, it was the first demonstration that pharmacological intervention can change the social structure of a primate group whose habits and relationships are not that much different from our own.

Meanwhile, two-year-old male rhesus monkeys with low brain serotonin were found to be more aggressive and more at risk of premature death than those with normal levels.[50] And recently, scientists at Columbia University have shown what happens if you knock out one of the serotonin receptors called 5-HT_{1B} in mice by genetic techniques.[51] The knockout mouse is used as a model to show what happens when the serotonin circuits involving this particular receptor are dead (because there is no gene there is no receptor). These mice show more impulsive aggression and get addicted to cocaine and alcohol quickly compared with normal counterparts.

We have already seen that low serotonin in humans is associated with cruelty to animals, aggressive behaviour in prison and suicide (see chapter 1). Now we will look at further evidence for this connection. For instance, attempts have been made to make predictions about the outcome of bad behaviour using tests for low brain serotonin. This is potentially useful, in distinguishing life-course persistent and adolescent behaviour, say, or pinpointing the most violent for special monitoring or treatment programmes.

A group of 29 disruptive American children had their serotonin levels tested and low levels did, overall, predict poor outcome.[52] In an adult study, which followed 114 male alcoholic violent offenders and arsonists from Finland after release from prison, low serotonin was found to be predictive of further offences.[53] Serotonin levels were measured at the start of the prison sentence and the men were followed up for an average of four and a half years after their release. These low-serotonin subjects also had a family history of parental alcoholism with violence; moreover their fathers had also tended to be absent from the home, while brothers were present, during the subjects' early childhood. (This raises the fascinating question of whether it is better for a child to have an abusive father out of the way or not.) These men certainly had a difficult background; how this interacts with serotonin is not yet known.

The serotonin saga is just beginning; with more sensitive tools for its investigation and a better understanding of brain chemistry, we will surely soon clarify the role it plays in aggression. And, better still, we could use this knowledge to predict who will become violent and so protect people from their actions.

Box 30   *Are you looking at me?*

Emil Coccaro of the Medical College of Pennsylvania – an expert in the neurochemistry of impulsive aggression – and his team looked at how a Prozac-like drug, paroxetine, interacts with the platelet serotonin transporter protein in aggressive individuals.[54]

Normally paroxetine and similar drugs bind tightly to transporter proteins and stop them being recycled by the pre-synaptic neurons (of which more in the next chapter). In this experiment, the paroxetine had a radioactive tag which meant the researchers could monitor what was happening to it. Most importantly, they could measure how much binding of the drug to transporter protein there was.

This revealed that the aggressive individuals had less of the transporter protein than normal controls. These people had been diagnosed with personality disorder, had a history of violence and tended to respond physically to provocation, real or imagined ('are you looking at me?'). At present, it is not too clear what this abnormality in serotonin transporter means. But, in the interests of cutting down on random, unprovoked violence, it merits further investigation.

Box 31   *One problem family*

The only gene linked to human aggression has been found in a troubled Dutch family; it adds another (incomplete) chapter to the serotonin saga. Fourteen males, through four generations, have shown a behavioural condition marked by borderline mental retardation and a history of exhibitionism, attempted rape and arson. As long ago as the 1940s, a concerned relative visited the whole family and interviewed each member about the problem, and said, 'From this I concluded that mental deficiency was hereditary in this kindred, and that it was transmitted by females. However, only males were affected.'[55]

Then, 30 years later, the family contacted Hans Brunner of the Department of Human Genetics at Nijmegen University Hospital in the hope of obtaining some scientific insight into their problem. DNA analysis of both affected and unaffected family members revealed that the problem was, as you might expect, on the X chromosome.[56]

Females have two X chromosomes: if one carries a defective gene there is a 50 per cent chance of it being transmitted to their offspring. If a boy receives the gene, it will be expressed because he only has this one X chromosome (the other is a Y chromosome). A girl will probably not be affected because she has two X chromosomes, one from the mother and the other from her father.

The gene in this case coded for monoamine oxidase (MAO), the enzyme which breaks down serotonin, dopamine and noradrenaline once they have been used within the synapse to transmit a message. The affected males had a mutation in this gene that meant they had no functional MAO at all from this gene. In the unaffected members, this region of DNA was entirely normal, which does strongly suggest causality. However, lack of MAO suggests that levels of serotonin and other transmitters in the synapses would be *higher* (because there was no enzyme to break them down) whereas above we have been looking at *lower* levels. Indeed, as we will see in the next chapter, inhibitors of MAO, which damp down its activity, in fact have a calming and antidepressant effect. Having no MAO and inhibiting its action should, you might think, have similar behavioural effects. It appears not. This does not invalidate this genetic study, though. Maybe this was a 'one-off' mutation peculiar to this family, but it again underlines the importance of serotonin in aggression and reminds us that there is still much to be written and explained in the serotonin saga.

Incidentally, the Dutch findings had a bearing on the Mobley case, described at the beginning of this chapter. The defence wondered if Stephen Mobley had a similar MAO deficiency, and Hans Brunner offered to test him – but the court would not allow it. The main reason given was that Stephen had a relatively normal IQ of 104, while low IQ seemed to be part and parcel of the Dutch problem, so it was unlikely the two families had this mutation in common.

A study of violent Swedish offenders, incidentally, noted lower MAO activity in their blood platelets, compared with non-violent offenders, so maybe this enzyme will turn out to be a key player in aggression.[57]

Cool, calm and collected

A low resting heart rate (pulse rate) is a sign of a strong cardiovascular system and a useful goal to aim for if you are trying to improve your level of fitness. Most top athletes have a resting heart rate below 50 beats per minute, compared with an average of around 70 beats per minute. But a low heart rate can have a more sinister connotation – it is linked with antisocial and aggressive behaviour, according to Adrian Raine of the University of Southern California, and co-workers.[58]

Antisocial types also tend to have low skin conductance responses; they do not get all nervous and sweaty when exposed to scary or emotional stimuli. (This so-called electrodermal response is the basis of the lie detector.) Both these physiological markers point to an underaroused SNS. In chapter 4, we saw how adrenaline and noradrenaline kick-start the body's response to stressors and produce familiar symptoms like racing heart, dry mouth and sweating. Aggressive and antisocial people seem to have a higher threshold than normal for this kind of arousal.

At first, this seems odd; surely explosively angry types get all worked up *more* easily than normal? Well, look at it this way: the hallmark of the psychopath is lack of guilt and disregard of the consequences. Anyone who can contemplate a violent act without feeling scared or squeamish may well be primed to act on impulse. Thus low arousal of the SNS could be the biological underpinning of the psychopath's emotional detachment. It may also suggest why some are high on novelty and sensation seeking: their nervous systems are, perhaps, hungry for stimulation and cannot get it from normal, everyday experience. This underarousal is probably an inherited trait, linked with a temperament high in sensation seeking and fearlessness.

Raine studied a group of 101 English 15-year-old boys and found the lowest resting heart rates in those later convicted of violent offences.[59] A larger study, of nearly 2000 boys and girls on the Indian Ocean island of Mauritius, suggested that this biological predisposition starts very early on. Low resting heart rate as young as three years old was linked to aggressive behaviour in adolescence.[60]

And it can work both ways. Further study of Raine's English schoolboys compared two subgroups. Both groups contained antisocial boys, but the first group did not progress to adult crime, while the second group did. Electrodermal and cardiovascular responses were higher in the first group, suggesting that normal arousal of the autonomic nervous system had a protective effect and stopped them from getting into trouble.[61] Again, as with the serotonin measures, we may one day be able to use these predictions to help prevent criminal behaviour in those at high risk of committing it.

Dead brain space?

Brain imaging research into violent behaviour is still very much at an early stage, but it is already providing some exciting insights. For example, a recent PET study by James Blair and his team at the Institute of Cognitive Neurology in London has uncovered something very interesting about the brains of antisocials.[62]

One key characteristic of such people, as we saw above, is lack of empathy. The research team checked this out by showing antisocials (in prison and special hospitals) pictures of sad faces: the kind of image that might give you a lump in the throat and start the tears welling up. They found that the antisocials just did not respond to the images in the usual way. The control group – non-antisocials who had committed murder – did respond, giving a baseline to the study.

Now the volunteers were given a PET scan while they looked at both sad and angry faces, so that brain activity could be recorded. The amygdala was found to be responsive to the sad faces (adding to its repertoire of emotional processing), and the orbitofrontal cortex was activated by angry expressions. The antisocials underreacted, as measured by amygdala activity on the PET scan, to sad expressions and also to fearful expressions, but they responded normally to angry expressions. Such individuals may therefore have sustained damage to the amygdala; the nature of the lesion is unknown, however, but could be defective connections to the frontal cortex linked to low serotonin levels.

One of the earliest studies of this kind, by scientists at the University of Texas, scanned the brains of four psychiatric patients who had a history of persistent and impulsive violence. Two showed no regret for their actions, while the other two did. All had decreased blood flow in their temporal lobe, as measured by a PET scan, but only the first two also showed a decrease of blood flow in the frontal lobe.[63] The temporal lobe – put crudely – links the 'thinking' cortex to the emotional brain, so maybe dysfunction here is not unexpected. Further studies have tended to confirm these early observations – those who show no remorse have physiological dead space in the frontal lobe – suggesting that circuits in this region may play a role in shaping our moral attitudes.

Adrian Raine has carried out further PET studies, on the brains of murderers pleading not guilty on grounds of insanity. Again, this study found reduced glucose metabolism (a marker of neuronal activity) in the pre-frontal cortex in the 41 murderers, who were compared with a group of normal controls.[64] Abnormalities were also found in brain areas involved in emotional processing, such as the amygdala and the thalamus. As Raine suggests, these findings, although preliminary, could be the 'initial indications of a network of abnormal cortical and subcortical brain processes that may predispose the violence in murderers pleading not guilty by reason of insanity'.

In this section we have surveyed the spectrum of stress, depression and antisocial behaviour. We now have at least some sense of where the science stands and where it may go in the future. Now it is time to look at how this huge burden of distress might be relieved.

PART III

How to Lighten Up

CHAPTER SEVEN

Pharmacological Fixes

In 50 years' time, the problem of depression will have been solved by science, because it is a chemical problem. Had I been born later than I was, I wouldn't have had to endure 40 years of mental illness – and the failure of my aspirations – because it would have been treated faster and more effectively. (Glyn Jones)

For those who place their faith in science and technology, antidepressants have revolutionized the treatment for depression, just as insulin gave new hope to people with diabetes, once considered a fatal disease. But, for some people, taking drugs to alleviate a problem of the mind is unacceptable, particularly when the depression has an obvious cause, such as bereavement or divorce. They may subscribe to the medieval view of medicine and believe that illness is some kind of punishment for past wrongs. Or they may simply not believe that depression is an illness at all.

But at least there *are* effective drug treatments for depression, for those who will take them. When it comes to crime and antisocial behaviour, there are far fewer pharmacological options.

Out of the blue

Antidepressants – a happy accident

People have always looked to drugs to relieve depression, such as alcohol, opiates and, as we shall see, herbs like St John's wort. In the first half of the 20th century depression bad enough to come to the attention of a psychiatrist was mostly treated with hospitalization and electric shock therapy.

Meanwhile, patients complaining of symptoms such as insomnia or anxiety might have been given barbiturates and, later, tranquillizers such as Valium or Librium.

We now know that, although these drugs do calm anxiety and induce sleep, in the long term they may make depression worse. Moreover, they are addictive, should not be mixed with alcohol and are very dangerous in overdose (the last thing you want when prescribing *anything* to a depressive who may be contemplating suicide). The only place tranquillizers have in primary care these days is for short-term relief of very severe anxiety and insomnia (helping someone deal with the upset of a bereavement just long enough to cope with the funeral, for example).

So, until the 1950s, there was no effective drug treatment for depression and nothing in the pipeline. We had antibiotics, insulin, painkillers, but nothing for mental illness. You either suffered in silence or you were locked up.

Until 1947, when the Ukranian emigré Selman Waksman introduced streptomycin, tuberculosis (TB) was still a greatly feared disease, because of its high mortality rate. Other anti-TB drugs followed, including one called iproniazid. It turned out not to be the best medicine for TB but it caught the attention of psychiatrist Nathan Kline, of Columbia University, because of its effect on patients' moods. In short, they became euphoric on iproniazid – way above what you would expect from the effects of remission of the TB.

Meanwhile, biochemist Albert Zeller of Northwestern University was looking for compounds that would inhibit the enzyme monoamine oxidase (MAO). He had shown that MAO broke down noradrenaline and serotonin once they had been used in the synapse. Inhibitors, he thought, would increase levels of these neurotransmitters in the brain by blocking the enzyme's action.

He came across iproniazid, on a random trawl of drug companies, looking for things to test, and it turned out to be a potent inhibitor of MAO. Tests on rats backed up Zeller's observations; iproniazid did, indeed, raise levels of noradrenaline and serotonin in the brain. What is more, it energized the rats (just as it did the TB patients). This effect was especially marked when their brains had first been depleted of the neurotransmitters by giving the drug reserpine.

Putting all these observations together led to Kline treating depressed patients in his private practice with iproniazid in 1956, to find they improved dramatically. Since the drug was already approved for TB in the United States, there were few barriers to its introduction for the treatment of depression. Within a year hundreds of thousands of patients were taking it. However, it was dropped almost as soon as it came onto the market – because a number of patients developed jaundice as a side effect.

Meanwhile Ronald Kuhn, in Switzerland, had been searching for antidepressants too, but from a different angle. He argued that a sedating, rather than an energizing, drug would do the trick. He was thinking of opium, which occasionally brought relief from depression, and the new major sedative, chlorpromazine, which calmed schizophrenics and is credited with the move towards care in the community.

In 1957, just a few months after iproniazid came onto the market for depression, Kuhn introduced imipramine. Chemically, imipramine resembled chlorpromazine because its molecules had three six-membered rings of atoms fused together; thus imipramine, and the related drugs that were later developed, are known as tricyclic antidepressants.

That takes care of two of the major classes of antidepressants: MAO inhibitors and tricyclics. Psychiatrists and their patients got by – mainly with tricyclics, which turned out to be the safer of the two types of drugs – until fluoxetine (Prozac) was introduced in 1987.

Unlike the earlier drugs, fluoxetine was no accident. It was a carefully crafted creation from the company Eli Lilly. But its history is still fascinating because the researchers behind it, Bryan Molloy and David Wong, began their careers in cardiology and antibiotics respectively. Their paths crossed at a lecture by Solomon Snyder, one of the founding fathers of biological psychiatry. Here they learnt about Snyder's development of synaptosomes. These are preparations of ground-up brain tissue (from experimental animals) that still contain functional nerve endings. This was an amazing new way of testing drugs that acted on synapses. The animal's brain was first exposed to the drug, then the synaptosomes were made. Then, you would expose the tissue to neurotransmitter – serotonin, say – and see how much of it was taken up in the presence of the drug.

Suitably inspired, Molloy and Wong went ahead to use the synaptosome technique to discover fluoxetine, a compound which acts only upon the serotonin system (we will see exactly how, below). Fluoxetine, and other drugs of this type, are known as selective serotonin reuptake inhibitors (SSRIs). Table 1 gives a complete list of all the drugs we mention in this chapter.

How do antidepressants work?

Around 70 per cent of patients prescribed an antidepressant will show a substantial improvement in their symptoms within three months. This tends to be true across the board, independent of the antidepressant used or the degree of depression being treated. It is a myth that depression with an obvious cause – such as divorce, or being fired – will not respond to medication.

Table 1. Antidepressant drugs in common use, sorted by type.

Type of drug	Examples (UK tradename in brackets)
TCA	imipramine (Tofranil); nortriptyline (Allegron); desipramine (Pertofran); amitriptyline (Tryptizol); dothiepin (Prothiaden); lofepramine (Gamanil); venlafaxine (Efexor); clomipramine (Anafranil)
SSRI	fluoxetine (Prozac); citalopram (Cipramil); paroxetine (Seroxat); nefazodone (Dutonin); fluvoxamine (Faverin); sertraline (Lustral)
MAO inhibitor	moclobemide (Manerix)
NARI	reboxetine (Edronax)
NASSA	mirtazapine (Zispin)

Note, venlafaxine and nefazadone are sometimes called 'atypical' antidepressants because they are thought to have a unique mode of action, having some SSRI and some TCA character. Here we have put them in the class they most resemble.

Key: TCA = tricyclic antidepressants; SSRI = selective serotonin reuptake inhibitors; MAO inhibitors = monoamine oxidase inhibitors; NARI = selective noradrenaline reuptake inhibitor; NASSA = noradrenaline and selective serotonin antidepressant.

This is obviously disappointing for the 30 per cent who do not respond to the first drug they are offered, but it compares reasonably well with the response rate found in drugs for other conditions, such as high blood pressure. And if one antidepressant does not seem to work, there are others which can be tried, either instead of, or in addition to, the first.

It is a bit surprising that the newer drugs like fluoxetine do not seem to be any more effective than those invented in the 1950s and 1960s.[1] In fact, some doctors argue that in some circumstances the older drugs might even be better, a point we will take up again below. However, there is more to a drug than its efficacy. The newer drugs are safer in overdose (very important in severe depression) and have fewer side effects.

All antidepressants, however, have a major drawback. For reasons that are still not very well understood, there is a time lag of one to four weeks before they kick in and the patient starts to feel a bit better (that is, if they are going to respond at all).

If someone leaves seeking help until they are feeling absolutely desperate, being told they will have to hang on for several more weeks before seeing any improvement can be devastating (although it is probably worse *not* to be forewarned of the time lag).

In fact, the changes in brain chemistry that the drug brings about probably start from day one. Early improvements, such as being a bit more active, might become apparent to those around the depressed person long before they notice any change themselves. Moreover, the symptoms are relieved in stages: sleep may improve, for instance, before feelings of guilt or anxiety are relieved.

However, many doctors believe that if someone shows no improvement at all after two weeks, there is little likelihood of the patient responding and they may as well try something else. Others advocate a more long-term approach and say the patient should really think in terms of months, rather than weeks, before the depression lifts.

Incidentally, a new drug, pindolol, appears to shorten the time lag before antidepressants take effect if taken in conjunction with them. Pindolol comes from the class of drugs known as the beta blockers, which are normally used to treat high blood pressure and heart failure. But in the context of depression, pindolol appears to help boost serotonin transmission.[2]

It is generally assumed that most antidepressants exert their effects by raising the levels of serotonin and noradrenaline within the synapses. But this assumes that depression is caused by depletion of these substances: the biogenic amine theory (as discussed in chapter 5). This is a circular argument. As the psychologist Dorothy Rowe puts it, 'Pneumonia is not caused by a lack of penicillin'. There must be more to it than this. For a start, if the levels of serotonin and noradrenaline in the brain are raised rapidly – as the evidence suggests – then why is there a time lag before patients feel better? And what about the role of other factors, like the HPA axis which controls the stress response and is so often out of balance in depression?

The bottom line is that we still do not really know what causes – or relieves – depression in humans. Depression is a far more complex and less well-understood disorder than say, diabetes. Here the disease is defined by the lack of a specific substance – the hormone insulin – and treatment simply consists of remedying the deficiency. The way antidepressants work is more complicated than this. They probably do raise serotonin and/or noradrenaline levels in the brain, although much of the evidence comes from animal studies, but do so by different mechanisms, depending on the class of drug. It is probably more accurate, too, to talk of levels of activity of brain *circuits* involving serotonin and noradrenaline rather than of levels of the neurotransmitters themselves. There are around 40 different antidepressants in common use; we will now take a closer look at the main types.

BOX 32   *The power of the placebo*

In trying to discover how antidepressants work, most researchers come up with increasingly sophisticated arguments in terms of neurotransmitters, receptors, and synapses. Others take the opposite view and say that, in fact, the drugs do not work at all. We just think they do.

You would probably be highly offended if your doctor fobbed you off with pink-coated sugar pills next time you needed a prescription. And if they actually did you any good, your faith in science and the medical profession would no doubt plummet to an all-time low. Yet, in clinical trials, up to 30 per cent of patients with depression given this type of dummy pill, known as a placebo, do get better.

Clinical trials are carried out to assess the efficacy, safety and side effect profile of new drugs. In a standard clinical trial, there are two groups of patients: one gets the new drug and the other a placebo. The difference in clinical response between the two groups is generally attributed to the pharmacological action of the drug. Put simply, the bigger the difference, the more effective the drug.

But if the placebo contains no active ingredient, surely it should have no effect on the patient at all? Well, life for pharmaceutical companies would be much simpler if that were the case, but there is more to taking a drug than just being exposed to its biologically active ingredients; the main complicating factor is human psychology.

Just being in a clinical trial – *any* kind of clinical trial – can be therapeutic in its own right. You get special attention from medical staff. First, they have to be especially thorough in their investigations because stringent controls will have been laid out in the study design. So participants may get extra care and time lavished on them. Second, the balance of power has been shifted a little, because you are doing them a big favour by agreeing to be in the trial at all (they may get a major publication from the results, or be invited to attend a big conference to give a talk). And finally, whether you are in a trial or not, taking any kind of treatment creates an expectation of recovery which is therapeutic in its own right. At least you are *doing* something.

Response to placebo in a clinical trial is made up, largely, of these three components. In trials of antidepressants, the difference between drug effect and placebo has been largely dependent on the severity of the depression. In very mild depression the difference may be minimal, with marked drug effects occurring mainly in major depression. Recently, Irving Kirsch of the University of Connecticut has carried out a meta-analysis of 19 different clinical trials of antidepressants covering over 2000 patients which led him to conclude that 75 per cent of the improvement brought about by an active drug was probably a placebo effect.[3]

Moreover, he speculates that the remaining 25 per cent could be an 'active' placebo effect, brought about by the experience of side effects which lead patients to believe they are taking a potent drug. A clinical trial is supposed to be 'blind': that is, neither patients nor investigators know whether they are on placebo or drug, in the interests of objectivity. But patients who have been on antidepressants before will be able to tell drug from placebo by the experience of side effects (placebos do not have side effects). It is estimated that 80 per cent 'know' which arm of the trial they are on purely from this experience. This unintentional unblinding of the trial will tend to exaggerate the differences between the drug and the placebo. Those in the first group will have positive expectations, because they know they are on an active drug. But those in the placebo group will have negative expectations, as they know they are acting as the controls. This is just the kind of subjective response that blinding a trial is meant to eliminate.

Kirsch's first study drew on trials from many sources and attracted criticism because of his methodology (plus the generalized wrath of the pharmaceutical industry for daring to suggest their products were not much better than expensive sugar pills). He is now embarking on a further study of 30 trials submitted to the US Food and Drug Administration of five new-generation antidepressants, including Prozac.[4] These should be good-quality uniform data, because of the strict guidelines the FDA imposes on trials. Watch this space.

The older generation

The tricyclic antidepressants (TCAs) like imipramine, nortriptyline and clomipramine are still quite widely prescribed. They block the reuptake of both noradrenaline and serotonin by the pre-synaptic neuron, which keeps these neurotransmitters in the synapse for longer (see Figure 8). Some TCAs have a stronger effect on noradrenaline than serotonin (and vice versa). For instance, desipramine only blocks the reuptake of noradrenaline, while clomipramine blocks noradrenaline more effectively than serotonin.

What may be more important in terms of therapeutic effect is the way the TCAs seem to remodel the synapse, by down-regulating (reducing the number of) receptors on the post-synaptic neuron. In fact the down-regulation of noradrenaline receptors is something researchers look out for in animal studies when they are testing new antidepressants.

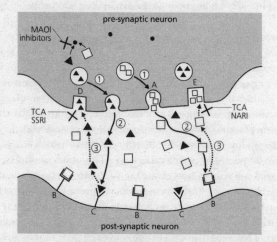

(Figure 8: How antidepressants work)
In normal neurotransmitter action, noradrenaline (white squares) and serotonin (black triangles) are released from vesicles in the pre-synaptic neuron (1) and travel across the synapse to receptor molecules on the post-synaptic neuron surface(2). Once the post-synaptic neuron has fired, they are then recycled to the pre-synaptic neuron (3). Tricyclic antidepressants (TCAs), selective serotonin reuptake inhibitors (SSRIs) and selective noradrenaline reuptake inhibitors (NARIs) block reuptake. Monoamine oxidase (MAO, black circles) is an enzyme found chiefly in the pre-synaptic neuron; it breaks down excess neurotransmitter leaking from vesicles in their resting state. MAO inhibitors act by blocking their action.
Key to labels: A is release site of neurotransmitters in synaptic gap: B is a noradrenaline receptor on the post-synaptic neuron surface: C is a serotonin receptor: D and E are serotonin and noradrenaline reuptake sites on the pre-synaptic neuron surface.

Like other body systems, the synapse likes to keep in balance; if it has more neurotransmitter molecules than it is used to, it will try to shift the balance back, by reducing the number of receptors they can bind to. If it turned up the number, or did nothing, then the system would become seriously out of balance. Maybe this shift by the synapse is responsible for lifting mood – we really do not know. But the brains of depressives and suicides sometimes show an *increase* in the number of serotonin receptors, a shift in the opposite direction.

As far as their overall effects are concerned, the TCAs can be divided into two groups. One consists of those, like amitriptyline and dothiepin, which have a predominantly sedating effect. These are especially suitable for depressed people who are agitated and anxious; if they are given at night, they may also help with sleep problems.

The other group, which includes imipramine, clomipramine and lofepramine, are stimulating rather than sedative in their effect and are best prescribed for people whose depression is characterized by lethargy and exhaustion. Indeed, if these patients get a sedating TCA they will probably feel the worse for it (perhaps the reason why many people on antidepressants complain of feeling like a 'zombie').

The TCAs can have some fairly severe side effects because they are relatively 'dirty' drugs, acting on many different brain circuits, not just those concerned with mood. Specifically, TCAs also tend to hit circuits powered by the neurotransmitter acetylcholine and a distinct pattern of side effects known as anticholinergic effects is often noted. Dry mouth (sometimes leading to tooth decay as the supply of antibacterial saliva dwindles), weight gain, dizziness, blurred vision and constipation are just some of the symptoms which add to the depressed person's burden.

Since the side effects tend to kick in before the benefits do, many people end up abandoning TCAs, feeling let down by the treatment they desperately hoped might make a difference. This is where a good relationship with the family doctor or psychiatrist might make all the difference. A doctor who is liked and respected enough to get away with a plea of 'look, just do this for me' may be able to get his or her patient to stick to the course till they recover.

An overdose of TCAs can be fatal and will be potentiated by the effects of alcohol – a very tempting combination for depressed people contemplating suicide. If the doctor still thinks a TCA is the right drug, he might have to ensure some kind of supervision, such as having a trusted family member take charge of the tablets.

So why on earth do doctors still give TCAs, when there are now antidepressants which are safer and have fewer side effects? Are they being driven by cost considerations? TCAs are relatively cheap (but that may change when the patent on Prozac runs out shortly and generic copies become available). Are people with mental health problems being given worse treatment than those with, say, cancer or heart disease?[5]

Maybe. But if a patient has found that a TCA has done the trick in a previous bout of depression, both he and the doctor may feel 'if it works don't fix it' and be reluctant to try a new drug. There is also some evidence that, particularly in severe depression, TCAs might even be more effective than other drugs. For instance, clomipramine was better than two different selective serotonin reuptake inhibitors (SSRIs), citalopram[6] and paroxetine,[7] and also more effective than moclobemide, which is an MAO inhibitor.[8]

Why this should be may, paradoxically, have something to do with the 'dirtiness' of these older drugs. So while acting on many brain circuits produces side effects, the fact that TCAs generally affect both serotonin and noradrenaline might boost their antidepressant effect, when compared with the SSRIs which only act on serotonin. In other words, maybe a two-pronged attack on the problem is just more effective.

Incidentally, lofepramine – one of the more stimulating drugs mentioned above – stands out among the TCAs, for having fewer side effects and being far less toxic in overdose.

The same is true of moclobemide (also mentioned above). The MAO inhibitors are the other older-generation drugs and were the first anti-depressants ever used. They block the action of the enzyme MAO, which breaks down serotonin and noradrenaline, and so increase levels within the synapse (see Figure 8). As with the TCAs, it is not known exactly how this relieves depression.

MAO inhibitors are not much used nowadays because they are very toxic when taken with certain types of food and drink, such as cheese, yeast extract, wine (especially red wine) and beer. The reason is that MAO in the liver normally breaks down tyramine, a substance found in high concentrations in these foods. But the older MAO inhibitors act on the liver enzymes, as well as those in the brain, and tyramine reaches the circulation instead of being broken down. It can cause a dangerous rise in blood pressure, via release of noradrenaline from nerve endings in the sympathetic nervous system, which may lead to a fatal stroke, or at best very bad headaches.

Indeed, before the food interaction was understood, many patients on MAO inhibitors did in fact die of brain haemorrhages in the 1960s.

Doctors and families faced the frightening prospect of impulsive suicidal patients eating themselves to death, literally, with a glass of Chianti and a slice of Stilton.

Moclobemide is a good example of how, sometimes, a dirty drug can be cleaned up. It acts specifically on MAO in the brain, leaving the liver enzyme alone, and so is relatively safe. Sometimes this class of drug proves useful: for patients who have not responded to other antidepressants, say, or for specific applications, such as the treatment of agoraphobia or somatization.

The Prozac revolution

Prozac (fluoxetine) hit the headlines in the 1990s – but not because it is a wonder drug, or at least not directly. Fluoxetine was a landmark because it was (relatively) free of side effects, and could be prescribed more widely. There are now many chemical 'cousins' of fluoxetine which have an equally good side effect profile, and some of the newer drugs are better still.

People with milder forms of depression and with related problems such as eating disorders, obsessive compulsive disorder and even shopping addiction found their lives being transformed by fluoxetine. Then paroxetine, another Prozac-like drug, became the first medication ever to be licensed for the treatment of social phobia (the clinical name for extreme and disabling shyness). The phrase 'better than well' was coined for the Prozac experience and there was talk of genuine personality change.

This is controversial, and one way of looking at it is this. We mentioned dysthymia in chapter 5: a low-level, chronic form of depression which is not terribly disabling, but gives a grey, flat aspect to people's lives. A dysthymic will have been feeling this way for as long as he can remember. Give him fluoxetine and he feels completely diferent, as his mood lifts for the first time ever. Maybe he could have felt this way on imipramine too, but he probably never got the opportunity to take it.

But there is no firm line in the sand between dysthymics and the rest of the population. A recent study, where normal volunteers were given a related drug, paroxetine, backs this up: those on the medication reported feeling more positive and being generally more sociable.[9] No wonder fluoxetine acquired a reputation as the 'happy pill' of the 1990s (taking the place of the tranquillizers Librium and Valium of the 1960s – at least in public perceptions). Indeed, Prozac was discussed so much in the media around this time that the company which discovered it, Eli Lilly, became concerned that depression, as a condition, was becoming trivialized (with stories of pets being given the drug, for instance).

Fluoxetine and related compounds like citalopram, fluvoxamine, nefazodone, paroxetine and sertraline are all classed as all SSRIs. Like the tricyclics, they block the neurotransmitter reuptake process but only for serotonin, not noradrenaline (see Figure 8). They also differ from the TCAs in that they do not down-regulate the noradrenaline receptors – so really, we are looking at a quite different class of drug, with a very specific type of action.

The SSRIs, as stated above, have fewer side effects than older drugs, and they are also much safer in overdose, which is why more and more doctors now prescribe them as first-line treatment for depression. Side effects that might occur include nausea, insomnia, anxiety and sexual dysfunction (loss of libido and erectile problems).

There had to be a backlash against Prozac. On 14 September 1989, 47-year-old Joe Wesbecker of Louisville, Kentucky, returned to the printing works where he had been employed for many years (having been on sick leave) and shot 20 of his co-workers, killing eight, before turning the gun on himself. At the post-mortem, traces of Prozac, which he had recently been prescribed, were found in his bloodstream, along with several other drugs.

Soon his family, and those of the dead and injured co-workers, were preparing lawsuits against Eli Lilly, claiming Prozac had turned Wesbecker violent. The claims were based on a paper by Martin Teicher, of Harvard Medical School, where he reported the occurrence of intense suicidal preoccupations among six depressed patients when they started Prozac (these faded when they came off the drug).[10]

This sounds paradoxical: we have already seen that it is *low* serotonin which is (sometimes) associated with suicide and violent behaviour. Prozac increases serotonin transmission, so you would expect people on it to be *less* (not more) violent. But we have seen other paradoxes like this. Remember the violent Dutch family in the last chapter: their genetic MAO defect should have made them happier and calmer (the same biochemical effect as an MAO inhibitor), not badly behaved. Maybe all this underlines how little we really know of the complexity of brain chemistry (and, say critics of mood-altering drugs, the folly of interfering with it).

But back to the Wesbecker case. It emerged that this man had a long history of mental illness, marked by suicide attempts and threats of violence against others. Maybe he would have gone on that killing spree whatever drug he had been on. Or Prozac could have interacted with one of the other drugs he was on, enhancing his violent propensities. Alternatively, maybe Wesbecker was just one of a few who *do* perhaps react badly to Prozac: after all, the drug does fiddle with serotonin metabolism. The brain – and the body – have, as we have seen, many mechanisms for maintaining the status quo. Maybe it turns down production of serotonin, in a few vulnerable people, to an abnormally low level in a response to its artificial increase by Prozac? As far as Wesbecker is concerned, though, we will never know what went wrong, for Eli Lilly made an out-of-court settlement with the plaintiffs.

Meanwhile, the Teicher report continued to stir up debate. You can argue, of course, that suicidal thoughts are a symptom of depression which is likely to emerge whatever drug is taken and should not really be considered as a side effect. When researchers from Eli Lilly reviewed the evidence in 1991 they found that Prozac was not linked with an increased risk of suicidal acts or thoughts among depressed patients.[11] But perhaps that is not very surprising.

There was more bad publicity for Prozac in 1997, on the death of Diana, Princess of Wales, and her lover Dodi Fayed in a road accident, for a postmortem revealed traces of the drug in the body of Henri Paul, the driver, who had also been killed after smashing the heavy-duty Mercedes into a Paris subway wall at high speed. We will never know the truth, but it is not impossible that Prozac – and drink – played a role in Paul's reckless and possibly even suicidal behaviour.

Party on with noradrenaline

It was perhaps inevitable that once researchers had come up with a selective *serotonin* reuptake inhibitor, they would try to do the same with noradrenaline. This line of thinking led to yet another class of anti-depressants: the selective noradrenaline reuptake inhibitors (NARIs). As the name suggests, these only block the reuptake of noradrenaline, leaving serotonin alone (see Figure 8). Reboxetine is the first of these new anti-depressants, and it stands out for the way it tackles the so-called negative symptoms of depression, such as social withdrawal. Depressed patients reported getting out and about more, resuming social activities, and generally increasing their interactions with other people after taking this drug.[12]

So attention is now shifting from the serotonin factor to look at the role noradrenaline plays in mood. It is beginning to look as if increasing serotonin transmission might brighten mood, while boosting noradrenaline has a beneficial, energizing effect on social functioning. The beauty of dissecting out the specific effects of the different neurotransmitters on mood is that doctors and patients can decide which antidepressant might be the most beneficial in their particular case. Where lethargy and social withdrawal are a big feature of the depression, treatment with a NARI might be more effective, while someone whose main problem is a persistent low, sad mood may benefit more from an SSRI.

Towards designer drugs

The complementary advantages of enhancing noradrenaline and serotonin may explain why the TCA antidepressants that act on both at once seemed to be more effective than SSRIs in the trials mentioned above. It would be nice to have all this in a drug, but without any significant side effects or toxicity. So along comes yet another new class of antidepressant, the noradrenaline and selective serotonin antidepressants (NASSAs), of which a drug called mirtazapine is the first example. These make the TCAs look like molecular blunderbusses and have a very specific and elegant mode of action.

First, they block noradrenaline autoreceptors on pre-synaptic neurons. A word of explanation here: the autoreceptor senses levels of neurotransmitter in the synapse and, if levels are sufficient, stops any further synthesis. Blocking the autoreceptor turns off this negative feedback loop and allows neurotransmitter synthesis to continue. This action makes more noradrenaline which, indirectly, boosts serotonin transmission, by acting on receptors on nearby serotonin neurons.

And that is not all. Mirtazapine also blocks two serotonin receptor subtypes, 5-HT_2 and 5-HT_3, leaving serotonin to interact with the 5-HT_1 subtype only. But side effects of anxiety, agitation and sexual dysfunction are associated with 5-HT_2 and nausea with 5-HT_3 binding by serotonin. Blocking this binding effectively eliminates the side effects, while keeping the mood-enhancing effects which you get from having serotonin bind to the 5-HT_1 receptor. This ability to hit just one receptor subtype out of several is how pharmaceutical companies are designing the side effect factor out of their drugs. Indeed, as you would expect, patients report very few SSRI-type side effects with mirtazapine and it seems to be as effective as clomipramine (the 'gold standard' in the trials mentioned above).[13]

Meanwhile, the TCA/SSRI story has continued to evolve, producing new drugs with a better side effect profile. Here we will mention just one, venlafaxine, which blocks the reuptake of noradrenaline and serotonin and has recently been approved for the treatment of general anxiety disorder (making it the first antidepressant ever to be licensed for this condition). This is a far cry from the 1960s, when anxiety disorders were invariably treated with benzodiazepine tranquillizers, such as Valium and Librium.

The benzodiazepines act quite differently from antidepressants; they plug into specialized receptors for a neurotransmitter called gamma-aminobutyric acid (GABA), so enhancing its effects in the brain. GABA is an inhibitory neurotransmitter and so has a calming effect on the circuits where it acts. Many benzodiazepine receptors are found in the parts of the brain where fear is thought to be generated, particularly the amygdala. So tranquillizers can reduce fear and anxiety, by a well-established biochemical mechanism.

However, we now know that benzodiazepine tranquillizers can create physiological and psychological dependence. People who stop taking benzodiazepines suddenly after long-term use may suffer a range of unpleasant symptoms, such as rebound insomnia, shaking, severe anxiety and palpitations, which can only be relieved by resuming the tablets. Moreover, alcohol acts at the GABA receptors too: if mixed with benzodiazepines it may produce a permanent inhibition of activity in neural circuits (leading to coma followed by death). So until venlafaxine, there was not much on offer, by way of useful medication, for anxiety disorders.

Flower power

Conventional pharmaceutical drugs are not the only route to easing depression. In recent years, there has been a revival of interest in a herbal remedy, hypericum, which has been used as an antidepressant since at least the first century AD. Hypericum is an extract from the yellow flowers of *Hypericum perforatum* or St John's wort, so called because it blooms around the birthday of St John the Baptist on 24 June. The plant grows on heathland and in woods in Europe, Western Asia and North Africa. In the Middle Ages physicians used it against 'dreadful melancholic thoughts' or 'to drive out the Devil'. Today, it is used extensively in Germany, where it is licensed for the treatment of anxiety and depression. In the UK it became the first (and so far only) antidepressant to be sold over the counter.

Unlike conventional antidepressants, hypericum contains a number of active ingredients of which, so far, two major ones – hypericin and a volatile oil called hyperforin – have been identified. Hypericum seems to have a novel mode of action, because it inhibits the reuptake of serotonin, noradrenaline *and* dopamine, at least in test tube experiments with mouse brain tissue.[14] It also appears to up-regulate the number of serotonin receptors in the frontal cortex of rats (the significance of this is not clear; such up-regulation is also seen in the brains of untreated depressed patients, but also seems to occur after successful treatment with ECT – another brain chemistry paradox!). No other antidepressant acts on all three mood neurotransmitters in this way.

Hypericum seems to be effective in treating mild to moderate depression compared with placebo and also has few serious side effects,[15] the most significant of which may be photosensivity (skin reaction following exposure to sunlight). It also scores well in comparison with conventional treatment, such as amitriptyline.[16]

Hypericum has been subjected to a small clinical trial in seasonal affective disorder (SAD) and found to be as effective as light therapy.[17] This was backed up by a larger, but more informal trial, which took place over the winter of 1997 and involved over 300 members of the UK SAD Association. They took an over-the-counter hypericum preparation over a period of eight weeks, either with or without light therapy (the conventional treatment for SAD).[18] The volunteers reported significant improvement in their symptoms of anxiety, loss of libido and insomnia, whether or not they added light therapy to the hypericum.

This is good news for people with SAD who may be looking for a more practical alternative to light therapy (which involves sitting in front of a light box for up to two hours a day). New trials are now underway; in the United States, the National Institute for Mental Health is recruiting volunteers to test the effectiveness of hypericum against SSRIs and placebo, while in Reading, UK, it is being trialled in women with premenstrual syndrome.

More data are needed on hypericum before it can be licensed widely as a treatment for depression. It will be useful for patients who do not want to take a conventional drug, but will accept a preparation seen as 'natural'; in other words, more patients will get the treatment they need. Some are already treating themselves with over-the-counter hypericum supplements, which is probably fine for mild depression. The problem with self-medication, however, is always that you may miss a serious or deteriorating illness (indigestion remedies could mask an stomach ulcer, or even cancer, for instance) and depression is no exception. So if the hypericum does not lead to an improvement within, say, a month – and especially if the depressive symptoms seem to be getting worse – a doctor should be consulted without delay.

A metal for mental stability

The antidepressant drugs we have discussed so far are all what pharma-
cologists call small organic molecules. That is, they are based on the
element carbon, in combination with hydrogen, oxygen, nitrogen and
maybe sulphur and phosphorus. In fact most drugs are organic molecules,
because they either mimic or interact with compounds found naturally in
the body, like enzymes.

But there are some exceptions – like the drug lithium carbonate, which
is used to relieve the symptoms of mania and to smooth out the mood
swings which occur in bipolar disorder. Lithium carbonate belongs to a
group of simple inorganic chemicals known as salts; its active component,
lithium, is a metal (in its pure form it is used in the batteries which power
laptop computers and mobile phones).

Until lithium came on the scene, people in the throes of acute mania had
to be treated by heavy sedation – first with barbiturates and then, from about
the 1950s, with the so-called major tranquillizers, like chlorpromazine.
These drugs, however, were really intended for the treatment of schizophrenia, and often plunged people with mania into a profound depression.

In the 1940s, the Australian psychiatrist John Cade was carrying out
research into depression and mania in a hospital in Bundoora, near
Melbourne. He became convinced of the existence of a mystery substance
which was overproduced in mania and underproduced in depression.
Treatment would consist in balancing the level of this compound, but first
Cade had to identify it. He began by examining the urine of his patients,
isolating various substances that might be the culprit, and injected them
into guinea pigs, to see what effect they had. Uric acid, a key component
of urine, was one obvious candidate, but it was not soluble enough to
inject. So Cade added some lithium to make the salt lithium urate, which
was soluble. To his surprise, lithium urate sedated the guinea pigs, without
sending them to sleep. He did not know if it was the lithium or the uric acid
that had the sedating effect, so he repeated his experiment with lithium
carbonate, and got the same result.

He then turned to his patients, and injected one, who had been in a state
of chronic mania for five years, with lithium. To his astonishment, the man
became calm within days of the injection and was soon able to return
home – a prospect previously unthinkable. Cade published his results in
1949, but the idea of lithium as a medication for mania did not really catch
on until it was taken up by the Danish psychiatrist Mogens Schou in the
1950s, after which it was introduced around Europe.

There was one problem: lithium carbonate is a common chemical, and so drug companies could not patent it (all the other antidepressants we have discussed were original, new compounds – save hypericin, of course, which has long been known). Lithium was never going to be a money-spinner, and this may have delayed its introduction into the United States until 1970.

There was more. Schou discovered that treating patients with lithium had the unexpected bonus of keeping them in remission, preventing future attacks of both mania *and* depression in up to 80 per cent of those taking it. This was a very unexpected finding, and it is still not fully understood how lithium can prevent both states. It appears to act on the neurons to make them less excitable and also stabilizes the balance between the neuro-transmitters (literally promoting mental stability).

However, lithium is not always an easy drug to take; it has a number of side effects, such as hand tremor, and the margin between a therapeutic and a toxic dose is quite narrow, compared with most drugs. Lithium is only prescribed by psychiatrists, and the patient needs to be monitored with regular blood tests.

The idea that bipolar disorder might arise from some form of irritable over-excitement of the neurons has led to the use of the anti-epileptic drugs carbamazepine and valproate to stabilize the condition. These might be added to lithium, or used instead of it.

Incidentally, the success of lithium in treating bipolar disorder again underlines the difference between this condition and major depression. Lithium is not an antidepressant and, conversely, antidepressants on their own do not relieve the depressive swings of bipolar disorder; in fact they can be dangerous, because they might precipitate an attack of mania.

Keeping the blues at bay

As we saw in chapter 5, depression tends to be a long-term – maybe even life-long – disorder. Up to 50 per cent of cases relapse, that is, experience the return of symptoms within six to nine months after an episode of depression has (apparently) cleared up. Over a longer time scale, 80 per cent of patients can expect to suffer recurrence of depression. However, there is lots of clinical evidence to suggest that extended treatment with antidepressant therapy can reduce the rates of relapse and recurrence.

This means that treatment – at the full dose – should continue for around six months after recovery from a bout of depression, to avoid relapse.[19]

If that sounds like a long time, consider this. Researchers at the University of Pittsburgh looked at people who had already been taking imipramine for three years and got one group to carry on for a further two years, while a second group was given a placebo. Of the eleven in the active treatment group, there were no recurrences of depression in the first year, and just one in the second. In the placebo group, though, six out of the nine patients experienced recurrences during the two-year period. Moreover, blood levels of imipramine were monitored in all the patients; the single patient who had a recurrence in the first group had a suspiciously low level, suggesting that this person was not taking the drug as directed.[20]

Of course, this was just a small study, but it has been supported by other research, which reveals that several of the newer antidepressants also have a protective long-term effect.[21] In the light of the evidence, people who have had two episodes of depression in five years, or three in their whole life, should probably consider taking medication for at least five years and, in some cases, maybe even for life.

A depressing prospect? Well, it is certainly a big commitment for the patient and a challenge for the doctor too. Non-compliance (failure to take drugs as prescribed) is an issue in any area of medicine, especially where long-term treatment is needed. For instance, one of the main reasons why there has been a rise in antibiotic resistance is that people do not take the full course of antibiotic treatment for an infection. Either they feel better within a few days and believe they do not need to take any more tablets or, as with TB, they will need to take medication for several months and may be too disorganized or just reluctant to bother (especially if there are associated side effects). This is worse than useless; the first few days of treatment kills the more sensitive bugs in a population of infecting bacteria, leaving the stronger, more resistant ones to thrive. If you are going to hit them, then hit them hard, should be the prescribing philosophy with infection.

Another situation where non-compliance is often found is with medication for high blood pressure. This is, on the whole, a condition that does not give rise to symptoms, but damages the circulatory system, setting the scene for later heart and kidney disease (that is why high blood pressure is known as 'the silent killer'). Medication can keep blood pressure within normal limits and so protects the circulation against these killer diseases. But if a blood pressure-lowering drug with side effects is prescribed, the treatment will feel worse than the (symptomless) disease and the patient may well abandon it.

Something similar may happen with antidepressants: once a bout of depression is over, the patient does not want to put up with side effects for several more months, never mind a lifetime. Moreover, there is a genuine fear attached to taking drugs which affect the mind; many people fear that antidepressants are addictive, possibly because they confuse them with benzodiazepine tranquillizers. Actually, antidepressants are *not* addictive (if they were, they would have a street value – like, for instance, capsules of the sleeping drug temazepam).

With the advent of newer drugs with fewer side effects, however, long-term treatment may be less problematic. And – going with the 'hit it hard' theory – it is also important to pick an antidepressant that wipes out all the symptoms of the depression from the first episode, rather than merely producing some kind of favourable response.[22] Here is where using one of the drugs that act on noradrenaline and serotonin might be better than just an SSRI: it may tend to do a more thorough job in promoting recovery.

BOX 33 *Drastic measures?*

Fifty years ago, electroconvulsive therapy (ECT) was practically the only treatment available for mental illness. The technique was first introduced by the Italian psychiatrist Ugo Cerletti in 1938. Its development grew from the observation that the condition of schizophrenics who also had epilepsy sometimes improved after a seizure. ECT involves inducing a seizure artificially, by passing a pulse of electricity through the frontal and temporal lobes of the brain.

After the above description of ever more sophisticated antidepressants, it may surprise you to discover that ECT is still used to treat depression and acute mania (it is no longer used in schizophrenia or, at least, it should not be). It appears to have a high success rate in very severe depression, where the patient has not responded to any of the drugs that have been tried; it would normally be used where the patient is acutely suicidal, has psychotic delusions or is refusing to eat and drink.

Dramatic improvement is quite common with ECT, and the treatment can be life-saving. But no-one knows quite how it works; put crudely, the shock may, somehow, jolt the brain back into balance. The treatment is generally applied to the frontal and temporal lobes of the brain where, as we saw in chapter 5, there may be underactivity of neurons in depression. It has been noted that ECT does up-regulate serotonin receptors (while it down-regulates noradrenaline receptors), so it can alter brain chemistry in the same way as antidepressants.

Still, the very idea does seem barbaric and, in the old days, it was distressing to see patients having violent seizures under ECT. Nowadays, an anaesthetic and a muscle relaxant are used, so the procedure is far less drastic. However, there is often some memory loss (usually reversible with time) and confusion associated with ECT treatment; this is minimized by applying the treatment to the non-dominant hemisphere of the brain (in most people, the right hemisphere) and so avoiding the areas that control language and, maybe, memory.

A potential alternative to ECT has emerged over the last ten years or so. Transcranial magnetic stimulation (TMS) involves inducing an electric current in the brain, by applying a magnetic field to it, through a metal coil placed on the scalp. A rapidly switching electric current is passed through the coil; this creates a rapidly changing magnetic field which, in turn, sends a pulse of electricity through the brain.

The underlying principle – electricity from a magnetic field – is known as electromagnetic induction. It was discovered by the British scientist Michael Faraday in 1821 and is the basis of the electricity supply industry (although Faraday felt sure no-one would find a practical use for his invention).

Applying TMS to the motor or visual cortex produces an obvious response: the subject either experiences involuntary limb movements or sees flashes of light. So we know it can stimulate brain activity. If the treatment is applied to the frontal lobes it may have an effect on mood, reportedly increasing sadness if applied to the left lobe, and happiness if applied to the right.[23]

This suggests it might be good for depression and there have, indeed, been several clinical trials, although the technique is very far from being established as a treatment. For instance, 70 patients with major depression were given either TMS or 'sham' TMS in ten sessions over a two-week period by Israeli researchers.[24] After this time, 17 of the 35 patients in the treatment group had dropped by over 50 per cent in their depression ratings, compared with only eight out of 32 in the sham treatment group.

A word about that 'sham' treatment: it is the equivalent of a placebo pill in a drug trial. The patients had the coil applied to their scalp, but in a direction in which no electric pulse could pass through their brain. So they thought they might be getting a treatment, but were not. If they had had no treatment at all, the trial would not have been double blinded and the results could have been biased.

The treatment was applied, in this case, to the right frontal lobe, although other trials have applied the pulse to the left lobe instead, apparently with similar results (yes, this does seem strange, given the observations above about mood changes in right and left lobes). The significance of this study is, perhaps, that 15 patients in the treatment group and 13 in the control group were ill enough to have been considered for ECT before the trial. Afterwards, only seven in the treatment group actually went on to receive it, compared with all 15 in the control group.

Side effects from TMS seemed minor: some discomfort from a twitching of the facial muscles during treatment, and headaches that could be relieved by paracetamol. But it is not yet known if the antidepressant effects of TMS are long-lasting. It is also not clear quite how TMS works – whether it is like ECT, or complementary to it in some way. Animal studies have shown that TMS can produce changes in neurotransmitters and receptors similar to those seen in ECT, however.[25]

From red to reasonable – pharmacology and bad behaviour

Ritalin – the discipline drug

Giving drugs to children – particularly drugs that affect the brain – is something that surely few parents or doctors do lightly. Yet, around four million American children and adults take a daily dose of Ritalin (methylphenidate) to treat ADHD: a number that has increased sevenfold since 1990.[26] In some classrooms, up to ten per cent of children may have a diagnosis of ADHD and be taking Ritalin. The drug is less popular in the UK, but even so, prescriptions are said to be doubling each year.

Ritalin is a stimulant which was originally used to keep people awake when they had the sleeping illness narcolepsy. It is thought to raise the levels of dopamine in the brain by binding the transporter molecule which normally recycles it to the pre-synaptic neuron, as part of the reuptake mechanism. Ritalin is, therefore, a reuptake inhibitor and (put simply) resembles Prozac, except that it works on dopamine. So it may be able to normalize the aberrant dopamine circuits in the ADHD brain (which, as we discussed in chapter 6, involve parts of the frontal cortex, basal ganglia and cerebellum which control memory, attention and learning).

Ritalin certainly has a calming effect on hyperactive children and this may create the mental space they need to learn (and it has an obvious calming effect too on the parents and children who have to deal with them). However, whether it has genuine long-term benefits remains uncertain. An expert panel convened by the United States National Institutes of Health in late 1998 concluded that children treated with Ritalin show almost no improvement in either academic achievement or social skills.[27]

Moreover, some researchers are concerned about the similarities between Ritalin, amphetamines and cocaine. PET scans carried out by Nora Volkow of the Brookhaven National Laboratory in New York revealed that Ritalin and cocaine, a potent drug of addiction, act in almost identical areas of the brain.[28]

So could Ritalin prime a young brain towards later cocaine addiction? Ten to 30 per cent of cocaine abusers are thought to have ADHD, but it is not obvious whether they are self-medicating because of the disorder (as people with depression sometimes turn to alcohol) or whether it is an effect of Ritalin.[29]

Current research shows the opposite. A study of three groups of boys suggested that Ritalin and other stimulant drugs in fact prevent those with ADHD from developing substance disorder.[30] The three groups were: boys with ADHD who had taken medication, boys with ADHD who had not, and boys without ADHD. The figures for later substance abuse were 25 per cent, 75 per cent and 18 per cent respectively, which suggests a marked protective effect if the condition is treated by stimulant medication. Note, too, how untreated ADHD leads to higher rates of substance abuse. But this study was quite small (only 56 boys in the Ritalin group) and there is the negative evidence compiled by the expert panel mentioned above to consider. These conflicting reports are disturbing; further investigations on bigger groups are needed to settle the question of just how effective Ritalin is both for treatment of ADHD and for protection against future problems.

Another twist to the Ritalin story comes from work with knockout mice. These animals lacked the dopamine transporter (DAT) gene, which has also been implicated in the genetics of ADHD. Their behaviour resembled that of hyperactive children in that they were 12 times more active than normal mice and incapable of learning their way around a maze because they got so easily distracted. This suggests they were a reasonable animal model in which to test out some drugs.

Ritalin worked like a dream (so did amphetamine and cocaine), calming the animals down and normalizing their behaviour. But the drugs did not alter the dopamine levels in the brain, which was rather surprising. The researchers wondered if the beneficial action of Ritalin was acting through serotonin, or some other neurotransmitter. When they tested Prozac, and other serotonin-enhancing drugs, on the hyperactive mice, they did indeed quieten down, as with Ritalin.[31] The implications of this work for humans are unclear, however, as this mouse model, while useful, is probably a gross over-simplification. But it does suggest that maybe using drugs that act on serotonin could be useful in ADHD and other disruptive behaviours.

Turning down aggression

To date, however, there has not been much research on medication that calms anger, aggression or violence. One drug which has met with some (limited) success is buspirone, a non-sedating tranquillizer which works by enhancing serotonin (though it is not an SSRI). For instance, in a small group of mentally retarded adults it reduced anxiety and aggression.[32] It also helps people whose violent behaviour is caused by brain injury.[33]

Prozac has been used to treat aggression, but not as much as you might think. In the 'angry' type of depression we looked at in chapter 1 fluoxetine did, indeed, eliminate the anger attacks and reduce feelings of hostility in 71 per cent of patients on the trial.[34] And it worked well in a small trial in antisocials with a history of impulsive aggression.[35] But the pharmacological treatment of bad behaviour is really in its infancy – for both scientific and political reasons. First, we would not necessarily expect serotonin-enhancing antidepressants to calm violent and antisocial behaviour, because the serotonin circuits involved in violence and depression are probably different (although they may overlap). More specific drugs will probably be needed, even if they still act on serotonin. Second, there are probably other transmitters and hormones involved and, as we saw in the last chapter, bad behaviour is very heterogeneous. The real problem is that drug treatments would probably be most effective if applied to younger people, before their problems get out of hand, and this raises all kinds of ethical issues (as with Ritalin treatment; and, incidentally, no-one has proved that the use of Ritalin has cut the adolescent or adult crime rate). And, while people are now more willing to believe that depression is a physical illness that can be treated by drugs, they are far from thinking the same about crime and antisocial behaviour. If we found a drug that would stop recidivism, would criminals want to take it? And if not, should they be forced to, in place of prison?

However smart the molecules we devise for manipulating mood and emotion, they can only reach their full potential if given alongside some kind of psychological support for the underlying problems. Talk therapy, therefore, is the subject of our next chapter.

CHAPTER EIGHT

Talking Treatments

Until now, we have focused very much on the biological aspects of both depression and 'bad' behaviour. But of course, these are also psychological disorders. So they should respond to psychological treatments. In practical terms this means psychotherapy – or talking treatment.

There are probably around 200 different types of psychotherapy of varying degrees of scientific and medical validity. What they all have in common is an attempt to establish a relationship – called the therapeutic alliance – between a trained professional and the patient (sometimes called the client) with the aim of dealing with the patient's problems.

You may think it is a sad reflection on modern society that we have to pay someone (either directly, or via the health service) to talk to about our problems. Surely a good friend or an older and wiser family member should be able to sort us out when we are down in the dumps or going off the rails? Well, we have already underlined the importance of social support in dealing with stress and depression. And we know how inadequate parenting can sow the seeds of delinquent behaviour.

But sometimes folk wisdom and common sense ('just pull yourself together'; 'it'll take you out of yourself') are counterproductive, while too much sympathy can lead to people dwelling on and so magnifying their problems. And sometimes friends and family are just too close to the problem to be of much use.

There is far more to good psychotherapy than just common sense and positive thinking. As we will see, in depression, certain forms of therapy can be as good as drugs in producing lasting improvement. Bad behaviour currently seems less amenable to therapy, but there is still great potential for effective psychological treatments in the future.

Dr Freud, I presume?

A therapist often subscribes to one particular school of psychotherapy, but if he (or she) is any good, he will have a wide range of therapeutic techniques at his fingertips and will not adhere too rigidly to the dogma of his training. And he should, these days, be aware of the role biological factors (as discussed in previous chapters) play in psychological disorders, even if he is not medically qualified.

Therapy can be given by a wide range of professionals: a psychiatrist, a clinical psychologist, a (non-medically) qualified psychotherapist or counsellor, a family doctor, a health visitor or practice nurse. Standards vary from place to place, but are not always as strict as they are for physical medicine. In other words you can be almost 100 per cent sure that someone who removes your gall bladder or prescribes insulin will be properly qualified to do so, but less certain of someone who is delving into your mind.

All forms of psychotherapy derive, directly or indirectly, from Sigmund Freud's theory of psychoanalysis, which was developed towards the end of the 19th century. Put simply, Freud thought that psychological problems like depression developed from unconscious conflicts arising during childhood. The work of psychoanalysis involves bringing the unconscious material into conscious awareness by various techniques, such as dream analysis and free association of thoughts. Thus the patient acquires insight into his psychological problems and may be able to resolve them.

As psychology, and knowledge of the brain, developed over the 20th century, psychotherapy also evolved into two main schools. Broadly speaking, the psychodynamic therapies – such as Jungian therapy and psychoanalysis – focus upon gaining insight into unconscious processes. (The word dynamic here refers to the conflict between unconscious forces.) The supportive therapies, such as behavioural training and cognitive therapy, are concentrated more upon conscious thought processes and often involve an element of learning.

In general, the psychodynamic therapies are more patient-centred, with the therapist taking a non-directive role (he may offer little advice or comment), while the supportive therapies are more of a two-way process where the therapist will offer more input and direction. Psychotherapy is not always one-to-one; it may be carried out in small groups, under the direction of one or more therapists. This is not just a cost-cutting exercise (although that is obviously a consideration), but can also be genuinely helpful to people whose problems are rooted in interpersonal conflicts and who need to learn new ways of relating to people.

The course of psychodynamic therapy is measure~~d~~
involve several sessions a week. It is rarely available t
services and there is not a great deal of evidence to suppoi
Maybe the Freudian model of psychological disorder is ~~i~~
the treatment cannot work (if it does, it is because of t~~h~~
between the therapist and client, which would happen anyw........ever
type of therapy was being used). Or it may be that the right ki~~nd~~ of studies
just have not been done yet.

In any case, it is hard to make a case for psychodynamic therapy in
depression because it is not really appropriate in terms of cost, availability,
or time scale for most people. If a time lag of four weeks before antidepressants work seems unbearable, how about a *year* before anything
happens in therapy?

Maybe the psychodynamic therapies are best for those who have come
through a depression and now want to understand themselves better? But
supportive therapies, specifically aimed at problem solving, seem to be
more appropriate as an actual cure for the condition.

The fourth way? A cognitive model of depression

Aaron Beck of the University of Pennsylvania was himself a psychoanalyst
before he developed cognitive therapy. In the context of therapy, cognition
refers to all the various higher mental processes and capacities, like
memory, learning, introspection, and analysis, which allow human beings
to interact with their environment in such a complex way.

Although the cognitive approach to depression has grown alongside our
understanding of the brain and mental processes, the Greek philosopher
Epictetus put forward the basic idea over two thousand years ago when he
said: '*People are disturbed not by events, but by the view they take of them.*' In other
words, our emotions, behaviours and motivations are all guided by the way
we think.

People with depression tend to think in an overly negative way about
themselves and the world around them. You could say that their problems
arise from a distortion of reality. This would tend to explain why, for
example, some people sink into clinical depression after a bereavement or
being fired. Obviously, most people would experience such events as
negative – but to the depressive, they appear more negative than to others
because of their cognitive response to them.

Beck started to analyse his own patients' thoughts and ideas and, eventually, discovered many characteristic aspects of cognition in depression.

..ese can be summed up in what he calls the cognitive triad: the depressive has a negative conception of himself ('I am useless'), of the world around him ('nothing ever goes right') and of the future ('I'll never get better'). Central to all depressive thinking is the concept of loss – of love, an over-idealized self-image, fulfilment, status, the future and so on.

Beck found that negative thinking even invaded the dreams of his patients. He studied the dreams of a group of depressed patients and compared them with those of a matched group of non-depressed patients (seeing him for other psychiatric conditions). The depressed patients had a higher proportion of dreams with negative outcomes than the control group. Beck wrote:

A typical dream of a depressed patient showed this content: the dreamer was portrayed as a 'loser'; he suffered deprivation of some tangible object, loss of self-esteem, or loss of a person to whom he was attached. Other themes in dreams included the dreamer's being portrayed as inept, repulsive, defective or thwarted in attempting to reach a goal.[1]

Beck's analyses also led to the identification of characteristic features of depressive thinking. Automatic thoughts, arising in conscious awareness but without prior reflection, bridge an (often neutral) event and an emotional response to it. Such negative thoughts fuel the continual inner stream of self-criticism which is such a prominent feature of depression. Then there is selective abstraction: the tendency to focus upon a single detail and block out the full picture (the criticisms in your work appraisal seem more significant than the praise). A related feature is arbitrary inference – jumping to negative conclusions. For instance, if an expected call from a friend does not come, it means that she no longer likes you, rather than that she is busy.

Overgeneralization is characteristic too: a single thoughtless act makes the depressive think that no-one cares for him. Similarly, thinking is often black and white: a failed test means you will *never* get your degree and one cancelled appointment means people *always* let you down. Note, too, the egocentric nature of this type of thinking: at its most extreme, it becomes delusional. Someone with a psychotic depression may believe he is responsible for a famine in a distant country, for instance.

It is not clear when and how this distorted thinking begins. Some people may be born temperamentally disposed towards negative thinking, and early life experiences, such as inadequate parenting, nudge them further in that direction. Nor do we know how this ties up with brain function; could underactivity in the frontal cortex regions mentioned in chapter 5 promote, or result from, such distorted thought processes?

It may not be complete, but the cognitive theory of depression can account for many of the symptoms of the condition. For instance, a depressed person fears he will fail at everything he tries and so becomes less active; he believes life is hopeless and not worth living, so begins to have suicidal thoughts – and so on. Negative thinking feeds on itself, perpetuating the depressed state: the affected person is less active, so achieves less, and this reinforces his negative self-image. Fortunately, just as these negative ideas were learned in the first place, so they can be unlearned and replaced with healthier and more adaptive thought patterns. This is where cognitive therapy comes in.

The cognitive approach offers another way of understanding depression and emotional disorders, and one which is perhaps more in keeping with the patient's dignity and self-image. This is because biological psychiatry tends to present emotional problems as arising from imbalances within the brain, while psychoanalysis sees the patient as being at the mercy of unconscious impulses. A third approach, behaviourism, which arose through the work of the American psychologist B.F. Skinner in the 1930s, likens human behaviour to that of animals and concentrates on the importance of conditioned responses (the importance of these in the emotion of fear was discussed in chapter 2). Behavioural therapy involves learning new responses, and is useful in treating phobias. However, the mind is treated as a 'black box' and little attention is given to thoughts and feelings.

By contrast with these three approaches, the cognitive approach gives more weight to the patient's inner experience, but without looking for hidden meanings. It is both easier for patients to understand than psychodynamic treatments, and easier to teach to other professionals. In recent years, the cognitive and behavioural approaches have merged, because there is an important learning component to cognitive therapy. For simplicity, we will continue to talk about cognitive therapy, although it is often also known as cognitive behavioural therapy.

Cognitive therapy for depression

If the circumstances are right, the negative thinking patterns of depression can be turned around in just a few months with a course of cognitive therapy – even if the patient has chronic depression. Treatment typically consists of between six and 20 sessions of around 45 minutes and is both structured and directed. The therapist will spend the first session outlining the ground rules, finding out about the patient, and agreeing goals to be worked upon together. There is no set plan, but often behavioural techniques are tried first, to get the depressed person more active and to relieve some of the symptoms. These are followed up with cognitive exercises which, it is hoped, will achieve the aim of the therapy: to produce long-lasting change in thinking patterns.

The behavioural techniques are simple, but powerful. Given that a severely depressed patient might lie in bed all day, ruminating on his problems, one common exercise is to make an activity schedule for the day, breaking tasks down into simple steps if necessary.

The therapist might also ask the patient to make lists – however minimal – of activities that gave pleasure, or small successes, to start to redress the balance in his negative thinking. These activities can start to chip away at the feelings of helplessness and hopelessness. Soon, the patient may begin to experience a little satisfaction and a certain sense of achievement, for a change.

Automatic thoughts lose their power once they are identified by a patient's introspection and the therapist's careful questioning. They will also explore alternative explanations for events in the patient's life: for instance, someone was disagreeable on the phone because they are having a bad day and it is not your fault. Ideas will also be tested against reality: 'I fail at everything' can become 'I could be better at presenting myself in meetings, but our customers appreciate my helpfulness on the phone'. In a nutshell, cognitive therapy is all about persuading the patient that his thoughts are just thoughts; they are not facts.

A skilful therapist will assess his patient's strengths and weaknesses from the outset and select the techniques he thinks will work best. The ultimate goal, remember, is to produce a permanent turnaround in the negative mind-set of depression. The fact that this can actually be done in cognitive therapy illustrates the power of the underlying theory.

Who benefits most from therapy?

Obviously, therapy is a welcome option for those who do not wish to take antidepressant drugs, either because of side effects or because they do not believe medication will offer the self-knowledge they seek in getting to the root of their problems. But, as we have said, therapy is a two-way process. However brilliant, caring, and empathic the therapist is, he will not make any progress with a depressed person who cannot (or, more likely, will not) keep his side of the bargain.

To benefit from any form of therapy – and cognitive therapy in particular – the patient needs to possess certain personal characteristics and abilities.[2] First, he should be willing to accept a certain personal responsibility (*not* blame) for his problems and, however depressed, at least accept the possibility of change.

The patient who insists, 'It's all due to a chemical imbalance in my brain', will probably not benefit much from therapy because of his attitude, and will do better on drug treatment. Therapy works best on the 'psychologically minded' patient, who has a certain level of insight into his thoughts and feelings. He should also be sharp enough intellectually to focus on a specific problem and adopt a problem-solving approach.

The patient should also be prepared to work at the tasks set by the therapist, which will be difficult for those who are used to being the passive recipient of medical treatment. And for all kinds of therapy, the patient needs to have at least minimal ability to engage in a meaningful relationship with others, so that a therapeutic alliance can be established with the therapist (this is why it is so hard to work with people with antisocial personality disorder). These qualities are more important than age, intelligence or social class. However, cognitive therapy has only been used extensively in the United States and Europe, to date, so it is not known whether it would need to be adapted to suit people from other cultures.

Pills for symptoms, talk for problems?

It is now well established that cognitive therapy can be as effective as drugs in treating depression and related conditions. In general, therapy is often the treatment of choice in mild depression, and drugs will usually be needed for the most severely ill patients. In between these two extremes it is hard to be prescriptive because new evidence is emerging all the time.

Beck and his co-workers were, naturally, among the first to trial the new therapy in the 1970s. Twelve depressed outpatients were assigned to therapy, and 18 to treatment with imipramine. At the end of 12 weeks, ten in the therapy group had recovered, one was markedly improved and the other moderately improved. None in the therapy group dropped out of the programme, but five in the drug treatment group did because of side effects or other reasons, suggesting that the therapy was the more acceptable treatment from the patient's point of view.

The patients in the therapy group showed a more rapid decrease in the degree of hopelessness experienced than the drug-treated patients; Beck thought this implied a decrease in suicide risk with therapy compared with drug treatment (and, of course, the risk is compounded with imipramine because of its danger in overdose). After six months of follow-up the therapy patients maintained their improvement and their clinical progress was better than that of the drug-treated patients.[3]

Further research confirmed the power of cognitive therapy. One particularly influential study was carried out by researchers for the US National Institutes for Mental Health and involved 239 patients with moderate to severe depression in three different sites, divided into four different groups. One got cognitive therapy, one got interpersonal therapy, one received imipramine, while the fourth was on a placebo – all for 16 weeks. Interpersonal therapy, as the name suggests, works specifically on personal relationship issues. The underlying theory is that depression arises from the lack of a satisfactory relationship with one's parents, which sets the scene for interpersonal difficulties in later life. Over 15–20 sessions, the therapist will focus on relationship issues around the depression (rather than delving too much into the past). From this, the patient learns how to deal more effectively with his relationships in the future.

Of the patients who entered the trial, 39 per cent in the cognitive therapy group recovered, compared with 34 per cent in the interpersonal therapy group, 32 per cent in the imipramine group and 26 per cent in the placebo group.[4] This shows that both forms of therapy are effective and comparable to drug treatment: but the rates of recovery overall are quite low and the placebo group also did relatively well. This is probably because the research team had a fairly stringent definition of recovery: no, or minimal, symptoms for at least eight weeks. Furthermore, the placebo group probably did well because, along with the imipramine group, they got something called clinical management, where they were able to discuss their treatment regularly with a clinician – which would have been therapeutic in its own right.

These patients were followed up for 18 months after the end of their treatment to see if the improvements were sustained. Unfortunately, they were not. Thirty-six per cent in the cognitive therapy group, 33 per cent in the interpersonal group, 50 per cent in the imipramine group and 33 per cent in the placebo group relapsed after their initial recovery. This suggests that none of the treatments had a long-lasting effect, although therapy seemed better than drugs (we now know, from other research discussed in the last chapter, that 16 weeks is not usually a long enough course for antidepressant treatment).

However, patients can do a lot better than this – if they are offered long-term maintenance therapy. Seventy-two outpatients who had already had at least one bout of depression, and were therefore at risk of relapse, were given 16 weeks of acute treatment followed by two years of maintenance in one of three different ways. They got either antidepressants for both phases, cognitive therapy for both phases, or antidepressants for the acute phase followed by maintenance therapy. After two years, the patients receiving therapy had done as well as those on medication: good news for people who find it hard to cope with the idea of taking drugs, even those with few side effects, long-term.[5]

Another study backs this up; 40 patients, also with recurrent depression, who had been successfully treated with drugs were given either maintenance cognitive therapy for 20 weeks, or routine counselling about their drug treatment. Over this time, the antidepressants were gradually withdrawn. Two years after the end of the programme, only 25 per cent of the therapy group had lapsed, compared with 80 per cent of the controls.[6]

Of course, this is a very small study, which needs to be replicated on a much larger scale, but the results are still quite impressive. The therapy was supplemented with lifestyle counselling, which underlined the importance of dealing with stressors such as lack of sleep and overwork (the kind of advice often given after a heart attack). For some people, this may have made all the difference.

An obvious question is whether the effect of therapy and antidepressants might be additive and you might, therefore, get a better cure rate if both are used. This has been addressed in several trials, with varied and interesting results. A group of outpatients with major depression were assigned to either cognitive therapy, imipramine, or both, for 12 weeks. Fifty-six per cent of the drug group, 62 per cent of the therapy group and 69 per cent of the group who got both recovered.[7]

Again, therapy seemed more effective than drug treatment, but there was only a modest advantage in having both. However, a more recent meta-analysis of all the data on combined drug–therapy treatments suggested that there was a distinct advantage to having both in the more severe, recurrent depressions, but not in mild depression.[8] This makes sense: just as drugs that work on both serotonin and noradrenaline sometimes seem to be more effective than a more specific medication (as discussed in the last chapter), so it could also be a good idea to have two lines of attack – therapy and drugs – in more severe and resistant forms of depression.

A new study presented to the American Psychiatric Association confirms the value of investing in both drugs and therapy to beat chronic depression. Known as the Serzone Chronic Depression Study, this is the largest study ever undertaken in this area. Six hundred and eighty-one patients depressed for at least two years showed an 85 per cent response rate (higher than usual) from a combination of the antidepressant nefazodone (Serzone) and psychotherapy, compared with 55 per cent for the drug alone and 52 per cent for therapy alone,[9] after 12 weeks of treatment. The therapy is a variant of cognitive therapy specifically designed for chronic depression by James P. McCullough of Virginia Commonwealth University and it is known as the Cognitive Behavioural Analysis System of Psychotherapy (CBASP).

Therapy remodels the brain

Perhaps it is not surprising that therapy can be as effective as drug treatments in psychological disorders. For we now know that successful therapy is associated with changes in brain activity which resemble those that occur after a course of medication. The evidence comes from studies of patients with obsessive compulsive disorder (OCD). This is a particularly distressing psychiatric condition in which patients are plagued by recurrent, unwanted thoughts (obsessions), which cause a state of perpetual nagging anxiety. The sufferer attempts to deal with the anxiety by acting out various meaningless rituals (the compulsive part of OCD) which may consume so much time and energy that they seriously impair normal functioning. The most common compulsive behaviours are repetitive hand washing and checking rituals (that 'did I turn the gas off?' worry – only magnified to the point where it is all-consuming).

Brain imaging suggests that in OCD a particular neural circuit, involving part of the frontal cortex, the thalamus (the brain's relay station for incoming signals) and a region called the caudate nucleus, is overactive. The caudate nucleus is one of the five basal ganglia that sit deep in the brain and control automatic behaviours, habits, and responses, such as having a daily shower, checking the doors and windows are locked when you leave the house and, in general, all those routine tasks that take over in OCD.

Normally this circuit lights up only when we are prompted to carry out these activities, but in OCD it is active all the time. OCD can be treated with fluoxetine and a good response to the drug is indicated by a damping down of overactivity in the caudate nucleus, as shown by a PET scan. The faulty perceptions of reality that drive OCD are obvious targets for modification by cognitive and behavioural therapies. When people respond – as they do – the PET scan again shows decreased activity in the caudate nucleus – physical proof that change has occurred.[10] Specifically the PET scan shows that the area is taking up less glucose, which shows that the neurons there are less active.

More recent research by the same team even suggests that brain imaging can predict which treatment will work best in individual patients. The diagnosis turned on the level of neuronal activity in the region of the frontal cortex involved in OCD. Those with the lowest pre-treatment activity, as measured by PET, did best on clomipramine treatment, while therapy was better for those with a higher level of activity.[11]

Special cases

Cognitive therapy may be particularly appreciated by women with post-natal depression who may not want to take drugs while they are breastfeeding. In a study based in the community, rather than in a psychiatric hospital, depressed mothers received counselling (based upon cognitive therapy) from specially trained health visitors for either one or six weeks. The counselling consisted of advice about child care, reassurance about parenting skills, encouragement to take part in activities that would improve mood, advice on recruiting practical support, and a regular review of behavioural targets. They also received either fluoxetine or a placebo – making four groups in all. Twelve weeks after starting the programme, the women in all four treatment groups had improved. Six sessions of counselling were better than one, fluoxetine was better than placebo, but there was no big advantage in getting both counselling and drugs.[12]

This is good news; women can choose the counselling option in post-natal depression and be drug-free while knowing that they are not depriving themselves (and their families) of a more effective treatment.

Therapy can give hope in even the most difficult cases. British psychiatrists recently revealed the results of a study of psychodynamic interpersonal therapy with patients who had previously failed to improve, despite long-term psychiatric treatment. Of the 110 patients recruited, 55 were assigned to eight weekly sessions of therapy, while the rest had remained under the care of their psychiatrist. Six months later, the therapy group seemed much improved both on their depression rating and in social functioning.[13] There was an economic angle to this study; the therapy group were noted to have cost the health services less than the control group during the follow-up period, suggesting that it may be worth investing more in therapy services to cut demand on health care in the long term.

We began by commenting that in severe depression, drug therapy is generally believed to be better than cognitive therapy. Now even that dictum has been turned on its head by the latest meta-analysis of the data. Reviewing the data on people with major depression who had received either medication or cognitive behaviour therapy, the researchers, from the University of Pennsylvania, found that there was really not much difference in the two approaches.[13] More good news for people who cannot – or will not – comply with medication programmes.

So therapy can help even the most chronic and severely depressed person. But, unlike drug therapy, talking treatment is not available on demand for everyone who can benefit. Not yet, anyway. But – more cause for optimism – it looks as if you may not need the full programme to get the benefits, for 'cut-down' and simplified versions of cognitive therapies are now being piloted in many community psychiatric programmes.

Short but sweet

Most doctors do not enter the profession merely to write out prescriptions. They would probably prefer to help someone with their consulting skills, rather than be seen as a legitimized drug pusher. This is what happened when a group of doctors tried talking to their patients for a change.

Back in the 1980s Dennis Gath and his team, based in Oxford, realized that the widespread habit of prescribing tranquillizers for emotional disorders was beginning to cause concern within the medical profession and wondered if there were not an alternative. So they tried giving distressed patients either the usual tranquillizers or brief counselling.

The six doctors who took part in the trials had no special training for this: they had to rely on whatever skills they already had in this direction. They could give as much counselling as they wanted over the six-month period of the trial, so long as it covered listening to the patient and assessing symptoms, explaining, reassuring and advising. In practice, most patients got about four 12-minute sessions and at the end of seven months they were assessed. Around 60 per cent in each group improved, which shows that even minimal attention from the doctor is as beneficial as tranquillizers (or maybe the patients would have got better anyway, without visiting the doctor?).[15]

Furthermore, there was no evidence that the patients not receiving tranquillizers felt cheated, or made up for the lack with increased consumption of tobacco, alcohol, or other non-prescribed drugs; nor did they visit the doctor more frequently.

But the doctors were concerned about the remaining 40 per cent or so who seemed to have more intransigent problems. So they devised a more structured treatment based upon problem solving. The plan was to offer four sessions, where the patient's problems would be identified in detail, then the patient was asked to think up as many potential solutions as possible. The most suitable was selected, and then patient and therapist (a psychiatrist in this study) together devised an action plan to be worked on before the next session. Patients referred by the family doctor were assigned either to the problem-solving group, or to a control group where they got whatever treatment the doctor would normally have given. At the end of the programme, the problem-solving group were much improved, compared with the controls.[16]

Encouraged by this, the Oxford team extended their research to patients with major depression. They set up three groups – 30 patients in a problem-solving therapy group, 31 receiving amitriptyline and 30 in a group receiving a placebo. The therapy group received one 60-minute session and five of 30 minutes over a 12-week period. After this time, 60 per cent of the problem-solving group had recovered, 52 per cent of the antidepressant group and only 27 per cent of the placebo group.[17]

So problem solving, which this time was administered by a psychiatrist and two research GPs, is slightly better than drugs – at least in this, admittedly small, study. Health professionals in primary care can readily be trained in these techniques and, over time, an investment of just a few hours over three months can bring positive results.

A larger study from Norway, involving 372 patients, tends to confirm these observations. All the patients got simple psychological treatment from their family doctors. This involved the doctor conveying a sense of hope and optimism and establishing a positive relationship with the patient with thorough discussions about the nature of the depression. The doctor might offer advice, such as suggesting increasing physical activity, but was not allowed to follow any specific type of therapy (such as a cognitive therapy programme). One group only got the therapy, another got sertraline (an SSRI) as well, while the third group were given mianserin, a drug like mirtazapine which acts on both serotonin and noradrenaline.

As you might expect and as we have already seen – more is better. Of the patients receiving only therapy, 47 per cent were substantially improved after 24 weeks, and these figures increased to 61 per cent with sertraline and 54 per cent with mianserin.[18] Actually, this is not quite as expected: the drug that acts on two neurotransmitter systems – mianserin – might have been expected to give the best results, but the differences are quite small. The take-home message is that even very simple therapy treatments given by a GP can have a major impact in alleviating depression.

Talking people out of bad behaviour

Cognitive therapy has now been applied to so many psychological conditions, such as eating disorders, sexual problems, OCD, hypochondria and even schizophrenia that it is tempting to believe that it ought to work with antisocial behaviour too. In theory – yes. Indeed, Beck has extended his system in order to treat ASP.[19] The goal is to get the patient to understand how his distorted belief system (he is always right, other people do not matter) is actually the source of problems such as unemployment, marriage breakdown and trouble with the law.

The necessary link between thoughts and behaviour is made by creating a very specific problem list to work on. In the case of impulsive aggression (whether or not in the context of ASP) the goal would be to get the person to create a tiny, reflective pause before lashing out. But it is very difficult to change the cognitive distortions that occur in personality disorder and, so far, success stories have been few and far between.

The reasons are not hard to find. Recall the personal criteria we outlined above for a patient to do well with cognitive therapy: insight, ability to form an intimate relationship, motivation and a sense of responsibility for his problems. But the *lack* of these qualities is the hallmark of the antisocial personality. So how can a therapist work with these people? It is a monumental challenge and one that should be undertaken by only the most experienced of practitioners. Even they may have to work hard to set aside feelings of revulsion and hostility which the client arouses in them (despite the superficial charm, many antisocial people are not particularly nice to know, particularly when they have committed violent crimes).

However, if the therapist can find a tiny chink in the client's personality armour, in the context of a highly structured programme directed towards changing antisocial behaviours, the results may be surprisingly positive. Apart from Beck's own work with antisocials, recent study of a small number of cases of ASP suggested that more positive behaviours and attitudes really can be fostered through short-term cognitive therapy.[20]

Sometimes the therapist can reach the antisocial client through tackling a co-existing problem. For instance, in one study a group of opiate addicts was assigned to either regular drug counselling or drug counselling and psychotherapy with a cognitive component. The patients were of four types: those with ASP, those with depression, those with ASP and depression, and a fourth group with no mental disorder, other than drug dependence. The patients with ASP alone did not improve with psychotherapy, but they did quite well if they also had depression – showing, for instance, a decrease in illegal activities.[21]

Cognitive therapy has also been given to people in prison. In one study a group of general offenders and sex offenders had weekly two-hour sessions over five weeks with the aim of restructuring faulty thinking and improving their social skills. Analysis showed some improvement in self-esteem among these inmates and, importantly, a decrease in aggression.[22]

Given the difficulties of treating adults with ASP, when behaviour patterns are fixed, it is probably best to target efforts at younger people at risk. The UK Home Office has conducted research into cognitive behavioural methods and concluded it was the most effective form of therapy for reducing antisocial behaviour in both young people and adults.[23] Results were best when factors that contributed directly to offending behaviour were targeted for change (rather than focusing on broad issues like home and school life) and the intensity and duration of the therapy programme were matched closely to the perceived risk of future offending.

Conduct disorder may also be amenable to therapy but, since this involves younger age groups, the parents may need to be involved directly in the treatment programme. Family therapy, parent management training, and problem-solving skills teaching have all met with some success, although the drop-out rates are high (having to attend therapy causes families all kinds of practical problems).

While cognitive therapy seems to reduce aggressive and antisocial behaviour in the short term, there is not much evidence of any long-lasting effect.[24] But even a temporary improvement might be good, because it might stabilize the behavioural problem and allow some useful 'social' learning to take place. Maybe that in itself can reduce the risk of problems in adult life.

Therapy, then, has an important role to play in psychological disorders. Compared with drug treatments, though, it requires greater participation on the part of the person affected. The reward for the work of therapy is long-lasting positive change and a feeling of achievement.

CHAPTER NINE

A Brighter Lifestyle

Until now, we have been looking at what medical professionals can do to ease the suffering caused by depression and bad behaviour. It is now time to look at what those affected can do for themselves through self-help and lifestyle changes.

You might think it is easy to change your lifestyle: after all, *you* are supposed to be in charge of your eating, exercise, and sleeping habits. And there appears to be a massive desire on the part of the general public to go down the self-improvement route: just look at the number of magazines, newspaper supplements, and popular books devoted to diet, fitness, and general well-being. Add to this the growing pickiness of people about their food (no additives, no preservatives, yes to organic but definitely no genetically modified organisms) and you may wonder why we do not all enjoy superb physical and mental health.

Unfortunately, there is a huge element of wishful thinking in our new-found health consciousness. Most people find it harder than they imagine to sustain 'healthy' habits. Your local gym probably has hundreds of members, most of whom join on New Year's Day, go a few times and then become too busy with work to keep up the routine. And what they do not tell you in slimming clubs and magazines, is that over 90 per cent of dieters put back all the weight they have lost within a few years.

So there is a huge gap between our aspirations and the reality. But does it really matter that we are getting fatter and unfitter (largely thanks to our work and car culture which, remember, are also our major stressors)? Did you know that 50 years ago, doctors thought it was impertinent to advise patients on their lifestyle? If someone had a heart attack, it was put down to bad luck, not too many fried breakfasts. Now the wall of a doctor's waiting room is a collage of posters urging you to eat fruit, drink sensibly and give up smoking. Patients are *expected* to help themselves these days.

Much health education has been directed towards the prevention of heart disease (and the evidence suggests that it is working, for death rates from heart disease have fallen both in the United States and in the UK in recent years). What is less clear is whether you can also help yourself to better mental health.

Food and mood

Feeding the brain

We have already seen that chemical imbalances in the brain may be linked with both depression and aggression (low serotonin, high cortisol and so on). It is tempting to think that maybe a 'natural' solution to depression would be to eat more foods high in serotonin, and so on. Unfortunately, it is not so simple. For a start, serotonin, noradrenaline and dopamine do not occur pre-formed to any great extent in most foods. (A weird exception is banana, which synthesizes all three and stores them in its peel.)

Instead, the body makes molecules, like neurotransmitters, by chemically transforming related compounds found in food. For neurotransmitters, the raw materials are the amino acids tyrosine (for dopamine and noradrenaline) and tryptophan (for serotonin). Amino acids are also the building blocks of proteins and are found, to a greater or lesser extent, in most foods.

The other way the body processes raw materials to get the chemicals it needs to function is to break them down. So, glucose, the fuel of the brain and the body (whose consumption is monitored in PET scanning), is a fairly simple molecule, produced from dismantling larger molecules like starch which occur in energy-rich foods. In general, we get ample supplies of all these raw materials from a varied diet (whether or not the food is processed, organic or, indeed, genetically modified).

Besides the big names – the neurotransmitters and hormones – there are thousands of backroom boys, whose job it is to fashion these star performers from the raw materials. Chiefly these are enzymes and vitamins, which often work together as a team, either elaborating or dismantling the contents of our daily diet into a form which the brain can use: serotonin from tryptophan, and so on. They themselves are made from raw materials (enzymes from amino acids, for instance).

Often, when brain chemistry is out of balance, it may be because of a genetic defect which means that one of these enzymes is not functioning correctly (or is not made at all). As we saw in chapter 5, the tryptophan hydroxylase enzyme (involved in making serotonin from tryptophan) appears to malfunction in some cases of depression because of a genetic defect. Consuming extra tryptophan-rich foods, like milk, would not help at all in such cases, for the problem is not in the raw material, but in the enzyme which is used to transform it.

Deficiencies and depression

Usually, the biochemical systems of the body can extract what is needed to feed the brain from a regular daily diet. Moreover, the machinery by which it does so is so complex that it cannot be easily manipulated by simplistic dietary interventions. Nevertheless, there is a pervasive belief that our diet is somehow deficient in certain components. Why else would health food shops and high street chemists alike display hundreds of different vitamin, mineral and herbal supplements? More importantly, is there any evidence that such supplements can improve your state of mind?

Actually, there is little hard scientific evidence about the effects of any aspect of diet on mental health. Partly, this is because any research on the links between nutrition and health is quite difficult to carry out in a reliable way. You cannot lock humans up in a lab for years at a time (the period you need to see trends emerging) and watch them eat. If the research is to be realistic, you need to look at the effects of real diets – which are quite complex and may also evolve over time – upon health. This means that your volunteers have to keep food diaries and remember everything they ate; not easy, even when you discount the tendency to fib a bit to make your diet sound better than it is.

Then again, cynics say that drug companies (which is where most of the money is) have a vested interest in not funding such research, because it will not bring patentable products. For instance, if depression was found to be due to vitamin B deficiency and people could be cured by taking a supplement instead, that would obviously hurt the sales of Prozac.

The studies that have been done are small and of varying quality. Here is a quick overview of a few of the better ones, just to illustrate that it seems worthwhile looking into the area of food and mental health in a more systematic way.

Vitamin B complex is a group of eight separate vitamins, all of which are involved in one way or another in the metabolizing of carbohydrate, fat and protein, and so play a role in keeping the brain (and body) well supplied with nutrients. It has long been known that people who are alcohol-dependent may become deficient in vitamin B_1 (thiamine); this occasionally leads to a potentially fatal brain disorder called Wernicke–Korsakoff syndrome. Other than this dramatic exception, B vitamin deficiency is uncommon. However, a study of a group of geriatric and younger patients with major depression showed that 28 per cent were deficient in vitamin B_2 (riboflavin), vitamin B_6 (pyridoxine) and vitamin B_{12} (cobalamin), but not in vitamin B_1 or folic acid.[1] Moreover, the more severe the depression, the worse the vitamin B_{12} status. Of course, it is not clear whether this link is causal: depression causes people to lose interest in food, so maybe the vitamin deficiencies arise *after* the illness takes hold.

It would be interesting to know if reversing the deficiency by giving vitamin supplements can improve depression; a couple of small studies have looked at this. In one, vitamin B_{12} deficiency was already known to be the cause of psychiatric problems in a group of 141 patients in a New York medical centre, even though they did not have symptoms of the usual anaemia. All of these patients responded very well to B_{12} injections.[2] Meanwhile, 33 per cent of a group of 123 patients with major depression or schizophrenia were found to have folic acid deficiency. The researchers, based at the Institute of Psychiatry in London, entered them into a double-blind trial, offering them either folic acid supplements or placebo, in addition to their usual treatment. The folic acid group showed good clinical and social improvement, suggesting that lack of the vitamin may play an important role in the development of these illnesses.[3]

Incidentally, there has recently been a lot of interest in the link between folic acid and the prevention of heart disease (folic acid seems to help keep the coronary arteries clear). Whether there is any link with folic acid deficiencies in depression remains to be seen. But selenium, an antioxidant mineral, may indeed play such a dual role. The antioxidants – which also include vitamins A, C and E as well as a plethora of substances in fruits, vegetables, tea and coffee – act as a force for good against free radicals. These are formed when oxygen molecules (essential to life, of course) are formed within the cell during normal metabolism. Think of them as vandals: these species have an unpaired electron and the laws of chemistry demand that electrons be paired up. So they roam through the cell, tearing electrons from delicate molecules like DNA and proteins, and wrecking them in the process. The accumulated damage contributes to heart disease, cancer, Alzheimer's and maybe other diseases of ageing. Antioxidants neutralize free radicals, taking them out of circulation before they can embark on their campaign of wanton destruction.

A small group of healthy men were given diets low or high in selenium. Those in the low group got hostile and depressed, which made the researchers wonder if low selenium could play a role in negative mood states.[4] In another small study, selenium supplements – tested against placebo – were found to result in mood elevation.[5] It would be very useful to see some far larger studies of this kind, to see if it would be worth adding vitamin and mineral supplements to standard treatment for depression.

Sweet nothings

Sometimes, however, it is what is in food rather than what is not which concerns people. Sucrose – commonly known as sugar – has often been blamed for mood swings and even violent behaviour. It is true that many processed and snack foods are high in (added) sugar (just check the label); when you eat them, the sugar is broken down very rapidly to glucose via the action of the hormone insulin. Blood sugar (that is, glucose in the blood) soars, only to plummet an hour or so after you have the snack, and the accompanying trough in energy and mood can be quite pronounced. If you have a complex carbohydrate snack instead, like toast, glucose is released more slowly and the blood sugar stays at a more constant level, which sustains you and keeps your mood on a more even keel.

Some people seem to be more sensitive to this effect than others, and sugar is sometimes said to make children hyperactive. However, when two groups of such sensitive children were monitored on diets high in sucrose, followed by one high in aspartame, an artificial sweetener, no significant differences were noticed in cognitive or behavioural functions between the two diets.[6] Of course, you can argue that the children were sensitive to both, but this is highly unlikely, as the two types of sweetener act in a completely different way in the body.

Food additives have been blamed for ADHD. Again the scientific evidence for this is conflicting, but in one fairly recent study, a beneficial effect was noticed when provoking foods were removed from the diet.[7] Seventy-eight children were placed on a 'few foods' elimination diet, and the behaviour of 59 of them did improve. The foods which parents blamed for the condition were then surreptitiously re-introduced and, sure enough, they did worsen behaviour in a subgroup of the children. The researchers concluded that child psychiatrists should listen more carefully to parents' views on how certain foods affected their offspring.

Coffee is often assumed to be bad for us (although recent research suggests it is rich in antioxidants) and it is true that it can rev up the sympathetic nervous system by stimulating adrenaline production. So it is surprising to learn that coffee is associated with a lowered risk of suicide. This emerged from a large ongoing health survey of nearly 87,000 nurses in the United States. Over the period of the trial there were 56 suicides in total. Women who drank two to three cups of coffee a day had 0.34 times the risk and those who drank four or more cups 0.42 times the risk of suicide compared with the non-coffee drinkers.[8] Of course, the absolute numbers of suicides involved are small, but the coffee effect is worthy of further investigation. It looks as if it was the caffeine in the coffee which had a long-term beneficial effect on mood.

To date there is not a great deal of hard evidence that the average daily diet has a huge influence – for good or bad – on mental health. Yet many complementary therapists, particularly so-called nutritionists, seem obsessed with the idea of 'cleaning up' one's diet and cutting out wheat, alcohol, dairy products, sugar, and processed foods. The benefits of a 'detoxifying' diet are probably more to do with the idea of taking good care of yourself, which raises self-esteem. But the notion that our food supply is somehow contaminated could (in its more extreme forms at least) be seen as a psychological problem in its own right – and one which is rarely confronted.

Nature's Prozac (again)

Prozac and the other SSRIs offer a sophisticated solution to low serotonin and depression, based upon our (still limited) understanding of what happens at the synapse. But why not take a simpler approach and give people serotonin itself? We considered briefly, above, the possibility of a high-serotonin diet – but there is another way.

The body transforms tryptophan into serotonin in a two-stage process. First, the enzyme tryptophan hydroxylase transforms it into an intermediate called 5-hydroxytryptophan (5-HTP) and then a second enzyme turns 5-HTP into serotonin. (Incidentally, you can be sure that the gene hunters are going to find links between this second enzyme – 5-HTP decarboxylase – and mood disorders, just as they did for its partner enzyme.)

Tryptophan itself was once used as a treatment for insomnia and depression, and was welcomed by people who preferred a natural treatment. But natural is not always best: tryptophan, and other amino acids, are manufactured by fermentation, where yeast or bacteria turn a raw material into a useful product. Fermentation, too, is a natural, biological process with a very long history. In the 1980s, many people in the United States (and a few in Britain) on tryptophan began falling ill with disabling fatigue, muscle weakness and inflammation of the heart and liver. The condition, known as eosinophilia myalgia, was traced back to a faulty batch of tryptophan which had been made in Japan – but not before 100 people had died.

What had happened was that the firm involved had decided to change the strain of microbe used to make the tryptophan, in an attempt to improve the process. Unfortunately, the new strain also produced a toxic contaminant, which was responsible for the illness. Once this was discovered, tryptophan was banned, although, ironically, it was not the tryptophan itself which caused the problem.

But recently there was good news for tryptophan fans (before the contaminant problem, 14 million Americans were taking it) when a 5-HTP supplement – the next best thing – was launched. 5-HTP is manufactured from a West African medicinal plant called *Griffonia simplicifolia*. It is being used to treat depression, anxiety, insomnia, OCD, migraine, and fibromyalgia, and even as a dieting aid.[9] Clinical trials suggest 5-HTP could be as effective as fluvoxamine, an SSRI.[10] Like St John's wort, the other 'natural' Prozac, 5-HTP can be bought over the counter for self-medication. It could be even more appealing to people who prefer natural medicine, because 5-HTP occurs naturally in the body whereas hypericum is a herb.

Nevertheless, 5-HTP still exerts a powerful biological effect and should not be mixed with other antidepressants. And of course, it should not be used as a substitute for expert medical attention in severe depression.

A fishy tale

A salmon steak once a week or, if you prefer, a daily dose of cod liver oil, is good for the health of your heart, because both contain omega-3 fatty acids. The important omega-3s are eicosapentaenoic acid (EPA) and docosahexaenoic acid (DHA). They keep the blood from clotting, which protects from heart attack and stroke, but they are also an important component of the membranes of synapses in the brain. And recently, an interesting story has begun to emerge about omega-3s, impulsive and hostile behaviour, stress, and depression.

First, a group of Japanese students were given either DHA-rich oil capsules or soya-oil placebo capsules from the end of their summer vacation until the middle of their final exams. They all took a psychological test that measured their feelings of aggression before and after the study period. There was no change in the group on DHA, but the control group reported a marked increase in aggression – presumably linked to exam stress.[11] And when mice were fed diets which either contained a regular amount of DHA or were deficient in it, the deficiency group showed more signs of stress and anxiety.[12]

This work opens up some intriguing lines of enquiry. Could the beneficial effects of omega-3s on the heart operate, in some way, through reducing the 'wear and tear' effects of stress on the cardiovascular system (the end result of which is to make blood less likely to clot)? And should we perhaps consider taking a fish oil supplement during stressful periods?

But the DHA story takes an uncanny twist when you start to look at people who are impulsive types. In both early-onset alcoholics[13] and violent, impulsive, angry people,[14] the higher the DHA the *lower* their brain serotonin, while the link was in the opposite direction for normal, healthy volunteers (more DHA meant more serotonin – more or less what was found with the Japanese students). What these findings mean is far from clear: taking them literally means that taking fish oils would make violent people *more* violent, while having the opposite effect in non-violent people.

And finally, omega-3s seem to be beneficial in bipolar disorder. When patients were given either fish oil or olive oil placebo in addition to their regular treatment, the omega-3 group had a significantly longer period of remission.[15] The researchers think the omega-3s may help dampen down overactive neuronal signalling pathways, acting in a similar way to lithium. This was only a small study, but if it is replicated on a larger scale it could lead to an inexpensive and acceptable way for bipolar patients to get more benefit from their treatment. Perhaps there is more scientific truth than we realize in the saying that fish is good for the brain?

On the move

We all know that exercise, like cod liver oil, is good for the heart, but did you know how effective it is as a cure for depression? This must be one of the best-kept secrets in psychiatry. There were over 1,000 papers on the benefits of exercise on mental health as early as 1984, yet only a few doctors are enlightened enough to hand out a book of swimming tickets in place of a prescription.[16]

Research has shown that aerobic (walking, running, and swimming) and anaerobic (stretching and toning) exercise is better than no treatment at all, for mild and moderate depression. Benefit comes from as little as five weeks of exercise – typically three sessions a week of 20–60 minutes – and it lasts for up to a year (especially if some form of physical activity is kept up). In some – but not all – studies, exercise has proved as effective as psychotherapy, including cognitive therapy. If it is done in conjunction with therapy, benefits are enhanced. There is less evidence about exercise compared with antidepressants. However, one recent report suggests exercise is better than nothing, but it is not as effective as clomipramine in the treatment of panic disorder.[17]

How can we account for the exercise effect? The favourite theory is that it releases endorphins, the body's natural painkillers, which home in on the same receptors in the brain as morphine and related compounds. The release of endorphins during physical exertion may be why sportsmen and women (and soldiers in battle) do not feel pain until they are out of the action. In depression, the pain is usually mental, rather than physical, but the endorphins seem to have an all-round 'feel-good' action.

Exercise, particularly aerobic exercise, also brings more oxygen to the brain; maybe this energizes the 'dead' areas found in depression. Whatever the mechanism, it probably works first through relieving stress and thereby preventing subsequent depression. It really is a pity that so many people drop out of their health clubs and keep-fit classes through the exhaustion and time pressure of a demanding job. So full marks to enlightened employers who provide exercise classes on the premises, or who subsidize fees for a gym.

Exercise out of doors may be especially good because of exposure to sunlight, which can raise serotonin levels. There are psychological reasons why exercise works, too. It is a distraction from the morbid thoughts and feelings that are the hallmark of depression; it gives a sense of achievement, particularly when specific goals are being aimed for ('ten more press-ups tomorrow'), which raises self-esteem. Like cognitive therapy, a structured exercise programme reverses the negative thought spiral of depression.

But, as with cognitive therapy, it can be hard to raise the motivation to exercise in someone who is very depressed. If you cannot even get out of bed, how will you manage a 20-minute brisk walk? It can only work if the doctor, or family, can somehow get the depressed person to build up their physical activity – even if the beginning is as small as a walk to the shops.

Equally, a bout of depression may sometimes be triggered by a break in exercise routine, through injury or illness, in someone who is physically active. And often an inability to continue with sports or exercise is a sign that depression is really talking hold. In his account *Malignant Sadness*, leading biologist Lewis Wolpert, a keen cyclist, comments how he became unable to ride his bike as he fell into despair.[18]

Obviously care must be taken in prescribing exercise to the physically unfit, but given that physical exercise is reckoned to be about five times cheaper than regular drug treatment for depression, there is surely a strong case for giving out gym memberships on prescription.

And so to bed

Sleep disturbances are a distinctive feature of depression. Typically, you wake early and cannot get back to sleep. Or, if anxiety and agitation are prominent, you will not be able to get to sleep in the first place. People with seasonal affective disorder often sleep excessively – 12 hours or more a night – like the hibernating animals whose state they seem to mimic. And for people with bipolar disorder, a night without sleep can often trigger a bout of mania (this is often seen in vulnerable students who stay up, cramming for exams). Conversely, lack of sleep may even jolt someone out of a profound depression – even though you might think lack of sleep would make them feel worse.

So it is hardly surprising that what is boringly called sleep hygiene is crucial to people prone to depression. In a nutshell, sleep hygiene is all about giving sleep a lot more respect. Some experts believe we are a chronically sleep-deprived society; this all started with Thomas Edison and the invention of the lightbulb (Edison believed too much time was wasted in sleep and so laid the foundations of the 24-hour society with the creation of artificial electric light). Other experts believe that the lie-in is an indulgent luxury, like overeating. The truth probably lies, as ever, between these two extremes, for sleep is a very individual thing. Some of us get by on five or six hours while others must have nine to function. The sad thing is that many people have no idea of their natural sleep rhythm, because they do not pay enough attention to their actual sleep needs.

Sleep hygiene involves trying to find out your individual requirements – by experimenting with an hour more, or less, sleep and seeing how you feel. Then, once you have discovered your optimum quota, you just make sure you get it (no more, no less) by following two simple rules. First, have a quiet hour before bed to ensure sleep comes easily. And second, get up at the same time every day and, if sleep starts to be a problem, be rigid about this to get your rhythm back in sync. It means sacrificing a lie-in at the weekend: if you get up at seven to go to work, you must be up at seven on Saturday too.

In the 1970s, Thomas Wehr and his colleagues at the US National Institute for Mental Health put forward the theory that the sleep cycles of depressives are out of sync with their biorhythms. In other words, they go to bed too long after their bodies have started to slow down for the night. Wehr found that if he got patients to advance their night's sleep – retiring at teatime and getting up just after midnight – there was a dramatic improvement in their mood. But his method never caught on, because it just was not very practical.

However, Mathias Berger and colleagues in Germany have, more recently, hit on a way of making this work. They studied 33 patients with major depression who had responded positively to sleep deprivation. After one night's total sleep deprivation, they entered a programme of sleep advance treatment for several days; they began by sleeping from 5 pm to midnight and the sleep period was advanced an hour each day until a sleep time of 11 pm to 6 am was reached. Sixty-one per cent of the patients maintained their improved mood during the sleep advance programme.[19] Then they gradually got back into a normal sleep routine by going to bed later each day. We do not yet know if the benefits of the programme were sustained, but it seems like a very promising approach.

Artistic licence

As with exercise, the benefits of the arts in alleviating stress and depression are often overlooked. But, intuitively, you will probably put on a CD of your favourite music – be it classical, jazz, or pop – when you feel upset or pressured. In fact the healing properties of music have been known for centuries; the Greek mathematician and all-round wise man Pythagoras recommended different tones and musical sequences to alter mood, while the Cherokee people have a repertoire of songs to treat a range of different ailments.

More recently, psychologists have looked at the complex relationship between music and brain activity. According to musicologist Elizabeth Miles, you can alter your state of mind by choosing music with a particular rhythm.[20] To lift your mood she suggests an uptempo beat teamed with inspirational lyrics, or any music associated with happy times. For stress relief you might go for something with soothing sounds, such as Chopin nocturnes or maybe pop ballads. If you can, play music while you do demanding work (well, surgeons do).

No doubt you already know this, but, as with exercise, people may neglect the music they love in stressful and difficult times. Maybe it is time to rediscover it?

Writing a journal can be enormously effective in tackling stress and depression. It need not be on the level of Virginia Woolf or Samuel Pepys: even a line a day, or a list of pros and cons around a difficult decision, can help clear the mind. The health benefits of writing in a journal have been underlined by a recent study. People with asthma and arthritis wrote about stressful events in their lives for just 20 minutes a day. They were compared with a control group who just wrote about their plans for the day (a practice which can, in itself, be very helpful, as we will see). The journal group experienced more improvements in lung function (in asthma) and pain (in arthritis) compared with their controls.[21] Maybe putting your feelings on paper somehow reduces the stress they cause? We do not know the mechanism, but it is intriguing that so many writers and artists (with their propensity for mood disorder, as we saw in chapter 5) kept personal journals and kept up extensive correspondence.

Film and theatre can relieve stress too. Many of the best stories involve pitting the hero or heroine against huge obstacles (which one can identify with, in a lesser way) which they find ways of overcoming. Although there are no formal scientific studies, stress expert Angela Patmore, of the University of East Anglia, suggests that seeing these scenarios played out on the stage or in the movies provides a good workout for the brain, subconsciously teaching it a new way of dealing with stress. So maybe when your friends say, 'Come and see the new *Star Wars*, it'll take you out of yourself,' they are not that far off the mark.

Naughty but nice

An appropriate amount of guilt keeps us more or less civilized and ensures we act with at least minimal concern for people around us. Too much guilt, though, destroys peace of mind in depression, while no guilt at all leads to the ruthlessness of ASP.

Is guilt all about personal relationships then? Well, no. Most people have their worst feelings of guilt about things like chocolate, fine wine, smoking, ice cream and other consumables. So much so, that one slimming club (which had better remain nameless) trades on this and uses the word 'sins' to describe calorific items you might allow yourself once or twice a day. This bizarre term even now appears on the menus in certain restaurant chains.

Alcohol, tobacco, sugar and caffeine have been around in one form or another for thousands of years. Common sense suggests we must get a lot of pleasure out of consuming them, much of which is to do with relieving stress (be honest, do you *really* want a stick of celery and a glass of mineral water halfway through the morning?). The evidence there is (and it is rather patchy) tends to back up the obvious: a cup of coffee, chocolate, a glass of good red wine or even a cigarette, will relax you and lift your mood.

But the possible benefits are extinguished if you cannot help feeling guilty (about your weight, or about your health) if you treat yourself to one of these items. Is this guilt *always* appropriate? It is impossible to say – for it is becoming increasingly difficult to assess the research into diet, alcohol and (maybe even) smoking, because it is so laden with value judgements, commercial concerns, and politics.

One organization which has taken up this issue is ARISE (the Association for Research into the Science of Enjoyment), an international coalition of psychologists and related professionals. They point out that the medical literature is dominated by negative concepts such as disease and stress. The argument goes that health is seen as the absence of illness, rather than as a positive quality in its own right, and the promotion of health and happiness has been neglected.

One recent study from ARISE shows that guilt, like stress, may harm your immune system. David Warburton, of the University of Reading, made measurements on the immune protein sIgA in saliva. In the first experiment, volunteers wrote an account of an event that had made them feel either happy or guilty, and were then asked to re-live it. They gave a saliva sample for sIgA before and after this test, as well as 45 minutes and three hours later. The positive mood induced (as ascertained by questioning the volunteers) by recalling the happy experience was linked with an increase in sIgA production, while recall of guilt was associated with no change.[22] In other words, thinking positive seems to boost your immune system. The take-home message is: find stress-relieving pleasures you can enjoy without guilt, if you want to get any genuine benefit from them.

Stress management in a nutshell

Big stress – bereavement, trauma, ill health or major losses – may well require professional counselling and support. But everyday pressures are easy to sort out – given just a couple of hours of serious self-analysis, a notebook, and an endless supply of sticky Post-It notes.

The key to your problem lies in just how hard you find it to free up those couple of hours for yourself. For stress management is all about successful *time* management.

Before you learn to do it better, you have first to discover where you are going wrong now. This means taking a time log for a week. Each 24 hours, write down the time you start and stop each different activity, including sleep (this useful exercise is borrowed from cognitive therapy).

For a balanced, minimum stress existence, the Health Education Authority suggests you spend 45–55 per cent of your time on personal needs, 25–30 per cent on work, including family responsibilities, and 20–25 per cent on leisure. Your personal needs (in case you have forgotten what these are) include sleep, shopping, washing, eating and domestic chores. Ten to one, if you are really feeling the effects of stress it is because work is dominating your time. If you *cannot* cut down – perhaps because you really love your job, or have a new baby (or both) – then if you at least commandeer one free hour a day, just for yourself, to do exactly as you please, you will soon feel a benefit.

But how do you get this balance? Briefly, by getting organized. Delegate as much work as possible (buy domestic help, if you can afford it, shop over the Internet, and so on). Refuse interruptions; if you work in an open-plan office, wear a baseball cap one way round if you are open to chat, the other way if you need to be left alone (do not be afraid of looking stupid – your colleagues will soon get the message and start doing the same).

And remember, technology is your servant, not the other way round. Use the answerphone to get two hours of uninterrupted work first thing, and do not accept trivial calls on your mobile phone. Minimize paperwork: the classic rule about handling each piece of paper once really works. And big tasks can be made to look less fearsome by chopping them up into stages, and then subdividing each stage into an even smaller chunk. Note the deadline in your diary and just work backwards.

In parallel with this, have a monthly plan, subdivided into a weekly plan of action and then each day (this is where the Post-It notes come in), make a list the night before, in order of priority, and even allotting times, of what you will do. Some people swear by the sense of achievement you get by ticking each item off as you do it.

It may all sound cold and clinical, as if life is reduced to a list, within a list, culled from a Master List, of things to do. But in a short period of time, it all becomes automatic.

Face it, don't fight it

There had to be a backlash against the stress management industry. Led by psychologist Angela Patmore of the University of East Anglia, the stress critics argue that an emphasis on stress *avoidance* may actually be harmful in encouraging learned helplessness.

Her own research has not found current stress management practice, with its emphasis on relaxation and fighting off stressors, to be particularly effective.[23] This is more or less in line with what we said in chapter 4, that stress itself is neutral and unavoidable; it is the way you deal with stressors that can be harmful.

So instead of avoiding stress you could walk headlong into it. Giving the brain a stress workout can toughen it up so it responds more easily to stress in the future. Some ideas include rehearsing stressful experiences through frightening films, dramatic music, and psychological drama. An employer may do more for his workers if he organizes parachuting or bungee jumps, rather than aromatherapy and yoga. We can also learn from survivors; instead of pitying people with PTSD we could admire them and ask how they cope. Or we could read inspirational memoirs and adventure stories. All these things may inoculate you against the harmful effects of stress.

The inoculation theory has resonances in other areas of life. Children are protected from paedophiles (who exist, obviously, although the chances of them attacking your child are still extremely rare) by ferrying them to and from school each day, where they would once have walked or taken a bus. Not only is this producing a generation of unfit youngsters, it also robs them of the chance to become streetwise.

In the area of physical health, the rise in asthma and other allergies has been attributed to homes which are too clean and hygienic. The immune system gets less chance than before to have a go at some bugs and thereby develop itself. Should an (innocent) allergen come along, the system over-reacts and you have hayfever, asthma or some other allergic condition.

Let us hope that the stress debate does not become too polarized, for the 'avoiders' and 'embracers' have a lot to learn from one another. We have now reviewed the main approaches to stress, depression and violence, so it is time to look to the future. Where might we be in 50 years' time?

PART FOUR

The Colour of the Future

CHAPTER TEN

Looking Forward: How Brain Science Could Change the Way We Live

The most bullish of the cognitive neuroscientists say the 21st century will see the end of all mental illness. Within 50 years, they say, we are sure to have the means to prevent, detect, treat and – in short – eliminate it. If social attitudes shifted, so that crime was seen as a brain disorder, this could also apply to bad behaviour.

Well, researchers do need a vision to motivate them, but you probably think this particular scenario is rather far-fetched. A world full of perfectly adjusted, law-abiding people? It sounds like social engineering gone (for want of a better word) mad. But before rejecting this vision out of hand, let us just look at if, and how, brain science could deliver this idealized world, or anything even close to it, within the next 50 years.

Genetic solutions

The Human Genome Project

They call it the Holy Grail of biology. The Human Genome Project is about the ultimate map, showing the identity and location of all the genes on the 46 human chromosomes. However, it will take many more years before the function of each one is identified, and longer still before the role each one plays is fully understood.

For genes do not operate in isolation or in a fixed manner. They interact with other genes and environmental factors; they can be turned on or off, or up and down, like a dimmer switch. So pinpointing a gene is only the first step in a long road towards enlightenment, and for genes that operate in the brain that road will be the longest, and hardest, of all. But, make no mistake, gene-based medicine is already with us, thanks to discoveries made in the last two decades.

Cystic fibrosis – a model for the future?

Already we can see how the identification of a gene has led to new ways of both diagnosing and treating disease – and to new ethical considerations. Let us look at how the discovery of the genetic defect that occurs in cystic fibrosis (CF) has changed the outlook for those who have the disease, since some of the same possibilities and problems may open up when genes influencing our behaviour are discovered.

CF is the commonest single-gene disorder in the Western world. Frequency varies between different populations, but it affects around one in 2500 in Northern Europe. The disease is characterized by sticky mucus in the respiratory system, which leads to frequent infection and severely impaired lung function. While most children born with CF now survive into adult life, it remains a serious and potentially fatal disorder.

In 1989, the identity of the gene that is mutated in people with CF was revealed. It goes by the unwieldy name of the cystic fibrosis trans-membrane regulator (CFTR). We all have this gene; it codes for a protein that, under normal circumstances, is part of the mechanism that pumps water and salt into and out of cells, so regulating the body's fluid balance. When the CFTR gene and its protein are mutated, insufficient water is pumped outward, leading to sticky mucus in the lungs and defective sweat glands: the hallmarks of CF.

The CFTR gene was identified using the gene-hunting experiments described in chapter 2. A similar approach has been used to track down genes involved in manic depression, as discussed in chapter 6. Once the CFTR gene had been found on chromosome seven, its DNA seqence was worked out, letter by letter.

The sequencing was an important breakthrough, because it enabled the researchers to compare the CFTR sequence in healthy people and people with CF and so identify the mutation leading to the disease. In fact, it turned out that there were many different mutations associated with CF; an individual family might be affected by any one of these.

From there, it was a relatively short step to developing a test for the mutations and this is now being applied in three main ways. First, anyone can now find out if they are a carrier, that is if they have one copy of a mutated CFTR gene – just by giving a saliva sample for DNA analysis. The CFTR is what we call a recessive gene. Like all genes it comes in pairs of alleles (one on each of the two chromosomes in a pair) and in this case you would need *two* mutated CFTR genes to get the disease. If you only carry one, you are said to be a carrier. You will not get CF, but if you marry another carrier you could have a child who would have a double dose of the mutated gene (one from each of you) who would, therefore, get the disease. In fact, you have a one in four chance of having an affected child if you are a carrier.

People with a dominant gene, like the gene which causes the fatal brain disorder Huntington's chorea, will get the disease if they have only one copy of the gene. However, even here, where genes look completely deterministic, there is variation in the age of onset, course, and severity of the disease. This suggests that even the Huntington's gene interacts with the environment (and other genes). So genes are never destiny, on their own.

Testing for carrier status of disease genes, or linked markers, has become increasingly common; such programmes are well underway for CF and several other single gene disorders.

BOX 34   *Genetic testing – recessive versus dominant*

The implications of genetic testing are quite different depending on the kind of gene you carry. If it is recessive, it will not affect the carrier's own health, but it may be passed on to the next generation, so the knowledge may influence decisions about having children.

If two carriers of CF go ahead and conceive a child, the testing process can be taken one step further. The foetus can be tested at an early stage of pregnancy and, if it is affected, the couple can opt for a termination or, if they decide to continue the pregnancy, prepare for the birth of an affected child.

There is another option, however. It is possible for eggs to be fertilized outside the womb by *in vitro* fertilization. Popularly known as the 'test tube baby' technique, this is more commonly used to by-pass blocked Fallopian tubes in cases of female infertility. One cell can be taken from a small group of eight-cell embryos, and the DNA analysed. Therefore, each embryo can be assessed for its genetic status. Only those bearing healthy genes will be transferred into the mother's womb; therefore the couple can embark on the pregnancy, knowing that the baby will be born free of the genetic disease. This is known as pre-implantation diagnosis. Alarmists *could* claim that this is genetic manipulation of future generations by the back door. But the procedure is technically quite demanding, and it is highly unlikely it will be offered to the general population in the near future – if ever.

For someone who may be carrying a dominant gene, because they know they have a family history of the disease, the consequences are more immediate. In, say, Huntington's chorea, the disease itself does not develop until middle age and there is (currently) no cure. So if you test positive in childhood or early adulthood, you have had the equivalent of a death sentence passed on you. If, however, your test results are negative, you have had the sword of Damocles removed. If you decide *not* to have the test, will you not always be wondering about the secret knowledge concealed in your genes?

What is more, the decision to test or not is not confined to the individual: the knowledge affects other blood relatives. A teenage boy whose maternal grandparent has Huntington's chorea may want to settle his own future by having the test. But if he is positive, it means his mother is too, and she may not have wanted the test herself. Should (or could) the boy keep the knowledge to himself? The signs are that people do not want to take this knowledge on board: the take-up for the Huntington's test has been far lower than was expected when it was introduced in 1993.

There are intermediate scenarios. The breast cancer genes, *BRCA1* and *BRCA2*, are not dominant genes *per se*, but they greatly increase the risk of developing breast or ovarian cancer in women whose families are affected by the disease. There are treatments available for these cancers, but they are not always effective.

Genetic testing throws up many practical and ethical dilemmas for those involved. Besides the impact on oneself, and the immediate family, there is also the issue of the use other parties might make of genetic information. In particular, employers and insurers could use it to discriminate against people carrying defective genes, unless strict ethical guidelines are drawn up.

At present, genetic tests are only carried out in specialist centres, where counselling and information are offered as routine. But the actual technology behind DNA testing is getting easier to use all the time. There will soon be little to stop direct marketing of DIY test kits, by mail order, or even over the Internet. This would enable people to determine their own genetic status (or even, surreptitiously, that of other people). Indeed DIY tests for a variant of the *ApoE4* gene linked with Alzheimer's disease are already available in the United States. The danger is that DNA analyses could easily be misinterpreted and misused when done outside a medical setting.

Behaviour genes – opportunities and ethical dilemmas

We have analysed the application of DNA technology to single gene disorders in some detail, because it highlights some potentially important issues in psychiatric genetics. Conditions such as depression and ASP disorder are not single gene disorders. They are likely to be influenced by many *susceptibility* genes, each of which will have a small effect in combination with the others. Furthermore, environmental influences will be at least equally important in their development.

But the multi-gene nature of depression and aggression does not mean that the technologies mentioned above could not, at least in theory, be developed for each relevant gene that is discovered. The way the technology is used may depend, very largely, on how gene-based medicine develops from the CF model.

Indeed, we are already well into the 'second wave' of discovery in gene-based medicine. Currently, many biotechnology companies are moving away from single gene disorders and are focusing their efforts, instead, on discovering genes involved in multi-gene physical disorders, such as heart disease, diabetes and cancer. These affect many more people, and so give the companies bigger markets for future diagnostic tests and drugs. Many of these companies are now building human DNA databases to look for susceptibility genes for both physical and mental illnesses. (The DNA samples, by the way, come from families recruited by clinicians associated with the companies with their full knowledge and consent, so it is all quite above board.)

The discoveries of the genes implicated in these disease processes will allow research and medical practice to develop in two parallel directions. First, population-based screening will allow preventative measures to be targeted more effectively. Already a variant in a gene that controls blood pressure is allowing doctors to pick out individuals who can benefit most, in terms of lowered blood pressure, from a low-salt diet.[1]

This new development is known as *pharmacogenomics* and it will also allow individual differences in the way people respond to a drug to be taken into account. We all have genes which determine how quickly a drug is broken down by the liver (and so how long it stays in the body), the likelihood of side effects and so on. Each person's pharmacogenetic profile could therefore personalize their prescription. It could show (one day) which antidepressant will give the best response and fewest side effects in a particular person. In short, pharmacogenomics will take the trial and error factor out of prescribing.

As far as genes involved in behaviour are concerned, we are nowhere near the population-based screening stage. At present, any testing for these genes is being done in a research context, with volunteers, to learn more about the role of that gene. Later, you might envisage tests being done in at-risk populations to see if they carry it.

This should only be done once the test can be shown to have a clear benefit, as with the blood pressure gene mentioned above. For instance, if people with a particular gene variant were shown to produce too much of the stress hormone cortisol, predisposing them to depression, they could be offered medication or psychotherapy to protect themselves.

What might turn out to be more useful, in psychiatric genetics, would be tests based on combinations of genes. Individual susceptibility genes are likely to be very common in the general population (unlike genes for single gene disorders which are rare). Researchers could tackle the difficult task of working out how the genes interact. Then they might be able to link different combinations of gene variants to actual risks of developing a mental disorder (something like: if you have A1, B3 and C9 you have a 30 per cent chance of bipolar disorder, but if you have A1, B3 and C11, the risk drops to ten per cent).

The risk assessment part of this is probably a very distant possibility, but the prospect of testing for many gene variants at once certainly is not. Already there are DNA 'chips' which can test thousands of genes in one go and, thanks to robotic technology, quickly and cheaply too.

Unfortunately, at present anyway, it is easier to see the downside – rather than the benefits – of this kind of testing. The information could be misused by employers, to select employees who will cope cheerfully with a heavy workload. It could also lead to less emphasis being placed upon social and cultural influences on behaviour. If 'problem' families are that way because of their genes, rather than from bad housing and poverty, will anyone bother to help improve their material circumstances?

It really should not be that way, if policy makers are made to realize that genes interact with the environment and may even make those involved *more* vulnerable to poor housing and so on. The message is we should do *more* to lessen psychosocial risk once we know about the genes, not less.

We just do not know what effect genetic knowledge could have on public attitudes. It could increase the stigma attached to mental and behavioural problems. On the other hand, it could have the benefit of *lessening* stigma; if a biological basis can be demonstrated, as for diabetes or kidney disease, then maybe society will be less inclined to blame the person. But, then again, the impact on the affected person is unpredictable. They may become more accepting of themselves, or they may adopt a fatalistic, even hopeless, attitude towards their behaviour and problems.

This is one of the main reasons why behavioural genetics is so controversial; indeed, a recent ethical enquiry by the Nuffield Council on Bioethics[2] found that many of those consulted thought such research should not be done at all, as it is thought to be mechanistic and demeaning to human dignity. Indeed, we must resist the trend to 'geneticization': the view that humans are just gene carriers, which has emerged from the sheer power of the new DNA technologies. The research needs to be carried out in an ethical and humanistic context. Before any such tests are put into the public domain, it will be necessary to weigh the cost–benefit equation very carefully. The Nuffield report recommends confidentiality, informed consent and that testing on children should be strongly discouraged: such guidelines are important in any genetic test but are perhaps even more significant where mental disorder is concerned.

This all sounds very ominous and difficult. But there are more immediate, and more obvious, benefits to come from the discovery of behavioural genes. Identifying these genes leads to a better understanding of the disease at a molecular level, in all its complexity. Put it this way, if gene A is involved in the sense that if it is mutated (dysfunctional) or absent, then it means protein A is needed for normal function: to synthesize a particular neurotransmitter essential in maintaining mood, say.

This will lead to new ideas for drug therapies – at its most simplistic, providing protein A itself to make up the deficiency. Returning to CF for a moment, this is precisely the approach that is used in gene therapy, only at one step removed. If a normal version of CFTR is missing, because the associated gene is missing, then a normal copy of the gene is supplied. This is the hope (some would say the hype) of gene therapy. Clinical trials of gene therapy for CF and other conditions, such as various forms of cancer, are already underway. There is, as yet, no prospect of gene therapy itself for mental disorder, but the uncovering of genes involved in behaviour could well lead to more precisely tailored drugs to tune up specific brain circuits, without side effects.

A further advantage of using genes to understand behaviour in terms of molecules is that it might enable us to rewrite, or even tear up, the DSM. If the same molecular pathways and genes turn out to be involved in, say, attention deficit and 'angry' depression, or anxiety and depression, then these seemingly disparate disorders can be better understood in terms of the common brain circuits. Already this is happening in brain imaging studies of anhedonia and violence – behaviours which are common to several different mental disorders.

Deeper into the brain

One advantage of genetics research is that it offers access to the brain in a non-invasive way. The other way into the brain is, of course, by imaging. Genetic studies will drive the imaging because genes for interesting receptors will start turning up; the people who do the imaging will want to try to locate these within neural circuits to find out what they do.

All the scanning technologies we discussed in chapter 2 are undergoing rapid development. The major improvements will be in the resolution of the images created by the scanner, that is, in the ability to make out details. Already Brodmann's classic map of the brain is being redrawn, allowing areas as small as one millimetre across to be distinguished. Armed with such a detailed map, neuroscientists may be able to pick up very subtle brain lesions (which are not currently detectable) and perhaps link these with mood or behavioural disorders.

Brain imaging has started to reveal the neural traces of stress, depression and crime, in terms of shrinkage of specific regions or changed patterns of activity. But, as yet, none of the scanning techniques is sufficiently sensitive to provide a diagnosis in individual cases. This will surely change, with increased understanding of brain systems and brain chemistry, coupled with better resolution of the instruments.

These diagnostic tests are more likely to focus upon the chemistry of the brain, rather than its structure. This new area of brain imaging is called functional neurochemistry (see also chapter 2) and, currently, it is all about looking at receptor molecules. These, you will remember, are located on the terminus of a 'receiving' neuron, and are the targets of neuro-transmitter molecules. When the neurotransmitter – serotonin, say – binds to one of its receptors, the neuron fires, carrying an electrical impulse through the neural circuit involved. There is (conflicting) evidence that some serotonin receptors might be up-regulated (that is, more numerous than normal) in depression. What is more, they get down-regulated (less numerous) on recovery. So it sounds as if looking at the density of serotonin receptors would be a good diagnostic test for depression.

However, making this a reality requires two big leaps forward over the next few years. First, we need to map out all the different types of serotonin receptors in the brain (there are probably 15 different subtypes) and get to know what the distribution is in a normal brain. Visualizing them is no problem: the neuroscientists use a radioactively tagged molecule, called a *radioligand*, which, like the normal neurotransmitter, homes in upon the receptor. The radioactive tag can easily be monitored, so it visualizes the sites of the receptors (see Figure 9).

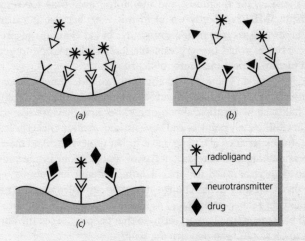

(a)

(b)

	radioligand
	neurotransmitter
	drug

(c)

(Figure 9: Functional neurochemistry in action)
Three ways of tracking brain chemistry: in A, the 'tagged' radioligand molecule sticks to receptors through chemical bonding, so that regions populated with receptor molecules 'light up': in B, neurotransmitters compete with radioligand for receptor binding sites – the more the neurotransmitter binds, the less the density of receptors 'occupied' by radioligand: C is similar to B, except that drug molecules compete for receptor binding with the radioligand. A drug which binds to this receptor will cause a marked decrease in radioligand binding, which can be detected by a scanner.

The receptor 5-HT_{1A} appears to be particularly important in depression; a new radioligand is now being used to visualize it, and to prepare a map showing exactly where it occurs in the brain.[3]

It may be possible to image even more of the synaptic action and look at what the neurotransmitters themselves are doing, because the neurotransmitter and the radioligand compete for the same receptor (Figure 9). If you did something to a patient to raise his serotonin, say, then more serotonin and less radioligand would bind to the receptor and this would be easy to monitor. Again we would like to know, using this technique, how neurotransmitter levels fluctuate in the normal brain.

The next big leap forward will be to make fMRI (which, you remember, requires no injection and relies on the magnetic properties of haemoglobin) act more like PET. At present, you can visualize receptors with PET, but not with fMRI, which just monitors blood flow. But you cannot gather enough data from PET, because it involves radioactivity, and patient exposure has to be limited. What is needed is some kind of way of introducing tagged molecules via fMRI, so that patients can be scanned in a routine way, for diagnosis, and monitored over time for response to treatment. fMRI is already useful in this way, because it can monitor whether a drug treatment improves, say, blood flow in the pre-frontal cortex – but it would be very valuable to extend its scope to get an all-round picture of the time course of depression.

But if scans *are* going to become more routine, much more patient education will be required. Already many patients needing routine MRI scans fail to show for their appointment, because they are scared. While scans are completely painless and have no known after-effects or long-term effects, the experience of having one is rather unnerving. And maybe there is also something a bit scary about having a doctor look inside your brain? Perhaps this is because we are all rather ill-educated about the brain generally. Certainly a big change in public attitudes may be needed if imaging is to realize its potential as a diagnostic tool. Maybe brain scans should become more of an art form, so that people can see the fascination of the mysterious organ beneath the skull?

Designer drugs

Many of the drug treatments we have discussed so far were discovered by accident. The search for new drugs today, however, leaves very little to chance. Computer graphics, robotics, and molecular biology between them are transforming the pharmaceutical industry.

Images of potential drug molecules are built on screen and their action on the target is simulated in virtual reality before any work is done on the lab bench. In the past, a chemist would spend weeks, if not months, painstakingly synthesizing just a few drug molecules. Now the computer graphic approach is complemented by a set of techniques known collectively as combinatorial chemistry. Using robots, and arrays of miniaturized test tubes, thousands of closely related molecules are synthesized together. These can be tested with sophisticated new screening systems and the best molecule for the job selected for further testing.

The whole idea is to get 'cleaner', more refined drugs, constructed to act only on one target, which will cut down on side effects. We saw in chapter

7 how antidepressants have been made which have a much more favourable side effect profile than older drugs – important, when people contemplate taking them long-term, or even for life.

What is more, there is a wider range of drugs available today. In the past, drugs have mainly been small organic molecules, such as pencillin and aspirin. Now, thanks to genetic engineering techniques, there are protein and peptide drugs, many of them based upon the body's own natural chemicals, like insulin. There is also the prospect of drugs that can 'turn off' genes (known as 'antisense' drugs). Furthermore, there are many new ways of delivering drugs: 'depot' injections, which last for weeks, patches, nasal sprays and inhalers, for example.

But there are few really new drugs that act on the brain. There is nothing for antisocial behaviour, for instance, and no choice of drugs for ADHD. These gaps arise from the limited nature of our understanding of the brain. New targets will come from discovery of brain genes and images of receptors, the two areas discussed above. Functional neurochemistry will be used to help develop these new drugs. Drug molecules can compete with radioligands, so we can see if they bind to receptors (Figure 9). You can use such techniques to see which receptors a drug hits and, if it is not specific enough, design a drug molecule which is. This approach is beginning to work for new drugs for treating schizophrenia, and for antidepressants.

Another challenge is the creation of animal models on which to test the drugs. It is difficult to find animal equivalents of disorders like depression and ADHD, because these behaviours are so complex. Nevertheless, some progress has been made by developing animals ('knockouts') which lack certain brain genes. For instance, mice lacking a CRF (corticotropin-releasing factor, one of the key stress hormones) receptor were less anxious in their behaviour than normal mice;[4] this may underline the importance of CRF in human worry and anxiety. In fact, drugs which rebalance the HPA axis in depression by blocking CRF receptors are already being discussed.[5] These mouse models will be extremely useful in their development.

The first generation of drugs that acted on the mind released people from lifelong imprisonment in mental hospitals. Is it too much to hope that the new wave may release people permanently from the misery of mental illness?

The human side

All the scientific advances in the world will not improve our mental health and crime figures, unless they go hand in hand with changes in the way we operate as a society. We do not have space here to review the wide range of schemes, projects and policies that aim to reduce the burden of depression and aggression on the individual and society. All we will say is that these are more likely to be successul if they take on board what we already know about the brain and behaviour.

Just one example illustrates this principle. Prison does not work, yet it would be a bold society that abandoned the principle of punishment by confinement (detention for the protection of the public is probably a different matter, as we discussed in chapter 6). There are stacks of scientific evidence that show that isolation, pain, fear, discomfort and association with deviant peers increase aggression. Prolonged isolation, for instance, leads to serotonin dysfunction and a dramatic increase in aggression in mice.[6]

Education, education, education

We have seen that children who will grow up with problems of depression or aggression can be identified as early as three years old, and we have seen proof of the vital importance of good parenting. So perhaps it is never too early to start educating children about how to live well. Pre-school education, especially with at-risk children, enhances their cognitive and social skills and gives them a good start which may protect them against current and future adverse influences.

Without wishing to sound patronizing, many adults could benefit from parent training. We are expected to train for professions and vocations, so why not parenthood? It does not come naturally to everyone. Training has been found to be effective in preventing delinquency – especially if it focuses upon praise and reward, how to play with children, discipline, setting limits and monitoring children's behaviour.[7] Good parent training does not neglect the adult's own needs; marital conflict and domestic violence can be reduced with anger management, problem-solving skills, and interpersonal skills, all of which will tend to enrich the home environment for at-risk children.

But the drop-out rate in parent training is quite high, for all kinds of reasons. Maybe, too, it is rather demeaning and stigmatizing to be told you need to learn how to be a parent, when you already have three children.

And anyway, if things reach this stage, much damage may already have been done. So maybe it would be better if these skills were taught routinely in schools. Certainly programmes which include anti-bullying initiatives and general social skills can be very successful. To this one could also add teaching children how to manage a workload, and raising awareness about the brain and its role in the emotions.

The world will be a far different place in 50 years time, and in so many ways. What should be most important is the knowledge we will then have about the human brain, the spectrum of our emotions, and why we behave as we do. The hope is that we can synthesize all this knowledge so that we can live happier, more peaceful lives. The study of the human brain has so much to teach us – and the story is just beginning.

Glossary

5-hydroxyindoleacetic acid (5-HIAA) A breakdown product of
  serotonin, often used as a marker for its presence
5-hydroxytryptophan (5-HT) Antidepressant food supplement
  extracted from a West African plant; precursor of serotonin
a stressor
Acetylcholine Neurotransmitter involved in memory and learning
  functions
Acute Stress Disorder Short-lived psychiatric disorder occuring
  within a month of exposure to trauma; may progress to PTSD
Adjustment Disorder Psychiatric disorder with symptoms of PTSD
  only in response to a lesser degree of stressor
Adrenaline A stress hormone produced by the adrenal glands
Allele A gene variant
Amygdala Almond-shaped structure in the centre of the brain which
  plays an important role in emotion
Anhedonia Clinical term for loss of pleasure or interest in life
Anterior cingulate gyrus An area of the brain which appears to be
  underactive in depression and overactive in mania; lies at the
  interface between the amygdala and the frontal cortex
Antibody A protein produced by the immune system, which reacts with
  a specific antigen
Anticholinergic effects Physiological side-effects such as drug mouth,
  dizziness, and weight gain caused by antidepressants acting upon
  acetylcholine circuits in the brain
Antigens Proteins on the cell surfaces of 'foreign' organisms, like
  invading bacteria, which trigger a response from the immune
  system
Antisocial Personality Disorder (ASP) Adult psychiatric disorder
  characterised by lack of empathy, aggressive/criminal behaviour
  and inability to tolerate boredom or frustration

Apolipoprotein E4 (ApoE4) gene A gene variant linked to Alzheimer's disease

Attention deficit hyperactivity disorder (ADHD) Childhood psychiatric disorder characterised by restlessness, short attention span and impulsive behaviour

Autonomic nervous system Part of the central nervous system which controls unconscious functions

Axon Long fibre of neuron, used to transmit electrical impulses

Basal ganglia Group of five nuclei at the base of the brain receiving many connections from the cortex and other brain areas

Biogenic amine theory The idea that depression arises from a deficit of the neurotransmitters serotonin, noradrenaline and dopamine in the brain

Bipolar disorder Also known as manic depression; a psychiatric disorder in which periods of depression alternate with periods of mania

Brain stem Structure at the base of the brain, joining it to the spinal cord

Carbamazepine An anti-epileptic drug also used in the treatment of bipolar disorder

Caudate nucleus One of the five basal ganglia; may be involved in ADHD

Central nervous system The brain and the spinal cord

Cerebellar vermis Part of the cerebellum thought to be involved in ADHD

Cerebellum Structure at the base of the brain which controls movement

Cerebral cortex The outer layer of the cerebrum, divided into four lobes

Cerebrum The largest and most highly developed part of the human brain, lying just beneath the skull; contains the neural structures for speech, vision, hearing, movement, sensation as well as for higher functions like personality, memory and thought

Cholestocystokinin (CCK) A molecule produced in both the brain and the gut, which is linked to the feeling of fullness; has also been linked to panic disorder

Chromosomes Thread-like structures within the nucleus of cells which carry the genes

Concordance The extent to which both twins of a pair show a given biological trait, such as a disease; used to estimate the genetic contribution to a disease

Conduct disorder (CD) Psychiatric disorder more often found in older children and teenagers, marked by antisocial and destructive behaviour

Coronary heart disease Disorder marked by build up of fatty deposits on the arteries that serve the heart

Corpus callosum Band of tissue joining the right and left hemispheres of the brain

Corpus striatum The largest mass of grey matter in the basal ganglia

Corticotropin releasing factor (CRF) Hormone released by the hypothalmus in response to a stressor

Corticotropin Hormone released by the pituitary gland in response to CRF

Cortisol A stress hormone produced by the adrenal glands

Cushing's disease A disorder caused by presence of a tumour somewhere in the HPA system and leading to overproduction of cortisol

Cyclothymia A mood disorder characterised by mood swings that are less severe than those seen in bipolar disorder

Cystic fibrosis transmembrane regulator (CFTR) A protein which is defective in cystic fibrosis; the corresponding gene was one of the first to be discovered in the context of inherited disease

Cytokine Molecule produced as part of the inflammatory response, responsible for symptoms like redness, swelling and so on

Dendrites Projections on a neuron, used to transmit electrical impulses

Dexamethasone suppression test (DST) A test which assesses the activity of the HPA axis

Diagnostic and Statistical Manual (DSM) The official classification of psychiatric disease produced by the American Psychiatric Association

Diencephalon The middle part of the brain, housing the thalamus and hypothalamus

Dizygotic twin Non-identical twin, arising from one of two fertilised eggs

DNA Deoxyribonucleic acid; the chemical which genes are made of

Docosahexaenoic acid (DHA) One of the important omega-3 fatty acids

Dopamine A neurotransmitter involved in mood, movement and many other brain

Dopamine transporter (DAT) A molecule involved in the transport of the neurotransmitter dopamine; abnormal levels may be involved in depression

Dopamine D4 receptor Molecule on surface of neurons which interacts with dopamine; abnormalities implicated in ADHD

Dysthymia Mild and chronic form of depression

Eicosapentaenoic acid (EPA) One of the important omega-3 fatty acids

Factitious disorder Psychiatric disorder involving feigning illness to get medical attention

Frontal lobe Region of the cerebral cortex in front of the ears; important in higher mental functions such as thought

Functional Magnetic Resonance Imaging (fMRI) Technique of imaging, recently developed, similar to MRI but providing functional, rather than structural, information

Functional neurochemistry The use of brain imaging to investigate brain chemistry, chiefly through visualising receptors on the surfaces of neurons

Gamma-aminobutyric acid (GABA) Inhibitory neurotransmitter and site of action of tranquillising drugs

General Adaptation Syndrome Theory of how the body and mind respond and adapt to stressors, made famous by Hans Selye

Glial cells. Cells which support and nourish neurons

Globus pallidus One of the five basal ganglia; may be involved in ADHD

Grey matter Tissue in the brain consisting mainly of cell bodies

Gyrus (pl Gyri) Ridge in the cerebral cortex bounded by sulci

High density lipoprotein (HDL) Also known as 'good' cholesterol; a protein which transports cholesterol away from the artery wall, so preventing build up of fatty deposits

Hippocampus Part of the brain involved in memory and learning

Homocysteine An amino acid whose build-up in the body has been linked to heart disease and Alzheimer's disease

Human Genome Project The plan to identify and locate all the 140,000 or so human genes

Hypericum The active ingredient of St John's Wort, a herbal antidepressant

Hyperkinetic disorder Alternative name for Attention-Deficit Hyperactivity Disorder

Hypothalamus The brain's 'thermostat' – a structure which regulates basic functions such as temperature and appetite

Hypothalamus-Pituitary-Adrenal (HPA) axis System of glands linking brain and body which generates the main hormonal response to a stressor

Intermittent explosive disorder Psychiatric disorder marked by sudden and extreme outbursts of anger

International Classification of Disease (ICD) The official classification of diseases produced by the World Health Organisation

Iproniazid An early antidepressant, originally developed for the treatment of tuberculosis

Kindling In depression, the sensitisation of the brain to further episodes of the disorder

Limbic region Area in the centre of the brain containing many structures concerned with emotion, such as the amygdala

Linkage analysis Technique of analysing the inheritance of disease within a family by tracking the inheritance of specific DNA patterns; can be used to identify genes responsible

Lithium A drug used in the treatment of bipolar disorder

Locus coerulus Tiny area in brain stem containing a high density of noradrenaline producing neurons

Low density lipoprotein (LDL) Also known as 'bad' cholesterol; causes deposition of cholesterol on the artery walls

Magnetic Resonance Imaging (MRI) Technique of imaging which provides structural information about the brain and other organs

Mania Excessive euphoria, optimism, extravagance and activity – out of all proportion to circumstances

Monoamine oxidase An enzyme which breaks down neurotransmitters sertonin, noradrenaline and dopamine

Monoamine oxidase inhibitors (MAOI) (for specific example, see Table 1) Type of antidepressant, not much used now, which stops breakdown of serotonin and noradrenaline and so raises their levels in the brain

Monozygotic twin Identical twin, arising from one fertilised egg splitting into two

Neuron Nerve cell

Neurotransmitter Brain chemical which allows communication between two neurons by flowing across the synapse between them

Neutrophil A cell of the immune system which helps in the repair of damaged tissue

Noradrenaline A neurotransmitter involved in mood regulation

Noradrenaline and selective serotonin antidepressants (NASSAs) (for specific examples, see Table 1) Newer type of antidepressant which acts on noradrenaline and serotonin

Noradrenergic Term describing receptors for noradrenaline

Nuclei In brain anatomy, structures consisting of grey matter organised in spheres of tissue

Nucleus accumbens A structure close to the amygdala which is involved in generating feelings of pleasure after food, sex or taking certain drugs

Obsessive compulsive disorder Psychiatric disorder characterised by anxiety, rituals, and repetitive thought patterns

Occipital lobe Region of the cerebral cortex at the back of the head; deals with visual signals

Omega-3 fatty acids Compounds found in fish oils which keep blood from clotting and are important in brain function

Oppositional defiant disorder (ODD) Childhood psychiatric disorder marked by abnormally severe disobedience and wilfulness

Organophosphates Inhibitors of enzyme that breaks down acetylcholine, found in nerve gases and pesticides; leads to uncontrolled firing of acetylcholine neurons

Panic disorder Psychiatric disorder characterised by intense anxiety occurring for no obvious reason

Parasympathetic nervous system Branch of the autonomic nervous system, whose actions oppose those of the sympathetic nervous system

Parietal lobe Region of the cerebral cortex at the top of the head; deals with body awareness, orientation and movement

Pharmacogenomics New branch of genetics dealing with an individual's susceptibility to disease and drug efficacy and side effects

Pituitary Gland in the centre of the brain which controls the endocrine (hormonal) system

Polymorphism Variation within a person's DNA which can be used in gene analysis

Positron emission tomography (PET) Technique of imaging which provides functional information (eg blood flow patterns) about the brain and other organs

Post-traumatic stress disorder A psychiatric disorder arising from exposure to trauma and characterised by anxiety, nightmares, flashbacks and emotional deadening

Pre-frontal lobe Region of the frontal lobe just behind the forehead, which is greatly expanded in the human brain compared to that of other species; thought to be involved in higher mental functions and rational behaviour

Radioligands Radioactively 'tagged' chemicals used in imaging for their ability to bind to receptors on brain cells and so provide a visual method of monitoring their activity

Receptor Molecule on a cell surface which can bind to an incoming molecule, such as a neurotransmitter; the act of binding triggers a biochemical response within the cell

Regional cerebral blood flow (rCBF) Blood flow patterns in area of the brain, measured by imaging and providing information about activity in that area of the brain

Reserpine A drug derived from the Indian snakeroot plant which decreases the levels of serotonin, noradrenaline and dopamine and can produce deep depression

Ritalin (methylphenidate) Drug used in ADHD

Selective noradrenaline reuptake inhibitors (NARIs) (for specific examples, see Table 1) Newer type of antidepressant which acts only on noradrenaline

Serotonin A neurotransmitter involved in mood and impulse control

Serotonin transporter (SERT) A molecule involved in the transport of the neurotransmitter serotonin; variants of the SERT gene have been implicated in depression

Somatisation disorder Psychiatric disorder characterised by bodily symptoms not explained by physical causes

Specific serotonin reuptake inhibitor (SSRIs) (for specific examples, see Table 1) Newer type of antidepressant which only acts upon serotonin

Substantia nigra Small structure in the brain stem highly populated with dopamine producing neurons

Sulcus (pl Sulci) Fissure dividing the cerebral cortex

Sympathetic nervous system Branch of the autonomic nervous system, whose actions oppose those of the parasympathetic nervous system

Synapse The gap between two neurons across which information flows via neurotransmitters

Synaptosome Preparation of ground-up brain tissue from animals which are used to investigate drugs that act on the brain

Tegmentum An area close to the substantia nigra, also involved in dopamine neurotransmission

Temperament The biological underpinnings of personality

Temporal lobe Region of the cerebral cortex above the ears; deals with sound, speech and some aspects of memory

Testosterone The main male sex hormone

Thalamus The brain's 'relay station' – a structure through which all incoming and outcoming information flows

T-lymphocytes Main cells of the immune system which attack invading organisms

Transcranial magnetic stimulation (TMS) A new method of treating depression involving the induction of an electric current in the brain, via the application of a magnetic field

Tricylic antidepressants (TCAs) (for specific examples, see Table 1) Older type of antidepressant which raises levels of serotonin and noradrenaline in the brain

Tryptophan hydroxylase (TPH) An enzyme involved in the production of serotonin; abnormalities in the corresponding gene have been linked with depression and violence

Tryptophan Amino acid obtained from the diet, used to synthesise serotonin; supplements used to treat depression and insomnia

White matter Tissue in the brain consisting mainly of axons

Notes and Further Reading

Chapter 1: Red Rage and Blue Gloom

Notes

1. *Daily Telegraph*, 4 September 1998.
2. *The Guardian*, 4 August 1999.
3. Moir, A. and Jessel, D., 1995, *A Mind to Crime: the Controversial Link Between the Mind and Criminal Behaviour*, London, Michael Joseph, p. 279.
4. Freud, S., 1917, 'Mourning and melancholia' in *On Metapsychology: the Theory of Psychoanalysis*, Volume 11, The Penguin Freud Library, London, Penguin, p. 261.
5. Kandel, D.B. and Davies, M., 1982, 'Epidemiology of depressed mood in adolescents', *Archives of General Psychiatry*, 39, 1205–12.
6. Rosenbaum, M. and Bennett, B., 1986, 'Homicide and depression', *American Journal of Psychiatry*, 143, 367–70.
7. Fava, M., 1998, 'Depression with anger attacks', *Journal of Clinical Psychiatry*, 59, 18–22.
8. Turner, R.J. and Beiser, M., 1990, 'Major depression and depressive symptomatology among the physically disabled: assessing the role of chronic stress', *Journal of Nervous and Mental Disease*, 178, 343–50.
9. van Praag, H.M., 1998, 'Anxiety and increased aggression as pacemakers of depression', *Acta Psychiatrica Scandinavica*, 393, 81–8.
10. Quiggle, N.L. et al., 1992, 'Social information processing in aggressive and depressed children', *Child Development*, 63, 1305–20.
11. Wolfersdorf, M. and Kiefer, A., 1998, 'Depression and aggression: a control study on the aggression hypothesis in depressive disorders based on the Buss–Durkee Questionniare', *Psychiatric Praxis*, 25, 240–5.
12. Bjork, J.M. et al., 1997, 'A positive correlation between self-ratings of

depression and laboratory-measured aggression', *Psychiatry Research*, 69, 33–8.

13. Gold, P.W. et al., 1988, 'Clinical and biological manifestations of depression', *New England Journal of Medicine*, 319, 413–19.

14. Sapolsky, R.M., 1996, 'Why stress is bad for your brain', *Science*, 273, 749–50.

15. Sheline, Y.I. et al., 1996, 'Hippocampal atrophy in recurrent major depression', *Proceedings of the National Academy of Sciences of the USA*, 93, 3908–13.

16. Gurvits, T. et al., 1996, 'Magnetic resonance imaging study of hippocampal volume in chronic, combat-related post-traumatic stress disorder', *Biological Psychiatry*, 40, 1091–9.

17. Bremner, J.D. et al., 1997, 'Magnetic resonance imaging-based measurement of hippocampal volume in post-traumatic stress disorder related to childhood physical and sexual abuse – a preliminary report', *Biological Psychiatry*, 41, 23–32.

18. Miczek, K.A. and Donat, P., 1989, 'Brain 5-HT systems and inhibition of aggressive behaviours', in *Behavioural Pharmacology of 5-HT*, P. Bevan et al., eds, Hillsdale NJ, Lawrence Erlbaum, pp. 117–44.

19. Mehlman, P.T. et al., 1994, 'Low CSF 5-HIAA concentrations and severe aggression and impaired impulse control in non-human primates', *American Journal of Psychiatry*, 15, 1485–91.

20. Kruesi, M.J.P. et al., 1990, 'CSF monoamine metabolites, aggression and impulsivity in disruptive behaviour disorders of children and adolescents', *Archives of General Psychiatry*, 47, 419–26.

21. Kruesi, M.J.P. et al., 1989, 'Cruelty to animals and CSF 5HIAA, *Psychiatry Research*, 28, 115–16.

22. Bioulac, B. et al., 1980, 'Serotoninergic dysfunction in the 47, XYY syndrome', *Biological Psychiatry*, 15, 917–23.

23. Linnoila, M. et al., 1983, 'Low cerebrospinal fluid 5-hydroxyindoleacetic acid concentration differentiates impulsive from non-impulsive violent behaviour', *Life Sciences*, 33, 2609–14.

24. Åsberg, M. et al., 1976, '5-HIAA in the cerebrospinal fluid: a biochemical suicide predictor?', *Archives of General Psychiatry*, 33, 1193–7.

25. Mann, J.J. et al., 1996, 'Attempted suicide characteristics and cerebrospinal fluid amine metabolites in depressed patients', *Neuropsychopharmacology*, 15, 576–86.

26. Moffitt, T.E. et al., 1998, 'Whole blood serotonin relates to violence in an epidemiological study', *Biological Psychiatry*, 36, 224–7.

27. Ballenger, J.C. et al., 1979, 'Alcohol and central serotonin metabolism in

man', *Archives of General Psychiatry*, 43, 446–57.

28. Fils-Aime, M.-L. et al., 1996, 'Early-onset alcoholics have lower cerebrospinal fluid 5-hydroxyindoleacetic acid than late-onset alcoholics', *Archives of General Psychiatry*, 53, 211–16.

29. Brown, G.I. and Linnoila, M.I., 1990, 'CSF serotonin metabolite (5-HIAA) studies in depression, impulsivity and violence', *Journal of Clinical Psychiatry*, 51:4 (supplement), 31–43.

30. Nemeroff, C., 1998, 'The neurobiology of depression', *Scientific American*, 278, 42–9.

31. Lidberg, L. et al., 1984, '5-hydroxyindoleacetic acid levels in attempted suicides who have killed their children', *Lancet*, 20 October, 928–9.

Chapter 2

Notes

1. Ekman, P., 1992, 'Facial expression of emotions; new findings, new questions', *Psychological Science*, 3, 34–48.

2. Plutchik, R., 1993, 'Emotions and their vicissitudes: emotions and psychopathology', in *Handbook of Emotion*, M. Lewis and J.M. Haviland, eds, New York, Guilford, pp. 53–65.

3. Smith, C.A. and Lazarus, R.S., 1990, 'Emotion and adaptation', in *Handbook of Personality: Theory and Research*, L.A. Pervin, ed., New York, Guilford, pp. 609–37.

4. LeDoux, J., 1998, *The Emotional Brain*, London, Phoenix.

5. LeDoux, J. et al., 1986, Interruption of projections from the medial geniculate body to an archi-neostriatial field disrupts the classical conditioning of emotional responses to acoustic stimuli in the rat', *Neuroscience*, 17, 615–27.

6. Snyder, S.H., 1996, *Drugs and the Brain*, New York, Scientific American Library, chapter 5.

7. Kramer, P., 1993, *Listening to Prozac: A Psychiatrist Explores Antidepressant Drugs and the Remaking of the Self*, London, 4th Estate, p. 134.

8. Damasio, H. et al., 1994, 'The return of Phineas Gage: clues about the brain from the skull of a famous patient', *Science*, 264, 1102–5.

9. Damasio, A.R., 1996, *Descartes' Error: Emotion, Reason and the Human Brain*, London, Papermac, chapter 3.

10. Adolphs, R. et al., 1998, 'The human amygdala in social judgement', *Nature*, 393, 470–4.

11. Grasby, P. et al., 1996, 'Psychopharmacology – *in vivo* neurochemistry and pharmacology', *British Medical Bulletin*, 52, 513–26.

12. Benjamin, J. et al., 1996, 'Population and familial association between the D4 dopamine receptor gene and measures of novelty seeking', *Nature Genetics*, 12, 81–4.

13. Lahoste, G. et al., 1996, 'Dopamine D4 receptor gene polymorphism is associated with attention deficit hyperactivity disorder', *Molecular Psychiatry*, 1, 121–4.

14. Lesch, K.P. et al., 1996, 'Association of anxiety-related traits with a polymorphism in the serotonin transporter gene regulatory region', *Science*, 274, 1527–31.

15. Rees, M. et al., 1997, 'Association studies of bipolar disorder at the human serotonin transporter gene', *Molecular Psychiatry*, 2, 398–402.

16. Williams, J. et al., 1997, 'Meta-analysis of association between the 5-HT2a receptor T102C polymorphism and schizophrenia', *Lancet*, 349, 1221.

Further Reading

Andreasen, N.C., 1997, 'Linking mind and brain in the study of mental illnesses: a project for a scientific psychopathology', *Science*, 275, 1586–93. Technical, but useful, overview of the status of brain imaging in current research.

Carter, R., 1998, *Mapping the Mind*, London, Weidenfeld and Nicolson, Beautifully illustrated overview of current research, with extracts from work of top neuroscientists.

Damasio, A. R., 1996, *Descartes' Error: Emotion, Reason and the Human Brain*, London, Papermac. More about Phineas Gage and Elliott from the neurologist who studied them, leading to new ideas about the relationship between emotion and thought.

Greenfield, S., 1997, *The Human Brain: a Guided Tour*, London, Phoenix. The brain in a nutshell by leading researcher and science popularizer.

LeDoux J., 1998, *The Emotional Brain: the Mysterious Underpinnings of Emotional Life*, London, Phoenix. A very readable account of research into emotion, covering his own work and others.

Weiner, J., 1999, *Time, Love, Memory: the Story of Genes and Behaviour*, London, Faber & Faber.

Chapter 3 Counting the Cost

Notes

1. Burton, R., 1997 [1651], *The Anatomy of Melancholy*, Kissinger Publishing Company.
2. *The Times*, 15 August 1995.
3. Binneveld, H., 1997, *From Shell Shock to Combat Stress: A Comparative History of Military Psychiatry*, trans. John O'Kane, Amsterdam, Amsterdam University Press.
4. Berrios, G.E. and Porter, R., 1995, *A History of Clinical Psychiatry: the Origin and History of Psychiatric Disorders*, London, Athlone.
5. Babington, A., 1997, *Shell Shock: a History of the Changing Attitudes Towards War Neurosis*, London, Leo Cooper.
6. Long, N. et al., 1996, 'Prevalence of post-traumatic stress disorder, depression and anxiety in a community sample of New Zealand Vietnam War veterans', *Australia and New Zealand Journal of Psychiatry*, 30, 253–6.
7. Stretch, R.H. et al., 1996, 'Post-traumatic stress disorder symptoms among Gulf War veterans', *Military Medicine*, 161, 407–10.
8. Goldstein, R.D. et al., 1998, 'War experiences and distress symptoms of Bosnian children', *Pediatrics*, 100, 873–8.
9. Servan-Schreiber, D. et al., 1998, 'Prevalence of post-traumatic stress disorder and major depressive disorder in Tibetan refugee children', *Journal of the American Academy of Child and Adolescent Psychiatry*, 37, 874–9.
10. Abdel-Khalek, A.M., 1997, 'A survey of fears associated with Iraqi aggression among Kuwaiti children and adolescents: a factorial study 5.7 years after the Gulf War', *Psychological Reports*, 81, 247–55.
11. Kearns, J., 1986, *Stress at Work: the Challenge of Change*, London, BUPA.
12. *The Sunday Times*, 18 May 1997.
13. Smith, A. et al., 1998, 'The scale of occupational stress', *Occupational Health Review*, May/June, 19–22.
14. Chambers, R. and Davies, M., 1999, *What Stress!*, London, Royal College of General Practioners, p. 131.
15. Hodgson, J.T. et al., 1993, *Self-reported Work-related Illness: Results From a Trailer Questionnaire on the 1990 Labour Force Survey in England and Wales*, Sudbury, HSE Books.
16. Jones, J.R. et al., 1998, *Self-reported Work-related Illness in 1995: Results from a Household Survey*, Sudbury, HSE Books.
17. Barsade, S. and Wiesenfeld, B., 1997, *Attitudes in the American Workplace*, New Haven, Yale University School of Management.

18. Shimizu, Y. et al., 1997, 'Employee stress status during the past decade (1982–1992) based on a nation-wide survey conducted by the Ministry of Labour in Japan', *Industrial Health*, 35, 441–50.

19. *The Sunday Times*, 18 May 1997.

20. Simkin, S., 1998, 'Stress in farmers: a survey of farmers in England and Wales', *Occupational and Environmental Medicine*, 55, 729–34.

21. Smith, A., 1998, 'Stress at work II: results from a pilot study', *Occupational Health Review*, September/October, 11–13.

22. Health and Safety Executive press release, 27 May 1999.

23. Cooper, C., 1998, 'The psychological implications of changing patterns of work', *RSA Journal*, 1/4, 74–8.

24. Worrall, L. and Cooper, C., 1997, *The Quality of Working Life*, London, The Institute of Management.

25. McHugh, N., 1998, 'Rationalization as a key stressor for public sector employees: an organisational case study', *Occupational Medicine*, 48, 103–12.

26. Miller, M.A. and Rahe, R.H.A., 1997, 'Life changes scaling for the 1990s', *Journal of Psychosomatic Research*, 43, 279–92.

27. Mumford, D.B. et al., 1997, 'Stress and psychiatric disorder in rural Punjab: a community survey of mountain villages in Chitral, Pakistan', *British Journal of Psychiatry*, 170, 299–307.

28. Mumford, D.B. et al., 1996, 'Stress and psychiatric disorder in the Hindu Kush: a community survey of mountain villages in Chitral, Pakistan', *British Journal of Psychiatry*, 168, 299–307.

29. Rozmbert, B. and Manderson, L., 1998, '"Nerves" and tranquillizer use in rural Brazil', *International Journal of Health Services*, 28, 165–81.

30. Wessely, S., 1995, 'The history of chronic fatigue syndrome', in *'Chronic Fatigue Syndrome'*, Stephen E. Straus, ed., New York, Marcel Dekker.

31. Berrios and Porter, *History of Clinical Psychiatry*.

32. Minois, G., 1999, *History of Suicide: Voluntary Death in Western Culture*, trans., Lydia G. Cochrane, Baltimore, Johns Hopkins University Press.

33. Üstün, T.B. and Sartorius, N., 1995, *Mental Illness in General Care*, London, John Wiley and Sons.

34. Murray, J.L. and Lopez, A.D., 1996, *The Global Burden of Disease*, Boston, Harvard University Press.

35. Press release, The European Dana Alliance for the Brain, 1998.

36. Essay on suicide statistics, April 1998, on www.rochford.org/suicide.

37. Befrienders International, 1995, *Study of Suicide Prevention within the European Community*, London, Befrienders International.

38. Diekstra, R.F.W., 1993, 'The epidemiology of suicide and parasuicide', *Acta Psychiatrica Scandinavica*, 371 (Supplement), 9–20.

39. Brown, P., 1997, 'No way out', *New Scientist*, 22 March, 34–7.
40. Diekstra: see note 38.
41. Office of National Statistics, analysis by the Samaritans, 25 April 1999; www.samaritans.org.
42. *The Guardian*, 8 June 1998.
43. Lewis, G., 1998, 'Suicide, deprivation and unemployment: record linkage study', *British Medical Journal*, 317, 1283–6.
44. *Our Healthier Nation*, White Paper, 1999 London, HMSO, July.
45. Farrington, D.P., 1995, 'The challenge of teenage antisocial behaviour', in *Psychosocial disturbances in Young People: Challenges for Prevention*, M. Rutter, ed., New York, Cambridge University Press.
46. www.theaa.co.uk/membership/fleet/fleet18.html.
47. Langley, J., 1996, 'Road rage is second biggest fear for drivers', *Daily Telegraph*, 17 July.
48. Jenkins, M.G. et al., 1998, 'Abuse of staff in accident and emergency departments: a survey of consultants in the UK and the Republic of Ireland', *Journal of Accident and Emergency Medicine*, 15, 262–5.
49. *British Crime Survey*, 1996, London, Home Office Research and Statistics Directorate.
50. Ibid.
51. Rutter, M. et al., 1998, *Antisocial Behaviour by Young People*, Cambridge, Cambridge University Press, chapter 4.
52. Smith, D.J., 1995, 'Youth crime and conduct disorders: trends, patterns, and causal explanations', in *Psychosocial Disorders in Young People: Time Trends and their Causes*, M. Rutter, and D.J. Smith, eds, Chichester, Wiley.
53. Rutter et al.: see note 51.
54. Nikiforov, I.V., *World Factbook of Criminal Justice* at blackstone.ojp.usdoj.gov.

Further Reading

Barker, P., 1991, *Regeneration*, London, Penguin. Booker Prize-winning account of shell shock in World War 1, centred around a fictionalized encounter between Siegfried Sassoon and W.H.R. Rivers.

Chapter 4: White-Out: Blinded by Stress

Notes

1. Beaumont, W., 1838, *Experiments and Observations on Gastic Juices and the Physiology of Digestion*, Edinburgh, Neill and Co.
2. Selye, H., 1956, *The Stress of Life*, New York, McGraw Hill.
3. Rahe, R.H. et al., 1964, 'Social stress and illness onset', *Journal of Psychosomatic Medicine*, 8, 35–44.
4. Miller, M.A. and Rahe, R.H., 1997, 'Life changes scaling for the 1990s', *Journal of Psychosomatic Research*, 43, 279–92.
5. Seligman, M., 1992, *Helplessness: on Development, Depression and Death*, New York, W.H. Freeman, pp. 112–21.
6. Marmot, M.G. et al., 1991, 'Health inequalities among British civil servants: the Whitehall II study', *Lancet*, 337, 1387–93.
7. Lepore, S.J. et al., 1993, 'Social support lowers cardiovascular reactivity to an acute stressor', *Psychosomatic Medicine*, 55, 518–24.
8. Greenwood, D.C. et al., 1996, 'Coronary heart disease; a review of the role of psychosocial stress and social support', *Journal of Public Health Medicine*, 18, 221–31.
9. Sapolsky, R., 1990, 'Adrenocortical function, social rank, and personality among wild baboons', *Biological Psychiatry*, 28, 862–78.
10. McGuire, M.T. et al., 1993, 'Life history strategies, adaptive variations, and behaviour–physiological interactions: the sociology of vervet monkeys', in *Sociophysiology*, P., Barchas, ed., New York, Oxford University Press.
11. Brunner, E., 1997, 'Stress and the biology of inequality, *British Medical Journal*, 314, 1472–6.
12. Sapolsky, R.M., 1997, 'The importance of a well-groomed child', *Science*, 277, 1620–1.
13. Meany, M.J. et al., 1988, 'Effect of neonatal handling on age-related impairments associated with the hippocampus', *Science*, 238, 766–8.
14. Liu et al., 1997, 'Maternal care, hippocampal glucocorticoid receptors, and hypothalamic-pituitary-adrenal responses to stress', *Science*, 277, 1659–62.
15. Wyman, P.A. et al., 1999, 'Caregiving and developmental factors differentiating young at-risk urban children showing resilient versus stress-affected outcomes; a replication and extension', *Child Development*, 70, 645–59.
16. Manuck, S. et al., 1995, 'The pathogenicity of behaviour and its

neuroendocrine mediation: an example from coronary heart disease', *Psychosomatic Medicine*, 57, 275.

17. Suomi, S., 1997, 'Early determinants of behaviour: evidence from primate studies', *British Medical Bulletin*, 53, 170–84.

18. Sapolsky, R.M., 1998, *Why Zebras Don't Get Ulcers: an Updated Guide to Stress, Stress-related Diseases and Coping*, New York, W.H. Freeman, pp. 280–3.

19. Weidner, G. et al., 1989, 'Hostility and cardiovascular reactivity to stress in women and men', *Psychosomatic Medicine*, 51, 36–45.

20. Price, V.A. et al., 1995, 'Relationship between insecurity and Type A behaviour', *American Heart Journal*, 129, 488–91.

21. Houston, B.K. et al., 1997, Social dominance and 22-year all-cause mortality in men', *Psychosomatic Medicine*, 59, 5–12.

22. Brisson, C. et al., 1999, 'Effect of family responsibilities and job strain on ambulatory blood pressure among white-collar women', *Psychosomatic Medicine*, 61, 205–13.

23. Tehrani, N., 1999, 'After the knock on the door, the hidden pain of road crash victims', The British Psychological Society Division of Counselling Psychology Annual Conference.

24. Anderson, I., 1999, 'Stressed-out: counsellors should focus on those who really need help', New Scientist, 24 July, p. 15.

25. Turnbull, G.J., 1998, 'A review of post-traumatic stress disorder, Part II, Treatment', *Injury*, 29, 169–75.

26. Page, W.F. et al., 1997, 'Persistence of PTSD in former prisoners of war', in *Post Traumatic Stress Disorder*, C.S. Fullerton and R.J. Ursano, eds, Washington, American Psychiatric Press.

27. Southwick, S.M. et al., 1997, 'Neurobiological alterations in PTSD: review of the clinical literature', in *Post Traumatic Stress Disorder*, C.S. Fullerton, and R.J. Ursano, eds, Washington, American Psychiatric Press.

28. LeDoux, J., 1998, *The Emotional Brain*, London, Phoenix, pp. 256–61.

29. Arnsten, A.F.T., 1998, 'The biology of being frazzled', *Science*, 280, 1711–12.

30. Klein, D.F., 1993, 'False suffocation alarms, spontaneous panics, and related conditions: an integrative hypothesis', *Archives of General Psychiatry*, 50, 306–17.

31. Kaufer, D. et al., 1998, 'Acute stress facilitates long-lasting changes in cholinergic gene expression', *Nature*, 393, 373–7.

32. Sapolsky, R.M., 1998, 'The stress of Gulf War syndrome', *Nature*, 393, 308–9.

33. Meisel, S. et al., 1991, 'Effect of Iraqi missile war on incidence of acute

myocardial infarction and sudden death in Israeli citizens', *Lancet*, 338, 660.

34. Leor, J. et al., 1996, 'Sudden cardiac death triggered by an earthquake', *New England Journal of Medicine*, 334, 413–19.

35. Gullette, E.C.D. et al., 1997, 'Effects of mental stress on myocardial ischemia during daily life', *Journal of the American Medical Association*, 277, 1521–26.

36. Marmot, M.G. et al., 1991, 'Health inequalities among British civil servants: the Whitehall II study', *Lancet*, 337, 1387–93.

37. Brunner, E.J. et al., 1996, 'Childhood social circumstances and psychosocial and behavioural factors as determinants of plasma fibrinogen', *Lancet*, 347, 1008–13.

38. Brunner, E.J. et al., 1993, Gender and employment grade differences in blood cholesterol, apolipoproteins and haemostatic factors in the Whitehall II study', *Atherosclerosis*, 102, 195–207.

39. Sapolsky, R.M. and Mott, G.E., 1987, 'Social subordinance in wild baboons in association with suppressed high density lipoprotein-cholesterol concentrations: the possible role of chronic social stress', *Endocrinology*, 121, 1605–10.

40. Shively, C.A. and Clarkson, T.B., 1994, 'Social status and coronary artery atherosclerosis in female monkeys', *Arterial Thrombosis*, 14, 721–6.

41. Manuck et al.: see note 16.

42. Stoney, C.M., 1999, 'Plasma homocysteine levels increase in women during psychological stress', *Life Sciences*, 64, 2359–65.

43. Bosma, H. et al., 1997, 'Low job control and risk of coronary heart disease in the Whitehall II (prospective cohort) study', *British Medical Journal*, 314, 558–65.

44. Cooper, C.L., 1998, 'The changing psychological contract at work', *Work and Stress*, 12, 97–100.

45. Marmot, M.G., 1983, 'Stress, social and cultural variations in heart disease', *Journal of Psychosomatic Research*, 27, 377–84.

46. Horsten, M. et al., 1999, 'Psychosocial factors and heart rate variability in healthy women', *Psychosomatic Medicine*, 61, 49–57.

47. Bobak, M. and Marmot, M., 1996, 'East–West mortality divide and its potential explanations; proposed research agenda', *British Medical Journal*, 312, 421–5.

48. Kristenson, M. et al., 1998, 'Attenuated cortisol response to a standardised stress test in Lithuanian and Swedish men: the LiVicordia study', *International Journal of Behavioural Medicine*, 5, 17–30.

49. Cohen, S. and Herbert, T.B., 1996, 'Health psychology: psychological

factors and physical disease from the perspective of human psychoneuroimmunology', *Annual Review of Psychology*, 46, 113–142.

50. Stone, A.A. et al., 1994, 'Daily events are associated with a secretory immune response to an oral antigen in man', *Health Psychology*, 13, 440–6.

51. Evans, P. et al., 1994, 'Stress, arousal, cortisol and secretory immunoglobulin A in students undergoing assessment', *British Journal of Clinical Psychology*, 33, 575–6.

52. Bachen, E.A. et al., 1995, 'Adrenergic blockade ameliorates cellular immune responses to mental stress in humans', *Psychosomatic Medicine*, 57, 366–72.

53. Kiecolt-Glaser, J.K. et al., 1991, 'Spousal caregivers of dementia victims: longitudinal changes in immunity and health', *Psychosomatic Medicine*, 53, 345–62.

54. Cohen, S. et al., 1991, 'Psychological stress and susceptibility to the common cold', *New England Journal of Medicine*, 325, 606–12.

55. Cohen, S. et al., 1998, 'Types of stressor that increase susceptibility to the common cold in healthy adults', *Health Psychology*, 17, 214–23.

56. Cohen, S. et al., 1999, 'Psychological stress, cytokine production, and severity of upper respiratory illness', *Psychosomatic Medicine*, 61, 175–180.

57. Cohen, S. et al., 1997, Chronic social stress, social status, and susceptibility to upper respiratory infections in non-human primates', *Psychosomatic Medicine*, 59, 213–21.

58. Kiecolt-Glaser, R. et al., 1999, Stress-related changes in proinflammatory cytokine production in wounds', *Archives of General Psychiatry*, 56, 450–6.

59. Petticrew, M., 1999, 'Cancer–stress link: the truth', *Nursing Times*, 95, 52–3.

60. Woolley, C.S. et al., 1990, 'Exposure to excess glucocorticoids alters dendritic morphology of adult hippocampal pyramidal neurons', *Brain Research*, 531, 225–31.

61. Margarinos, A.M. and McEwen, B.S., 1995, 'Stress-induced atrophy of apical dendrites of hippocampal CA3c neurons: involvement of glucocorticoid secretion and excitatory amino acid receptors', *Neuroscience*, 69, 89–98.

62. Sapolsky, R.M. and Pulsinelli, W., 1985, 'Glucocorticoids potentiate ischemic injury to neurons: therapeutic implications', *Science*, 229, 1397–1400.

63. Sapolsky, R.M. et al., 1985, 'Prolonged glucocorticoid exposure reduces hippocampal neuron number: implications for ageing', *Journal of Neuroscience*, 5, 1222–7.

64. Starkman, M.N. et al., 1992, 'Hippocampal formation volume, memory

dysfunction, and cortisol levels in patients with Cushing's syndrome', *Biological Psychiatry*, 32, 756–65.

65. Gurvits, T.V. et al., 1996, 'Magnetic resonance imaging study of hippocampal volume in chronic, combat-related post-traumatic stress disorder', *Biological Psychiatry*, 40, 1091–9.

66. Bremner, J.D. et al., 1997, 'Magnetic resonance imaging-based measurement of hippocampal volume in post-traumatic stress disorder related to childhood physical and sexual abuse – a preliminary report', *Biological Psychiatry*, 41, 23–32.

67. Sheline, Y.I. et al., 1996, 'Hippocampal atrophy in recurrent major depression', *Proceedings of the National Academy of Sciences of the USA*, 93, 3908–13.

Further Reading

Brunner, E., 1997, 'Stress and the biology of inequality', *British Medical Journal*, 314, 1472–6. A useful summary of the role stress plays in the relationship between socio-economic class and health, by one of the authors of the important Whitehall II study.

Cohen, S. and Herbert, T.B., 1996, 'Health psychology: psychological factors and physical disease from the perspective of psychoneuroimmunology', *Annual Review of Psychology* 47, 113–42. A review of stress, the immune system and disease.

Lazarus, R.S., 1999, *'Stress and Emotion: a New Synthesis'*, New York, Springer. A world expert explores the latest trends.

Sapolsky, R.M., 1996, 'Why stress is bad for your brain', *Science* 273 749–50. A review of hippocampal damage and exposure to glucocorticoids.

Sapolsky, R.M., 1998, *Why Zebras Don't Get Ulcers: An Updated Guide to Stress, Stress-related Diseases and Coping*, New York, W.H. Freeman and Company, A comprehensive and readable introduction to the science of stress by one of the world's leading experts.

Selye, H., 1978, *The Stress of Life: Revised Edition*, New York, McGraw Hill. The classic work on stress.

Chapter 5: Blue Mood, Grey World: The Problem of Depression

Notes

1. Kessler, R.C. et al., 1994, 'Lifetime and 12-month prevalence of DSM-III-R psychiatric disorders in the United States; results from the National Comorbidity Survey', *Archives of General Psychiatry*, 51, 8–19.

2. Paykel, E.S. et al., 1992, 'Recognition and management of depression in general practice: consensus statement', *British Medical Journal*, 305, 1198–202.

3. Jones, G., 1989, 'One step away from the final darkness', *New Scientist*, 4 March, 62–3.

4. Jamison, K.R., 1996, *An Unquiet Mind*, London, Picador, p. 150.

5. Wolpert, L., 1999, *Malignant Sadness: The Anatomy of Depression*, London, Faber & Faber, p. vii.

6. *Ibid.*, p. 6.

7. Tolstoy, L., 1996, *Confession*, trans. David Patterson, New York, W.W. Norton & Co.

8. Ford D.E. et al., 1998, 'Depression is a risk factor for coronary heart disease in men: the precursors study', *Archives of Internal Medicine*, 158, 1422–6.

9. Hippisley-Cox, J. et al., 1998, 'Depression as a risk factor for ischemic heart disease in men: population based case control study', *British Medical Journal*, 316, 1714–19.

10. Watkins, L.L. and Grossman, P., 1999, 'Association of depressive symptoms with reduced baroflex cardiac control in coronary heart disease', *American Heart Journal*, 137, 453–7.

11. Forsen, L. et al., 1999, 'Mental distress and risk of hip fracture: do broken hearts lead to broken bones?' *Journal of Epidemiology and Community Health*, 53, 343–7.

12. Regier, D.A. et al., 1990, 'Comorbidity of mental disorders with alcohol and other drug abuse; results from the Epidemiologic Catchment Area (ECA) study', *Journal of the American Medical Association*, 264, 2511–18.

13. Slater, E. and Mayer, A. 1959, 'Contributions to a pathography of the musician Robert Schuman,' *Confinia Psychiatrica*, 2, 65–94; quoted in adapted form in Redfeld Jamison, *Touched with Fire*, p. 146.

14. Schildkraut, J.J. et al., 1994, 'Mind and mood in modern art, II: Depressive disorders, spirituality, and early deaths in the abstract

expressionist artists of the New York School', *American Journal of Psychiatry*, 151, 482–8.

15. Post, F., 1994, 'Creativity and psychopathology. A study of 291 world-famous men', *British Journal of Psychiatry*, 165, 22–3.

16. Post, F., 1996, 'Verbal creativity, depression and alcoholism: an investigation of one hundred American and British writers', *British Journal of Psychiatry*, 168, 545–55.

17. Jamison, K.R., 1989, 'Mood disorders and patterns of creativity in British writers and artists', *Psychiatry*, 52, 125–34.

18. Richards, R.L. et al., 1988, 'Creativity in manic-depressives, cyclothymes, their normal relatives and control subjects', *Journal of Abnormal Psychology*, 97, 281–8.

19. McGuffin, P. et al., 1996, 'A hospital-based twin register of the heritability of DSM-IV unipolar depression', *Archives of General Psychiatry*, 53, 129–136.

20. Bertesen, A. et al., 1977, 'A Danish twin study of manic-depressive disorders', *British Journal of Psychiatry*, 130, 330–51.

21. Bowlby, J., 1988, *A Secure Base: Clinical Applications of Attachment Theory*, London, Routledge, chapter 2.

22. Harrington, R. and Harrison, L., 1999, 'Unproven assumptions about the impact of bereavement on children', *Journal of the Royal Society of Medicine*, 92, 230–33.

23. Cassano, G.B. et al., 1992, 'The importance of measures of affective temperaments in genetic studies of mood disorders', *Journal of Psychiatric Research*, 26, 257–68.

24. Caspi, A. et al., 1996, 'Behavioural observations at age 3 years predict adult psychiatric disorders: longitudinal evidence from a birth cohort', *Archives of General Psychiatry*, 53, 1033–9.

25. Suomi, S.J., 1997, 'Early determinants of behaviour: evidence from primate studies', *British Medical Bulletin*, 53, 170–84.

26. Seligman, M.E., 1992, *Helplessness: on Development, Depression and Death*, New York, W.H. Freeman, pp. 79–106.

27. Lloyd, C., 1980, 'Life events and depressive disorder reviewed; events as precipitating factors', *Archives of General Psychiatry*, 37, 541–8.

28. Brown, G.W. and Harris, T., 1978, *Social Origins of Depression: a Study of Psychiatric Disorders in Women*, London, Tavistock.

29. Jamison, K.R., *Touched with Fire, Manic-Depressive Illness and the Artistic Temperament*, New York, Free Press, p. 86.

30. Deb, S. et al., 1998, 'Minor head injury associated with risk of psychiatric problems', *Journal of Neurology, Neurosurgery and Psychiatry*, 65, 899–902.

31. Bode, L. et al., 1996, 'First isolates of infectious human Borna disease virus

from patients with mood disorders', *Molecular Psychiatry*, 3, 200–12.

32. *The Observer*, 1999, 'New lads to new sads', 14 March.

33. Egeland, J.A. et al., 1987, 'Bipolar affective disorders linked to DNA markers on chromosome 11', *Nature*, 325, 783–7.

34. Kelsoe, J.R. et al., 1989, 'Re-evaluation of the linkage relationship between chromosome 11p loci and the gene for bipolar affective disorder in the Old Order Amish', *Nature*, 342, 238–43.

35. Risch, N. and Botstein, D., 1996, A manic depressive history, *Nature Genetics*, 12, 351–3.

36. Kovacs, M. et al., 1997, 'A controlled family history study of childhood-onset depressive disorder', *Archives of General Psychiatry*, 54, 613–23.

37. Kelsoe, J.R. et al., 1996, 'Possible locus for bipolar disorder near the dopamine transporter on chromosome 5', *American Journal of Medical Genetics*, 67, 533–40.

38. Furlong, R.A. et al., 1998, 'Analysis and meta-analysis of two serotonin transporter gene polymorphisms in bipolar and unipolar affective disorders', *American Journal of Medical Genetics*, 81, 58–63.

39. Vincent, J.B. et al., 1999, 'Genetic association of serotonin system genes in bipolar affective disorder', *American Journal of Psychiatry*, 156, 136–8.

40. Bellevier, F. et al., 1998, 'Association between the tryptophan hydroxylase gene and manic depressive illness', *Archives of General Psychiatry*, 55, 33–7.

41. Kirov, G. et al., 1999, 'Tryptophan hydroxylase gene and manic depressive illness', *Archives of General Psychiatry*, 56, 98–9; McQuillan, A. et al., 1999, 'No allelic association between bipolar affective disorder and the tryptophan hydroxylase gene', *Archives of General Psychiatry*, 56, 99–101.

42. Nakamura, N. et al., 1999, 'Variations in the human homologue of a fruit fly gene are associated with mood and panic disorder', *Molecular Psychiatry*, 5, 155–62.

43. Kennedy, J.L. et al., 1999, 'A genetic marker of panic disorder', *Molecular Psychiatry*, 4, 284–5.

44. Åsberg, M. et al., 1976, 'Serotonin depression: biochemical subgroup within the affective disorders?' *Science*, 191, 478–80.

45. D'haenen, A.H. et al., 1992, 'SPECT imaging of serotonin 2 receptors in depression', *Psychiatry Research*, 45, 227–37.

46. Lucki, I., 1998, 'The spectrum of behaviours influenced by serotonin', *Biological Psychiatry*, 44, 151–62.

47. Cloninger, R.C., 1987, 'A systematic method for clinical description and classification of personality variants: a proposal', *Archives of General Psychiatry*, 44, 573–88.

48. Nemeroff, C.B., 1998, 'The neurobiology of depression', *Scientific American*, 278, 42–9.
49. Arborelius, L. et al., 1999, 'The role of corticotropin-releasing factor in depression and anxiety disorders', *Journal of Epidemiology*, 160, 1–12.
50. Duman, R.S. et al., 1997, 'A molecular and cellular theory of depression', *Archives of General Psychiatry*, 54, 597–606.
51. Post, R.M. et al., 1986, 'Conditioning and sensitisation in the longitudinal course of affective illness', *British Journal of Psychiatry*, 149, 191–201.
52. Shah, P.J. et al., 1998, 'Cortical grey matter reductions associated with treatment-resistant chronic unipolar depression. Controlled magnetic resonance imaging study', *British Journal of Psychiatry*, 172, 527–32.
53. Sheline, Y. et al., 1998, 'Amygdala core nuclei volumes are decreased in recurrent major depression', *Neuroreport*, 9, 2023–8.
54. Kumar, A. et al., 1998, 'Late-onset minor and major depression: early evidence for common neuroanatomical substrates detected by using MRI', *Proceedings of the National Academy of Sciences of the USA*, 95, 7654–8.
55. Bench, C.J. et al., 1995, 'Changes in regional cerebral blood flow on recovery from depression', *Psychological Medicine*, 25, 247–61.
56. Drevets, W.C. et al., 1997, 'Subgenual prefrontal cortex abnormalities in mood disorder', *Nature*, 386, 824–7.
57. Mayberg, H.S. et al., 1999, 'Reciprocal limbic-cortical function and negative mood: converging PET findings in depression and normal sadness', *American Journal of Psychiatry*, 156, 675–81.
58. For expert comment, see Drevets, W.C., 1998, 'Functional neuroimaging studies of depression: the anatomy of melancholia', *Annual Review of Medicine*, 49, 341–61, and Nemeroff, C.B. et al., 1999, 'Functional brain imaging: twenty-first century phrenology or psychobiological advance for the millennium?', *American Journal of Psychiatry*, 156, 671–3.

Further Reading

Barondes, S.H., 1998, *Mood Genes: Hunting for Origins of Mania and Depression*, London, Penguin. About the genetics of mood disorders by a biologist.
Berman, J., 1999, *Surviving Literary Suicide*, Boston, Massachusetts University Press. Professor of English presents unique chronicle of student responses to suicide in literature; a fascinating update of the *Young Werther* theme which advances understanding of the death wish.
Lott, T. 1996, *The Scent of Dried Roses*, London, Penguin. Award-winning and insightful account of writer's experience of depression and his mother's suicide.

Jamison, K.R., 1994, *Touched with Fire: Manic-Depressive Illness and the Artistic Temperament*, New York, Free Press. The definitive account – scholarly, yet readable.

Jamison, K.R., 1995, *An Unquiet Mind: A Memoir of Moods and Madness*, London, Picador. Frank personal account of manic depression by one of the world's leading experts, who also suffers from the disorder.

Rowe, D., 1989 Depression: *The Way Out of Your Prison*, London, Routledge. One of the best self-help books written by leading psychologist.

Styron, W., 1991, *Darkness Visible*, London, Picador. Pulitzer Prize-winning author writes eloquently about his experience of depression.

Sutherland, S. 1998, *Breakdown: A Personal Crisis and a Medical Dilemma*, Oxford, Oxford University Press. Update of a classic account of breakdown and manic depression by psychology expert with personal experience.

Wolpert, L., 1999, *Malignant Sadness: The Anatomy of Depression*, London, Faber & Faber. Seeking to understand his own depression, expert biologist Wolpert surveys the field.

Whybrow, P.C., 1997, *A Mood Apart: A Thinker's Guide to Emotion and its Disorder*, London, Picador. Account of manic depressive disorder by a psychiatrist.

www.mentalhealth.com: a useful web site with details of the DSM-IV (American) and ICD-10 (European) diagnostic classifications, treatments, personal experiences, magazine articles, and most cited journal articles, plus useful links.

Chapter 6: Red Mist: Inside the Criminal Mind

Notes

1. Denno, D.W., 1996, 'Legal implications of genetics and crime research,' in *The Genetics of Criminal and antisocial Behaviour*, Ciba Foundation Symposium 194, G.R. Bock and J.A. Goode, eds, Chichester, John Wiley & Sons.

2. Lorenz, K., 1966, *On Aggression*, New York, Harcourt Brace.

3. Wolfgang, M.E. et al., 1972, *Delinquency in a Birth Cohort*, Chicago, University of Chicago Press.

4. Norman Chester Centre for Football Research, 21 June 1999, on www.le.ac.uk.

5. Zoccolillo, M. et al., 1992, 'The outcome of childhood conduct disorder: implications for defining adult personality disorder and conduct disorder', *Psychological Medicine*, 22, 971–86.

6. Taylor, E., 1998, 'Understanding hyperactivity – a moving target', *MRC News*, Spring, 8–11.

7. Taylor, E. et al., 1996, 'Hyperactivity and conduct problems as risk factors for adolescent development', *Journal of the American Academy of Child and Adolescent Psychiatry*, 35, 1213–26.

8. Mannuzza, S. et al., 1993, 'Adult outcome of hyperactive boys: educational achievement, occupational rank, and psychiatric status', *Archives of General Psychiatry*, 50, 565–76.

9. Biederman, J. et al., 1996, 'A prospective 4-year follow-up study of attention-deficit hyperactivity and related disorders', *Archives of General Psychiatry*, 53, 437–46.

10. Barkley, R.A., 1998, 'Attention-deficit hyperactivity disorder', *Scientific American*, September, 44–9.

11. Barkley, R.A., 1997, 'Advancing age, declining ADHD', *American Journal of Psychiatry*, 154, 1323–5.

12. Biederman et al.: see note 10.

13. Castellanos, F.X. et al., 1996, 'Quantitative brain magnetic resonance imaging in attention-deficit hyperactivity disorder', *Archives of General Psychiatry*, 53, 607–16.

14. Gill, M. et al., in press, 'Confirmation of association between ADHD and a dopamine transporter polymorphism', *Molecular Psychiatry*.

15. Swanson, J.M. et al., in press, 'Association of the dopamine receptor D4 (DRD4) gene with a refined phenotype of ADHD – a family approach', *Molecular Psychiatry*.

16. Gojone, H. et al., 1996, 'Genetic influences on parent reported attention related problems in a Norwegian general population twin sample', *Journal of the American Academy of Child and Adolescent Psychiatry*, 35, 588–96.

17. Levy, F. et al., 1997, 'Attention-deficit hyperactivity disorder: a category or a continuum? Genetic analysis of a large-scale twin study', *Journal of the American Academy of Child and Adolescent Psychiatry*, 36, 737–44.

18. Hartmann, T., 1999, *Attention-Deficit Disorder: a Different Perception*, Glass Valley, CA, Underwood Books.

19. Farrington, D.P., 1995, The challenge of teenage antisocial behaviour, in *Psychosocial Disturbances in Young People: Challenges for Prevention*, M. Rutter, ed., New York, Cambridge University Press, pp. 83–130.

20. Moffitt, T.E., 1993, 'Adolescence-limited and life-course-persistent antisocial behaviour: a developmental taxonomy', *Psychological Review*, 100, 674–701.

21. Phillips, M., 1998, 'Forget psychiatry, stop psychopaths', *Sunday Times*, 25 October.

22. Geddes, J., 1999, 'Suicide and homicide by people with mental illness', *British Medical Journal*, 318, 1225–6.

23. Shaw, J. et al., 1999, 'Mental disorder and clinical care in people convicted of homicide: national clinical survey', *British Medical Journal*, 318, 1240–44.

24. Wessely, S.C., 1994, 'The criminal careers of incident cases of schizophrenia', *Psychological Medicine*, 24, 483–502.

25. Steadman, H.J. et al., 1998, 'Violence by people discharged from acute psychiatric in-patient facilities and by others in the same neighbourhoods', *Archives of General Psychiatry*, 55, 393–401.

26. Link, B.G. and Stueve, A., 1998, 'New evidence of the violence risk posed by people with mental illness', *Archives of General Psychiatry*, 55, 403–4.

27. Institute of Psychiatry press release, 21 April 1999.

28. Caspi, A. et al., 1996, 'Behavioural observations at age 3 years predict adult psychiatric disorders', *Archives of General Psychiatry*, 53, 1033–9.

29. Gibbs W.W., 1995, 'Seeking the criminal elements', *Scientific American*, March, 77–83.

30. Lynam, D.R., 1996, 'Early identification of chronic offenders: who is the fledgling psychopath?', *Psychological Bulletin*, 120, 209–34.

31. Lyons, M.J., 1996, 'A twin study of self-reported criminal behaviour', in Bock, and Goode, eds, *Genetics of Criminal Behaviour* (see note 1).

32. Bohman, M., 1996, 'Predisposition to criminality: Swedish adoption studies in retrospect', in Bock, and Goode, eds, *Genetics of Criminal Behaviour* (see note 1).

33. Cadoret, R.J. et al., 1995, 'Genetic–environmental interaction in the genesis of aggressivity and conduct disorders', *Archives of General Psychiatry*, 52, 916–24.

34. Miles, D.R. and Carey, G., 1997, 'Genetic and environmental architecture of human aggression', *Journal of Personality and Social Psychology*, 72, 207–17.

35. Moffitt, T.E. and Caspi, A., 1999, 'Findings about partner violence from the Dunedin multidisciplinary health and development study', National Institute of Justice, Research in Brief, Washington, US Department of Justice.

36. Caspi, A. et al., 1995, 'Temperamental origins of child and adolescent behaviour problems: from age three to age 15', *Child Development*, 66, 55–68.

37. Raine, A. et al., 1994, 'Birth complications combined with early maternal rejection at age 1 year predispose to violent crime at age 18 years, *Archives of General Psychiatry*, 51, 984–8.

38. Raine, A. et al., 1996, 'High rates of violence, crime, academic problems, and behavioural problems in males with both early neuromotor deficits and unstable family environments', *Archives of General Psychiatry*, 53, 544–9.

39. Brennan, P.A. et al., 1999, 'Maternal smoking during pregnancy and adult male criminal outcomes', *Archives of General Psychiatry*, 56, 215–19.

40. Fergusson, D.M., 1999, 'Prenatal smoking and antisocial behaviour', *Archives of General Psychiatry*, 56, 223–4.

41. Widom, C.S., 1989, 'The cycle of violence', *Science*, 244, 160–5.

42. Johnson, J.G. et al., 1999, 'Childhood maltreatment increases risk for personality disorders in early adulthood', *Archives of General Psychiatry*, 56, 600–6.

43. Moffitt and Caspi: see note 35.

44. Conger, R.D. et al., 1995, 'It takes two to replicate: a mediational model for the impact of parents' stress on adolescent adjustment', *Child Development*, 66, 80–97.

45. Fergusson, D.M. and Lynskey, M.T., 1996, 'Adolescent resiliency in family adversity', *Journal of Child Psychology and Psychiatry*, 37, 281–92.

46. Ito, T.A. et al., 1996, 'Alcohol and aggression: a meta-analysis on the moderating effects of inhibitory cues, triggering events, and self-focused attention', *Psychological Bulletin*, 120, 60–82.

47. Rossow, I., 1996, 'Alcohol-related violence: the impact of drinking patterns and drinking context', *Addiction*, 91, 1651–61.

48. Browne, K.D. and Pennell, A., 1998, *Effects of Video Violence on Young Offenders*, Home Office Research and Statistics Directorate, Research Findings No 65, London, The Home Office.

49. Raleigh, M.J., et al., 1991, 'Serotonergic mechanisms promote dominance acquisition in adult male vervet monkeys', *Brain Research*, 559, 181–90.

50. Higley, J.D. et al., 1996, 'Excessive mortality in young free-ranging male non-human primates with low cerebrospinal fluid 5-hydroxyindoleacetic acid concentrations', *Archives of General Psychiatry*, 53, 537–43.

51. Brunner, D. and Hen, R., 1997, 'Insights into the neurobiology of impulsive behaviour from serotonin receptor knockout mice', *Annals of the New York Academy of Sciences*, 836, 81–105.

52. Kruesi, M.J. et al., 1992, 'A 2-year prospective follow-up study of children and adolescents with disruptive behaviour disorders. Prediction by cerebrospinal fluid 5-hydroxyindoleacetic acid, homovanillic acid and autonomic measures?', *Archives of General Psychiatry*, 49, 429–35.

53. Virkkunen, M.D. et al., 1996, 'A prospective follow-up study of alchoholic violent offenders and fire setters', *Archives of General Psychiatry*, 53, 523–9.

54. Coccaro, E.F. et al., 1996, 'Impulsive aggression in personality disorder

correlates with tritiated paroxetine binding in the platelet', *Archives of General Psychiatry*, 53, 531–6.

55. Brunner, H.G., 1996, 'MAOA deficiency and abnormal behaviour: perspectives on an association', in Bock and Goode eds, *Genetics of Criminal Behaviour* (see note 1).

56. Brunner, H.G. et al., 1993, 'Abnormal behaviour associated with a point mutation in the structural gene for monoamine oxidase A', *Science*, 262, 578–80.

57. Belfrage, H. et al., 1992, 'Platelet monoamine oxidase activity in mentally disordered violent offenders', *Acta Psychiatrica Scandinavica*, 85, 218–21.

58. Raine, A. 1996, 'Autonomic nervous system factors underlying disinhibited, antisocial and violent behaviour', *Annals of the New York Academy of Sciences*, 794, 46–59.

59. Raine, A. et al., 1990, 'Relationships between central and autonomic measures of arousal at age 15 years and criminality at age 24 years', *Archives of General Psychiatry*, 47, 1003–7.

60. Raine, A. et al., 1997, 'Low resting heart rate at age 3 years predisposes towards aggression at age 11 years: Evidence from the Mauritius Child Health Project', *Journal of the American Academy of Child and Adolescent Psychiatry*, 36, 1457–64.

61. Raine, A. et al., 1995, 'High autonomic arousal and electrodermal orienting at age 15 years as protective factors against criminal behaviour at age 29 years', *American Journal of Psychiatry*, 152, 1505–600.

62. Blair, J., 1999, 'Psychopathy's sad face', *MRC News*, Winter/Spring, 12–15.

63. Volkow, N.D. and Tancredi, L., 1987, 'Neural substrates of violent behaviour. A preliminary study with positron emission tomography', *British Journal of Psyschiatry*, 151, 668–73.

64. Raine, A. et al., 1997, 'Brain abnormalities in murderers indicated by positron emission tomography', *Biological Psychiatry*, 42, 496–508.

Further Reading

Baumeister, R.F., 1997, *Evil: Inside Human Violence and Cruelty*, New York, W.H. Freeman.

Black, D.W., 1999, *Bad Boys, Bad Men: Confronting antisocial Personality Disorder*, New York, Oxford University Press. The first comprehensive account of APD, from a psychiatrist long fascinated by the condition.

Bock, G.R. and Goode J.A. (eds) 1996, *The Genetics of Criminal and antisocial*

Behaviour, Ciba Foundation Symposium 194, Chichester, John Wiley & Sons.

James, O., 1995, *Juvenile Violence in a Winner–Loser Culture: Socio-Economic and Familial Origins of the Rise of Violence against the Person*, London, Free Association Books. A clinical psychologist develops the theme that inequality lies at the root of the rise in violence in the UK seen since 1987.

Masters, B., 1996, *The Evil That Men Do*, London, Doubleday.

Moir, A. and Jessel D., 1995, *A Mind to Crime: the Controversial Link Between the Mind and Criminal Behaviour*, London, Michael Joseph.

Niehoff, D., 1999, *The Biology of Violence: How Understanding the Brain, Behaviour and Environment Can Break the Vicious Circle of Aggression*, New York, The Free Press. A neuroscientist's view of the background and latest scientific developments.

Rutter, M. et al., 1998, *Antisocial Behaviour by Young People*, Cambridge, Cambridge University Press. A comprehensive, timely and readable review of current research into antisocial behaviour.

Watson, L., 1995, *Dark Nature: a Natural History of Evil*, Hodder and Stoughton. An account of the anthropology of evil.

Chapter 7: Pharmacological Fixes

Notes

1. For a recent overview, with debate and comments, see Spigset, O. and Mårtensson, B., 1999, 'Drug treatment of depression', *British Medical Journal*, 318, 1188–91.

2. Puzantian, T. and Kawase, K., 1999, 'Does the addition of pindolol accelerate or enhance the response to selective serotonin reuptake inhibitor antidepressants?', *Pharmacotherapy*, 19, 205–12.

3. Kirsch, I. and Sapirstein, G., 1998, *Prevention and Treatment* (a peer-reviewed on-line journal published by the American Psychological Association at journals.apa.org/prevention) 1, article 0002a, posted June 26.

4. Enserink, M., 1999, 'Can the placebo be the cure?' *Science*, 284, 238–40.

5. Manning, C., 1999, 'Some further thoughts', eBMJ (electronic version of the *British Medical Journal*), 8 May.

6. Danish University Antidepressant Group, 1986, 'Citalopram: clinical effect profile in comparison with clomipramine. A controlled multicentre study', *Psychopharmacology*, 90, 131–8.

7. Danish University Antidepressant Group, 1990, 'Paroxetine: a selective serotonin reuptake inhibitor showing better tolerance, but weaker antidepressant effect than clomipramine in a controlled multicentre study', *Journal of Affective Disorders*, 18, 289–99.

8. Danish University Antidepressant Group, 1993, 'Moclobemide: a reversible MAO-A-inhibitor showing weaker antidepressant effect than clomimpramine in a controlled multicentre study', *Journal of Affective Disorders*, 28, 105–16.

9. Knutson, B. et al., 1998, 'Selective alteration of personality and social behaviour by serotonergic intervention', *American Journal of Psychiatry*, 153, 373–9.

10. Teicher, M.H. et al., 1990, 'Emergence of intense suicidal preoccupation during fluoxetine treatment', *American Journal of Psychiatry*, 147, 207–10.

11. Beasley, C.M. et al., 1991, 'Fluoxetine and suicide: a meta-analysis of controlled trials of treatment for depression', *British Medical Journal*, 303, 685–92.

12. Montgomery, S.A., 1998, 'The place of reboxetine in antidepressant therapy', *Journal of Clinical Psychiatry*, 59 (supplement 14), 26–9.

13. Burrows, G.D. and Kremer, C.M.E., 1997, 'Mirtazapine: Clinical advantages in the treatment of depression', *Journal of Clinical Psychopharmacology*, 17, (supplement 1), 34S.

14. Müller, W.E. et al., 1997, 'Effects of hypericum extract (LI60) in biochemical models of antidepressant activity', *Pharmacopsychiatry*, 30, 102–7.

15. Linde, K. et al., 1996, 'St John's wort for depression – an overview and meta-analysis of randomised clinical trials', *British Medical Journal*, 313, 253–8.

16. Wheatley, D., 1997, 'LI60, an extract of St John's wort, versus amitriptyline in mildly to moderately depressed outpatients – a controlled 6-week clinical trial', *Pharmacopsychiatry*, 39, 77–80.

17. Kasper, S., 1997, 'Treatment of seasonal affective disorder (SAD) with hypericum extract', *Pharmacopsychiatry*, 30, 89–93.

18. Wheatley, D., 1999, 'Hypericum in seasonal affective disorder (SAD)', *Current Medical Research and Opinion*, 15, 33–7.

19. Paykel, E., 1996, 'Tertiary prevention: longer-term drug treatment in depression', in *'The Prevention of Mental Illness in Primary Care'* T. Kendrick, et al., eds, Cambridge, Cambridge University Press, pp. 281–93.

20. Kupfer, D.J. et al., 1992, 'Five-years outcome for maintenance therapies in recurrent depresssion', *Archives of General Psychiatry*, 49, 769–73.

21. Thase, M.E., 1999, 'Redefining antidepressant efficacy toward long-term recovery', *Journal of Clinical Psychiatry*, 60 (supplement 6), 15–19; Versiani,

M. et al., 1999, 'Reboxetine, a unique selective NRI, prevents relapse and recurrence in long-term treatment of major depressive disorder', *Journal of Clinical Psychiatry*, 60, 400–406.

22. Stahl, S.M., 1999, 'Why settle for silver, when you can go for gold? Response vs recovery as the goal of antidepressant therapy', *Journal of Clinical Psychiatry*, 60, 213–14.

23. Pascual-Leone, A. et al., 1996, 'Lateralized effect of rapid-rate transcranial magnetic stimulation of the prefrontal cortex on mood', *Neurology*, 46, 499–502.

24. Klein, E. et al., 1999, 'Therapeutic efficacy of right prefrontal slow repetitive transcranial magnetic stimulation in major depression', *Archives of General Psychiatry*, 56, 315–20.

25. George, M.S. et al., 1999, 'Transcranial magnetic stimulation: applications in neuropsychiatry', *Archives of General Psychiatry*, 56, 300–311.

26. 1998 'Pay attention: who really benefits from drugs given to hyperactive kids', Anon., *New Scientist*, editorial, 28 November.

27. Motluk, A., 1998, 'Are drugs really the answer for hyperactive kids?', *New Scientist*, 28 November, 24.

28. Volkow, N. et al., 1995, 'Is methylphenidate like cocaine? Studies on their pharmacokinetics and distribution in the human brain', *Archives of General Psychiatry*, 52, 456–63.

29. Motluk, A., 1998, 'Calm before the storm: will the hyperactive children of today be the drug addicts of tomorrow?', *New Scientist*, 18 April, 18–19.

30. Biederman, J. et al., 1999, 'Pharmacotherapy of attention-deficit hyperactivity disorder reduces risk for substance use disorder', *Paediatrics*, 104, e20.

31. Marx, J., 1999, 'How stimulant drugs may calm hyperactivity', *Science*, 283, 306.

32. Ratey, J. et al., 1991, 'Buspirone treatment of aggression and anxiety in mentally retarded patients: a multiple-baseline, placebo lead-in study', *Journal of Clinical Psychiatry*, 52, 159–62.

33. Stanislav, S.W. et al., 1994, 'Buspirone's efficacy in organic-induced aggression', *Journal of Clinical Psychopharmacology*, 14, 126–30.

34. Fava, M, et al., 1993, 'Anger attacks in unipolar depression, Part 1: Clinical correlates and response to fluoxetine treatment', *American Journal of Psychiatry*, 150, 1158–63.

35. Coccaro, E.F. and Kavoussi, R.J., 1997, 'Fluoxetine and impulsive aggressive behaviour in personality-disordered subjects', *Archives of General Psychiatry*, 54, 1081–8.

Further Reading

Cornwell, J., 1996, *The Power to Harm: Mind, Murder and Drugs on Trial*, London, Penguin. Insightful and balanced: the inside story of Joe Wesbecker's killing spree, blamed on an adverse reaction to Prozac.

Healy, D., 1998, *The Antidepressant Era: A Comprehensive History of Psychiatric Drugs*, Cambridge MA, Harvard University Press. The definitive account: detailed and comprehensive.

Kramer, P., 1993, *Listening to Prozac: A Psychiatrist Explores Antidepressant Drugs and the Remaking of the Self*, London, 4th Estate. The classic book on Prozac, depression and personality written by a leading psychiatrist: hard science woven round fascinating case histories.

Rosenthal, N., 1998, *St John's Wort: Your Natural Prozac*. London, Thorsons. Psychiatrist's helpful guide for those taking St John's wort.

Snyder, S.H., 1996, *Drugs and the Brain*, New York, Scientific American Library. Very readable introduction to the whole range of drugs – from therapeutic to recreational – which affect the brain.

Chapter 8: Talking Treatments

Notes

1. Beck, A., 1976, *Cognitive Therapy and the Emotional Disorders*, London, Penguin, p. 125.
2. Blenkiron, P., 1999, 'Who is suitable for cognitive behavioural therapy?' *Journal of the Royal Society of Medicine*, 92, 222–9.
3. Beck (see note 1), p. 304.
4. Shea, M.T. et al., 1992, 'Course of depressive symptoms over follow-up. Findings from the National Institute of Mental Health Treatment of Depression Collaborative Research Program', *Archives of General Psychiatry*, 55, 816–20.
5. Blackburn, I.M. and Moore, R.G., 1997, 'Controlled acute and follow-up trial of cognitive therpay and pharmacotherapy in out-patients with recurrent depression', *British Journal of Psychiatry*, 171, 328–34.
6. Fava, G.A. et al., 1998, 'Prevention of recurrent depression with cognitive behavioural therapy: preliminary findings', *Archives of General Psychiatry*, 55, 816–20.
7. Hollon, S.D. et al., 1992, 'Cognitive therapy and pharmacotherapy for depression: singly and in combination', *Archives of General Psychiatry*, 49, 774–81.

8. Thase, M.E. et al., 1997, 'Treatment of major depression with psycho-therapy or psychotherapy–pharmacotherapy combinations', *Archives of General Psychiatry*, 54, 1009–15.

9. Brown University News Bureau press release, May 18 1999.

10. Schwartz, J.M. et al., 1996, 'Systematic changes in cerebral glucose metabolic rate after successful behaviour modification treatment in obsessive compulsive disorder', *Archives of General Psychiatry*, 53, 109–13.

11. Brody, A.L, et al., 1998, 'FDG-PET predictors of response to behavioural therapy and pharmacotherapy in obsessive compulsive disorder', *Psychiatry Research*, 84, 1–6.

12. Appleby, L. et al., 1997, 'A controlled study of fluoxetine and cognitive behavioural counselling in the treatment of post-natal depression', *British Medical Journal*, 314, 932–6.

13. Guthrie, E. et al., 1999, 'Cost-effectiveness of brief psychodynamic-interpersonal therapy in high utilisers of psychiatric services', *Archives of General Psychiatry*, 56, 519–26.

14. DeRubeis, R.J. et al., 1999, 'Medications versus cognitive behavioural therapy for severely depressed outpatients: mega-analysis of four randomised comparisons', *American Journal of Psychiatry*, 156, 1007–13.

15. Gath, D. and Mynors-Wallis, L., 1997, 'Problem-solving treatment in primary care' in *The Science and Practice of Cognitive Behaviour Therapy*, D.M. Clark and C.G. Fairburn, eds, Oxford, Oxford University Press, pp. 415–31.

16. Ibid.

17. Mynors-Wallis, L. et al., 1995, 'Randomised controlled trial comparing problem-solving treatment with amitriptyline and placebo for major depression in primary care', *British Medical Journal*, 310, 441–5.

18. Malt, U.F. et al., 1999, 'The Norwegian naturalistic treatment study of depression in general practice (NORDEP). 1: Randomised double blind study', *British Medical Journal*, 318, 1180–84.

19. Beck, A.T. et al., 1990, *Cognitive Therapy of Personality Disorders*, New York, Guilford Press, chapter 8.

20. Davidson, K.M. and Tyrer, P., 1996, 'Cognitive therapy for antisocial and borderline personality disorders: single case study series', *British Journal of Clinical Psychology*, 35, 413–29.

21. Woody, G.E., 1985, 'Sociopathy and psychotherapy outcomes'. *Archives of General Psychiatry*, 42, 1081–6.

22. Valliant, P.M. and Antonowicz, D.H., 1991, 'Cognitive behavioural therapy and social skills training improves personality and cognition in incarcerated offenders', *Psychological Reports*, 68, 27–33.

23. Vennard, J. et al., 1997, 'Part 1: the use of cognitive behavioural approaches with offenders: Messages from the research', in *Changing Offenders' Attitudes and Behaviour: What Works?*, Home Office Research Study, no. 171, London, HMSO, pp. 1–35.
24. Kazdin, A.E., 1997, 'Practitioner review: psychosocial treatments for conduct disorder in children', *Journal of Child Psychology and Psychiatry*, 36, 161–78.

Further Reading

Beck, A.T., 1976, *Cognitive Therapy and the Emotional Disorders*, London, Penguin. Very readable overview by the pioneer of this treatment.

Clark, D.M. and Fairburn, C.G., eds, 1997, *The Science and Practice of Cognitive Behaviour Therapy*, Oxford, Oxford University Press. A useful reference text.

Greenberger, D. and Padesky, C.A., 1995, *Mind Over Mood*, New York, Guilford Press. Probably the best of the self-help cognitive therapy workbooks.

Chapter 9: A Brighter Lifestyle

Notes

1. Bell, I.R. et al., 1991, 'B complex vitamin patterns in geriatric and young adult inpatients with major depression', *Journal of the American Geriatric Society*, 39, 252–7.
2. Lindenbaum, J. et al., 1988, 'Neuropsychiatric disorders caused by cobalamin deficiency in the absence of anaemia or macrocytosis', *New England Journal of Medicine*, 318, 1720–8.
3. Godfrey, P.S. et al., 1990, 'Enhancement of recovery from psychiatric illness by methylfolate', *Lancet*, 336, 392–5.
4. Hawkes, W.C. and Hornbostel, L., 1996, 'Effects of dietary selenium on mood in healthy men living in a metabolic research unit', *Biological Psychiatry*, 39, 121–8.
5. Benton, D. and Cook, R., 1991, 'The impact of selenium supplementation on mood', *Biological Psychiatry*, 29, 1092–8.
6. Wolraich, M.L. et al., 1994, 'Effects of diets high in sucrose or aspartame on the behaviour and cognitive performance of children', *New England Journal of Medicine*, 330, 301–7.

7. Carter, C.M. et al., 1993, 'Effects of a few food diet in attention deficit disorder', *Archives of Diseases in Childhood*, 69, 564–8.

8. Kawachi, I. et al., 1996, 'A prospective study of coffee drinking and suicide in women', *Archives of Internal Medicine* 156, 521–5

9. 'The natural alternative to Prozac, *Beyond Nutrition*, Autumn, 1998, pp. 7–9.

10. Poldinger, W. et al., 1991, 'A functional dimensional approach to depression: serotonin deficiency as a target syndrome in a comparison of 5-hydroxytryptophan', *Psychopathology*, 24, 53–81.

11. Hamazaki, T. et al., 1996, 'The effect of docosahexaenoic acid on aggression in young adults. A placebo-controlled double-blind study', *Journal of Clinical Investigation*, 97, 1129–33.

12. Hamazaki, T. et al., 1999, 'Administration of docosahexaenoic acid influences behaviour and plasma catecholamine levels at times of psychological stress', *Lipids*, 34, (supplement), S33–7.

13. Hibbeln, J.R. et al., 1998, 'Essential fatty acids predict metabolites of serotonin and dopamine in cerebrospinal fluid among healthy control subjects, and in early and late-onset alcoholics', *Biological Psychiatry*, 44, 235–42.

14. Hibbeln, J.R. et al., 1998, 'A replication study of violent and non-violent subjects: cerebrospinal fluid metabolites of serotonin and dopamine are predicted by plasma essential fatty acids', *Biological Psychiatry*, 44, 243–9.

15. Stoll, A.L. et al., 1999, 'Omega-3 fatty acids in bipolar disorder; a preliminary double-blind, placebo-controlled trial', *Archives of General Psychiatry*, 56, 407–12.

16. Tkachuk, G.A. and Martin, G.L., 1999, 'Exercise therapy for patients with psychiatric disorders: research and clinical implications', *Professional Psychology Research and Practice*, 30, 275-82 (www.apa.org/journals/pro/pro303275.html).

17. Broocks, A. et al., 1998, 'Comparison of aerobic exercise, clomipramine, and placebo in the treatment of panic disorder', *American Journal of Psychiatry*, 155, 603–9.

18. Wolpert, L., 1999, *Malignant Sadness: The Anatomy of Depression*, London, Faber & Faber, p. vii.

19. Berger, M. et al., 1997, 'Sleep deprivation combined with consecutive sleep phase advance as a fast-acting therapy in depression: an open pilot trial in medicated and unmedicated patients', *American Journal of Psychiatry*, 154, 870–2.

20. Miles, E., 1999, *Tune Your Brain: Using Music to Manage Your Mind, Body and Mood*, Berkley Publishing Group: www.tuneyourbrain.com.

21. Smyth, J.M., 1999, 'Effects of writing about stressful experiences on symptom reduction in patients with asthma or rheumatoid arthritis: a randomized trial', *Journal of the American Medical Association*, 281, 1304–9.
22. www.arise.org, 1998.
23. Patmore, A., 1998, *Killing the Messenger: The Pathologising of the Stress Response'*, University of East Anglia.

Further reading

Chambers, R. and Davies, M., 1999, *What Stress! The Once in a Lifetime Programme That Will Help You Control Stress in Your Workplace*, London, Royal College of General Practioners, One of the best of the self-help books on stress: common sense and professional advice on stress in a practical workbook format.

Christensen, L., 1996, *Diet Behaviour Relationships: Focus on Depression*, Washington, American Psychological Association. Psychologist reviews research in this area.

Miles, E., 1999, *Tune Your Brain: Using Music to Manage Your Mind, Body and Mood*, Berkley Publishing Group: www.tuneyourbrain.com.

Thayer, R.E., 1996, *The Origin of Everyday Moods: Managing Energy, Tension, and Stress*, New York, Oxford University Press. Psychology professor offers all-round lifestyle guide.

Chapter 10: Looking Forward: How Brain Science Could Change the Way We Live

Notes

1. Cohen, J., 1997, 'Developing prescriptions with a personal touch', *Science*, 275, 776–80.
2. Nuffield Council on Bioethics, 1998, 'Mental disorders and genetics: the ethical context', London, Nuffield Council on Bioethics.
3. Ito, H. et al., 1999, 'Localization of 5-HTIA receptors in the living human brain using [carbonyl-11C] WAY-100635 PET with anatomic standardization techniques', *Journal of Nuclear Medicine*, 40, 102–9.
4. Contarino, A. et al., 1999, 'Reduced anxiety-like and cognitive performance in mice lacking the corticotropin-releasing factor receptor 1' *Brain Research*, 835, 1–9.
5. Nemeroff, C.B., 1998, 'Psychopharmcology of affective disorders in the

21st century', *Biological Psychiatry*, 44, 517–25.

6. Valzelli, L. and Bernasconi, S., 1979, 'Aggressiveness by isolation and brain serotonin turnover changes in different strains of mice', *Neuropsychobiology*, 5, 129–35.

7. Rutter, M. et al., 1998, *Antisocial Behaviour by Young People: Preventative Strategies at a Predelinquency Phase*, Cambridge, Cambridge University Press, pp. 327–8.

Further Reading

Blank, R.H. 1999, *Brain Policy: How the New Neuroscience Will Change Our Lives and Our Politics*, Washington DC, Georgetown University Press. Insightful overview of how brain science should affect public.

Plomin, R. and Rutter, M., 1998, 'Child development, molecular genetics, and what to do with genes once they are found', *Child Development*, 69, 1223–42. Useful discussion of issues raised by behavioural genetics, by two leading researchers.

Ridley, M., 1999, *Genome*, London, 4th Estate. All you need to know about the Human Genome Project.

Index

INDEX